Universities, Innovation and the Economy

In the twenty-first century, universities are part of systems of innovation spanning the globe. While there is nothing new in universities' links with industry, what is recent is their role as territorial actors. It is government policy in many countries that universities, and in some countries national laboratories, stimulate regional or local economic development. They are expected to be at the heart of networked structures contributing to the growth of productive knowledge-oriented clusters.

Universities, Innovation and the Economy explores the implications of this expectation. Its purpose is to situate this new role within the context of broader political histories, comparing how countries in Europe and North America have balanced the traditional roles of teaching and research with that of exploitation of research and defining a territorial role.

Helen Lawton Smith highlights how pressure, both from the state and from industry, has produced new paradigms of accountability that include responsibilities for regional development. This book utilizes empirical evidence gained from studies conducted in both North America and Europe to provide an overview of the changing geography of university–industry links.

Helen Lawton Smith is Reader in Management, School of Management and Organisational Psychology, Birkbeck, University of London, UK, and Director of Research, Oxfordshire Economic Observatory, Oxford University.

Routledge studies in business organizations and networks

Universities, Innovation and the Economy

Helen Lawton Smith

Routledge
Taylor & Francis Group

LONDON AND NEW YORK

First published 2006
by Routledge
2 Park Square, Milton Park, Abingdon, Oxon OX14 4RN

Simultaneously published in the USA and Canada
by Routledge
270 Madison Ave, New York, NY 10016

Routledge is an imprint of the Taylor & Francis Group, an informa business

© 2006 Helen Lawton Smith

Typeset in Times by Wearset Ltd, Boldon, Tyne and Wear
Printed and bound in Great Britain by TJI Digital, Padstow, Cornwall

British Library Cataloguing in Publication Data
A catalogue record for this book is available from the British Library

Library of Congress Cataloging in Publication Data
A catalog record for this book has been requested

ISBN10: 0-415-32493-9 (hbk)
ISBN10: 0-203-35805-8 (ebk)

ISBN13: 978-0-415-32493-9 (hbk)
ISBN13: 978-0-203-35805-4 (ebk)

Contents

Illustrations

Figures

Tables

Preface and acknowledgements

Universities are now universally seen as sources of wealth creation. At the one extreme this means that they are mandated through legislation and financial 'incentives' to drive economic development, at the other they are seen as catalysts without which local high-tech economic development would not have developed. The reality is more complicated than either. The book is an attempt to explore that reality.

This task would not have been possible without the help and support of many people. I am particularly grateful to Tim Cook and Tom Hockaday of Isis Innovation, Oxford University, for their support, patience and data and to Catherine Quinn, Jeremy Whiteley, Nigel Thrift also of Oxford University for their help on points of information. In the US, I would like to thank Alan Attaway, Nancy Davis, Andrew Lane and Teresa Fan of the University of Louisville for their kind help with the Louisville case study, and Joseph Montemarano, Princeton University for his advice and information. Philip Shapira, Alan Hughes and Jeff Saperstein are thanked for their kind permission for use of their material. John Banks did sterling work on copy-editing, but any mistakes are my responsibility. Finally I would like to thank Rob Langham, Commissioning Editor at Routledge, for his help in seeing the project through.

This book is dedicated to Jeff Park for his love and inspiration.

Abbreviations

ATP	Advanced Technology Program (US)
AUTM	Association of University Technology Managers (US)
CEC	Commission of the European Communities
CIS	Community Innovation Survey
CPD	Continuing Professional Development
DoD	Department of Defense (US)
DTI	Department of Trade and Industry
EC	European Commission
EPO	European Patent Office
EPSCoR	Experimental Program to Stimulate Competitive Research (US)
ERA	European Research Area
EU	European Union (post-Maastricht Treaty 1991)
FY	Financial year
GERD	Government Expenditure on Research and Development
HE	Higher education
HEFCE	Higher Education Funding Council for England
HEIs	Higher education institutes
HEIF	Higher Education Innovation Fund (UK)
HESA	Higher Education Statistics Agency (UK)
IPR	Intellectual Property Rights
ISAP	International Association of Science Parks
KIS	Knowledge-intensive services
MCA	Medicines Control Agency
MNCs	Multinational companies
MoD	Ministry of Defence (UK)
MIT	Massachusetts Institute of Technology
NIS	National Innovation System
NIH	National Institutes of Health (US)
NSB	National Science Board (US)
NSF	National Science Foundation (US)
OECD	Organization for Economic Co-operation and Development
OST	Office of Science and Technology

PROs	Public Research Organisations
RAE	Research Assessment Exercise (UK)
R&D	Research and development
RDAs	Regional Development Agencies
RIS	Regional Innovation System
RTD	Research and Technological Development
S&E	Science and engineering
S&T	Science and technology
SMEs	Small and Medium-Sized Enterprises
TTO	Technology Transfer Office
USPTO	US Patent and Trademark Office
VC	Venture capital

Introduction

> Universities are at the heart of our productive capacity and are powerful
> drivers of technological change. They are central to local and regional eco-
> nomic development and produce people with knowledge and skills. They
> are at the hub of business networks and industrial clusters of the know-
> ledge economy.
>
> (Lord Sainsbury 2002 announcing the new Faraday Partnerships)

This statement by the UK's Minister of Science and Technology ideologi-
cally and politically places universities at the centre of economic development per se and of contemporary local and regional economies.
Academics researching in this field have made similar statements. For
example, Leifner *et al.* (2004, 23) state that 'A society's economic competitiveness is dependent on the performance of its higher education
institutions' and Godin and Gingras (2000) argue that, despite a real diversification of the loci of production of knowledge, 'universities still are at
the heart of the system and all other actors rely on the expertise'. In
answering the question 'what is the role of universities in knowledge-based
capitalism?' Florida and Cohen (1999, 590) argue that 'Science has
emerged as an alternative to engine of economic growth to the classic
triumvirate of land, labour and capital, the traditional sources of wealth'.

This statement raises a number of questions. For example, what kinds
of roles do universities play in economic development? One answer is that
'The best of the world's research universities are uniquely the sources of
vitality, understanding and skills in highly developed societies' (Kodama
and Branscomb 1999, 4). Is this role unique to universities? The European
Commission (EC) (2003a) finds that it is. In setting out its view of the role
and uniqueness of universities, the Report claims, 'The knowledge society
depends for its growth on the production of new knowledge, its transmission through education and training, its dissemination through information
and communication technologies and on its use through new industrial
processes or services'. Universities take part in all three processes and are
'at the heart of the Europe of Knowledge' (page 4). Thus as Florida and

Cohen (1999, 593) argue, the shift from industrial capitalism to knowledge-based capitalism makes the university ever more critical as a provider of resources such as talent, knowledge and innovation. State intervention, therefore, is justified because the role for policy makers is to 'introduce governance systems to make technological interactions and technological communications possible' (Antonelli and Quere 2002, 1051) reducing the interaction deficit within and across national (and regional) innovation systems (Geuna *et al.* 2003) thereby improving the distribution power of the innovation system (David and Foray 1995).

The 'triple helix' model of university–industry–government relations developed by Etzkowitz and Leydesdorff (1997) encapsulates this notion of interdependence and institutional change. It denotes 'a transformation in the relationship among university, industry and government as well as within each of these spheres' (Etzkowitz 2003, 295). It has gained common currency in both policy and academic discourses because of its articulation of a convergence in missions and strategies within each of these three spheres (Georghiou and Metcalfe 2002). It is also 'a significant shift in the social contract' between universities and society (Martin, B. 2003, 25).

Such a convergence in missions at regional and local as well as national levels amounts to what Charles (2003) describes as an 'instrumental position'. It is based on the underlying assumption that proximity is causal in improving the efficiency by which the process of innovation occurs – innovation being defined as 'the process of transforming an invention into something commercially useful and valuable' (Miller and Morris 1999). Now the key economic actor is increasingly expected to be a cluster of firms emanating from or at least closely associated with a university or other knowledge-producing institution (Etzkowitz 2003). The pervasiveness of Porter's (1990, 1998) cluster concept is a major factor in this narrative, giving as it does a clear policy strategy to local or regional policy makers by suggesting that local linkages are a key factor in economic competitiveness. This position is increasingly being challenged, however, as assumptions are questioned about the economic significance of intra-regional linkages, including those of between universities and local firms, as evidence casts doubt on the connection, or indeed the existence of strong patterns of local linkages and indeed whether they are desirable in an increasingly internationalized economy (Malmberg and Power 2004). As the book will show, the impacts of universities, many of which will be at a regional or local scale, will vary considerably over time, over space between sectors, between firms of different sizes and that both academics and policy-makers need to be more aware of these variations.

The background to the now normative position that universities are creators of wealth is the slowdown in productivity growth and associated decline in competitiveness of firms in high-technology industries in the later 1970s and early 1980s which has been blamed on the decline in the rate of technological innovation (see Poyago-Theotoky *et al.* 2002). These authors find that concerns were especially strong in the US at Federal and state level. This brought about a new wave of thinking in technology policy in which university–industry partnerships were at the forefront. In the UK, for example, since the 1980s, three different governmental and academic discourses have been constructed around enterprise and innovation. The first discourse in the 1980s within the loose framework of Thatcherite policies was about individuals and entrepreneurship. Second, in the 1990s, this was joined by the national policy agenda of the valorization of public-sector research. Third, the debate has been about enterprise – valorization and regional development (Lawton Smith 2003a).

As Europe strives to compete with the US (and the US with China), current initiatives established to integrate European higher education systems – the European Research Area and European Higher Education Area – are designed to overcome the European paradox: a strong science base but poor performance in technological and industrial competitiveness (EC 1996 and EC 2003b, 413). This Europeanization of member states' higher education system is designed to increase internal equity and the EU's competitive position versus the US through harmonization. There is to be closer interaction not only between public research/universities and industry but also between different parts of the public research system in order to reduce fragmentation and compartmentalization of EU public research (EC 2003b, 428). France's dirigiste system is very different from the UK's laissez-faire system and from the German decentralized regional system.

It is a combination of the lack of integration of science and technological systems across member states, a confusion of institutional arrangements and objectives and weaknesses in particular fields, that has put Europe behind the US. Riccaboni *et al.* (2003) find that it is variations in the organizations in upstream R&D processes between the US and Europe as a whole that are responsible for differences in performance and the greater integrative capacity among the diverse kinds of actors and organizations. It is not just the structure with respect to institutional rules, but what is done within that structure, for example rules regulating terms and conditions of employment (Steinmueller 2003). With respect to technological advance, the US has relative strengths as measured through scientific or technological output indicators; R&D or economic performance indicators are in information and computer sciences and mechanical and electronic engineering, areas where the EU15 is weak (EC 1994). Thus the US, more so than Europe, is spending more on the very R&D-intensive competition (for example in sectors such as advanced organic chemicals and telecommunications equipment) that needs more science inputs and requires high levels of both government and industry expenditure on R&D (Grupp 1995).

This book came about because of my unease with the uncritical position of the territorial role as the latest of the multiple roles that universities are required to perform. This disquiet sits alongside numerous articles that have appeared in the UK's national press about the problematic position that universities and individual academics have been placed in with regard to the ownership and control of intellectual property created during the course of research funded by industry. It seems to me that the techno-economic prioritization pays insufficient attention to the evidence or the consequences of the policy of 'encouraging' universities to increase the amount of industrial research they undertake.

What therefore does the book set out to do? It sets out to record paradigm shifts articulated in policies that are a response to and further reinforce trends already taking place and in which universities are being repositioned in society's expectations in relation to industry. It compares developments in Europe with those in the US, the world's largest economy and the yardstick for measurement for the rest of the world. It explores the incentives for change, which are being remade in the contemporary political economy. It also shows how universities are sites of conflict faced with a number of tensions such as those between the balance of effort of teaching and research, with regard to ethical issues about what kinds of scientific research should be undertaken and legal issues over ownership of intellectual property versus openness within the academic process. It is generally the case in countries belonging to the Organization for Economic Development (OECD) that the share of Government Expenditure on Research and Development (GERD) funded by governments has decreased with that share being largely taken over by industry.

Why should the relationship between universities, innovation and economic development be examined? What do we mean by economic development? What is the justification for the now central importance of universities' territorial role? There seems to be two main answers. First, the topic is of relevance to the formulation and implementation of public policies when decisions are made on how to boost innovation – which is now in its various guises as the knowledge economy, the 'new economy' and so on. Economic development more generally is 'actions taken with the express intention of enhancing economic prosperity, for individuals, communities and employers' (MacKinnon 1998, 6).

The book's primary focus then is the role of universities in enhancing that prosperity through participation in the innovation process on which the prospects for economic development lie. Knowledge production, transfer of scientific and engineering technologies, the mechanisms by which they are transferred including intellectual transfers, the formation of new firms and the labour markets associated with those technologies collectively form that contribution to technological advance. The book sets the university's territorial role into perspective by examining the broader nature of the relationship and identifying what aspects of that relationship are significant at regional/local levels in the abstract and in the particular. Successful universities are often a defining characteristic of successful places although, as studies from the 1980s have shown, this is not necessarily causal. Indeed, the focus on universities and clusters has been recent. Hall (1984, 12) notes that in Britain, 'with the possible exception of Cambridge, the presence of a major university has not been a major factor in the development of high-tech industry'. The focus on the territorial role, however, is not meant to be prioritized above important changes in the way universities are required to function, such as the impact of the current funding regime on the kinds of research being undertaken.

The focus is primarily on science and engineering-based industries. There is little here about services, about banking or insurance, and other financial industries even though economies cannot be understood without reference to the global finance industry (Clark 2004). Nor is it in the scope of this book to discuss the wider contribution of universities to sustainable development including the effects on the built environment and social and community development – which are integral to the relationship of a university with its locality – nor other aspects of economic relationship arising from the close relationship with quality of life and intellectual climate of localities and regions and which are central to universities' position within society (see Florida 1999). Glasson (2003) highlights many other potential effects of a university on its local community – providing further examples of the extended model of universities, particularly with regard to sustainable development issues such as the built environment and social and community development.

Moreover, while universities' role is to be of benefit to society through these various means, the impact is not one-way. Formal and informal relationships have multiple feedback effects not only on the universities (and public laboratories) and the individual scientists and engineers and how they conduct their internal affairs but on the relationship with civil society and the 'value' of universities as well as with industry. In the UK, for example, as the pressure on universities to engage more fully in the innovation process increases, it is recognized that the real problem is investment by industry and typically does not reflect a lack of supply in scientific knowledge (see HM Treasury 2003; Coombs and Metcalfe 2000; Polt 2001; Hughes 2003). Therefore, a major concern of innovation policy is to maximize the economic impact of public investment in research, for example by providing inputs to as much private R&D as possible (Arundel and Geuna 2004, 7).

Second, many aspects of the functioning of the university–industry relationship in market economies in general and the territorial role are not fully understood. As is the case of the study of industrial organization (Scherer and Ross 1990), theory, data and methodologies which reveal the different aspects of that relationship are becoming available. Thus a number of ways of looking at universities and increasingly formalized assessments such as recruitment of students and performance targets of academics are possible. Evaluation is increasingly becoming central to the policy-making process (Kuhlmann 2003). We need to know what measures are used and the limitations of indicators which rank performance of countries, regions/localities, universities and academics. This is a crucial issue in this debate. In spite of the current enthusiasm for universities' central position in knowledge-based capitalism (Florida and Cohen 1999), the 1998 OECD Report 'The University in Transition' concludes that firms do not rely on universities and other public research organizations (PROs) for their innovation activities. How clear, then, is the evidence that universities provide more than a minor input into innovation (Arundel and Geuna 2004)? Measurement is always going to be inexact. As Patel (2002) points out, some contributions of academic research to technological practice will be *direct*, when such research leads to applicable discoveries, engineering research techniques (such as computer simulations) and instrumentation. Others will be *indirect*, when research training, background knowledge and professional networks contribute to business firms' own problem-solving activities – in particular, to the experimental engineering research, design practice, production and operation that will be mainly located there. Moreover, the relative importance of these contributions varies across industries and across scientific disciplines. In this book it will be argued that far too much attention has been paid to the contribution universities make to economic development such as spin-offs, patents and licensing as means for technology transfer, and that insufficient attention has been paid both in Europe and in the US to the contribution of universities to local and regional labour markets, through graduated students (undergraduates, post-grads and continuing professional development (CPD)).

The variability of the impact of universities is examined. The territorial role here refers to explicit relationships within the university's geographical hinterland, whether each institution sees that to be the locality, city, region or nation state (see OECD 1998). For example, economists often describe the regional scale as the nation state (see for example Geuna and Nesta 2003). For Krugman (1991) the relevant geographical unit of observation for the link between knowledge inputs and innovative output is the city. And not only do national innovation systems vary, the uniqueness of each university necessarily means that in their territorial role each has its own characteristics. As the case studies show, Stanford is a world away from the University of Louisville, which in turn is radically different from Princeton – but they all have significant and different positions in the university–economy interface.

In organizing these discussions the book draws perspectives from a range of literatures, primarily geography, economics and business and management, to examine how political processes work alongside regulatory and legal processes and have been embedded in institutional change over the last 150 years. Most of the evidence is desk-based research with the exception of the case studies of European universities in Chapter 7 and two of the three US universities in Chapter 8 where interviews were conducted with university faculty. It is clear from this brief discussion that relationships between the universities and economies are multi-paradigmatic with co-existing paradigms that sometimes complement each other, sometimes compete and are sometimes contradictory.

The following eight chapters attempt to capture the complexity of the relationship between universities innovation and economic development. Chapter 1 briefly reviews the history of university–industry interaction and sets out a conceptual framework, comprising eight paradigms, which are used to frame the analysis for the remaining chapters. Chapter 2 sets out the conceptual explanations for why the university's territorial role might be developed and why it is also problematic. It discusses what the expectations of what the universe of linkages might be and what role proximity plays in those. A threefold distinction is made between the co-presence of universities and economic activity, linkages which arise from proximity, and those which are orchestrated as a result of policy initiatives which place universities within a system of local governance. Chapter 3 examines the evidence for the impact of universities on economic development, defining what indicators are used, the useful and limitations of those tools and what the results tell us. Chapter 4 is about universities in innovation systems in Europe and describes the main trends and discusses how, although the territorial role has become universal, there is considerable diversity in the form that this takes. Chapter 6 discusses the contribution of universities to innovation and economic development through the development and enhancement of labour markets. In Chapter 7, case studies of the twin towns of Oxford and Grenoble illustrate similarities but also diversity in relationships between the science base and economic development arising from historical and current political policy interventions, local dynamics and institutional strategies. Chapter 8 takes the same approach as Chapter 7 to the US, comparing three universities, Stanford, Louisville and Princeton. As the chapter demonstrates, there are tensions within the US system showing that similar questions are being asked to those in the UK about the expectations placed on universities to deliver economic development. To conclude, Chapter 9 revisits the eight paradigms to review the evidence on the relationship between universities, innovation and economic development per se and to highlight the complex interdependent factors which shape relationships between universities and their geographical hinterlands.

1   New paradigms in the twenty-first century

Introduction

The long history of close collaboration between the university and industry dates back at least to the eighteenth century in Europe and to the nineteenth century in the US. The contemporary policy emphasis on the territorial role in which universities are encouraged to be entrepreneurial and spin-out new firms, to engage more closely with firms in their immediate hinterland and to take on social responsibilities, reflects the current prioritization of regionalism and clusters which is to be found throughout the world.

In this chapter, the context and drivers of the quality and extent of relationship between universities and economic development are explored, beginning with a brief history of the universities' economic development role. This shows that although much is new in the form that relationships take, many of the current practices and modes of interaction were found in nineteenth- and twentieth-century Europe and the US – and in some cases even earlier. From this overview, a number of paradigms are derived which will be used as the analytical framework for the rest of the book.

A historical perspective

Universities' involvement in civic and industrial projects in Europe dates back to at least the eighteenth century. Schwerin (2004) details how in Scotland the construction of the improved steam engine by Glasgow University's instrument maker James Watt in 1765 was soon applied to factory steam engines and later facilitated the construction of steamships. The demand for skilled workers for machinery for the cotton industry and steam power prompted the founding of the University of Strathclyde in 1896. Its focus on engineering and technology transfer complemented the ancient university of Glasgow. A close relationship between Clyde shipbuilding industry and the Glasgow universities existed from the 1820s with a handful of academics taking key positions within the local innovation system (page 28). In nineteenth-century Britain universities were also involved in actions to improve public health in growing and insalubrious towns and cities as well as safety and working conditions in mines and factories (Pavitt 2003, 91).

In the US, public universities were established expressly with a primary motive of engaging with industry (Adams 2002, 275). The Morrill Act 1862 granted land for the establishment of one college in a state with its primary objective the teaching of courses in agriculture and mechanical arts. By the end of the nineteenth century, industries were able to draw on the growing number of schools of applied science and technology, such as the Sheffield Scientific School at Yale and the Massachusetts Institute of Technology as well as government academies such as the US Military Academy (Charles and Howells 1992). Universities have played a central role in the US system of innovation. Prior to the establishment of the modern corporate laboratory, the university was the main source of expertise (Kodama and Branscomb 1999, 5).

The current debate about these relationships has a long history. B. Martin (2003, 8) traces the development of the contemporary 'social contract' between science and the university and the state. He finds that the Humboldt university model spread from Germany to other parts of Europe in the nineteenth and twentieth centuries (although not to France and England) and others have suggested that this model was still influential in the US as late as 1930 (Herbst 2004, 15). Under the Humboldt social contract, the government assumed primary responsibility for funding the university, the key characteristic of the model was the unity of teaching and research – the assumption that both functions had to be conducted within the same institution – and was characterized by a high level of autonomy for both individuals and institutions, which formed a key characteristic of the Vannevar Bush agenda, conditions which Powers (2003) argues are still critical today.

Yet as well as the mission to undertake fundamental research, German universities also undertook research largely directed by industry, especially the chemical industry. In both Europe and the US the rapid rise of the chemical and pharmaceutical industries was associated with successful collaboration with academic scientists. Moreover, although American firms and universities worked together, this was not on the same scale and intensity as in Germany until the interwar period (see the discussion in Charles and Howells 1992, 11). This is related to the evolution of science-based industry in the late nineteenth and twentieth centuries, in particular the rise of the industrial R&D laboratory (Florida and Cohen 1999, 593).

In the twentieth century, in the UK and the US, systemic government policy and practice, like other major changes in government policy and expenditure, have taken place during wars as the government has taken on greater responsibility for functions that would otherwise be uncoordinated (Yarrow and Lawton Smith 1993). In the UK, for example, in the middle of the First World War, in 1916, the Department for Scientific and Industrial Research established the 'Application of Scientific Research to Trade and Industry' (Philips 1994, 40). In the US, the Naval Consulting Board brought together industry, government and academics to help organize US naval research (Charles and Howells 1992). There too major collaborative initiatives in pharmaceuticals manufacture, petrochemicals and synthetic rubber were launched during the Second World War, and the National Advisory Committee on Aeronautics, founded in 1915 and absorbed into NASA in 1958, made important contributions to aircraft design throughout its existence. Likewise university–industry research collaboration was well established in the 1920s and 1930s and contributed to the development of the academic discipline of chemical engineering, transforming the chemical industry (Mowery 1998) as well as being in the van of the creation of new fields of technological knowledge which then drive new industries (Rosenberg and Nelson 1994).

History and structure

The close relationship between US universities and industry, particularly between the Land Grant universities and industry, dates back to the nineteenth century. Following the formation of Land Grant universities established under the 1862 Morrill Act, that relationship took the form of practical collaboration and the provision of vocational skills for a wide range of professions important to local communities (Rosenberg and Nelson 1994, 324). Even as early as the 1880s, universities such as MIT, a Land Grant university which was established as a technical university in 1861, were providing trained engineers for growing firms such as General Electric and Westinghouse, introducing its first courses in 1882 (Saxenian 1994). The tradition of Land Grant universities undertaking generic industrial research has remained. For example, in the early 1980s, 37 universities were performing research for local and regional forest product industries (Rosenberg and Nelson 1994). This field, with agriculture, particularly with the advent of bioengineered seeds and plants, areas in which Land Grant universities specialize, maintains the link (Powers 2003).

This was unlike centralized systems such as France, as universities chose their own route to working with industry, an autonomy which has remained (Etzkowitz 2003; Rosenberg and Nelson 1994). This autonomy can be traced back to the European, particularly German model, adopted by many of the early universities. The nineteenth century German model of a single professor representing a discipline surrounded by permanent staff of assistants broke down to be replaced with a model in which departments comprised professors of different grades with relative autonomy, with support staff. Throughout the twentieth century schools of engineering such as at Stanford provided leadership in engineering and applied science research. Rosenberg and Nelson find that universities played a critical role in the emergence of the discipline of chemical engineering and aeronautical engineering and more recently in computer science and engineering and biotechnology. They also argue that scholars did not come to dominate universities – as was the case in European universities.

US universities underwent two major transformations from the nineteenth century (Etzkowitz *et al.* 2000). The first was the 'first academic revolution' associated with the paucity of research funds in the context of the new role of research. Until the 1920s this was of the hands-on problem-solving kind. Therefore the success of universities depended on responsiveness to the demands of the local communities. The second was in the post-Second World War period when 'similar pressures were brought to bear on universities, so encouraging the need to secure additional income, the wider, and more fundamental impact of the knowledge-based economy ... which ensured this process was of a qualitatively distinct order to that of the previous century'.

The Vannevar Bush social contract (1945 to the end of the 1980s), published in Bush's 1945 report, 'Science, the Endless Frontier', was based on state support for science and university autonomy – the separation of scientific communities from the rest of society (Geuna *et al.* 2003), the maintenance of defence R&D, public support for medical R&D and for federal government to assume responsibility for supporting basic research. R&D to improve existing products and processes became almost exclusively the province of industry in fields where firms had strong R&D capabilities (Rosenberg and Nelson 1994). This research policy which also had its parallels in Europe was about winning new scientific knowledge (Pavitt 2003, Martin, B. 2003, Edqvist 2003). B. Martin (2003, 9) describes the characteristics of the Bush social contract as:

- high level of autonomy for science
- decisions on what should be funded should be left to scientists
- basic research was best done in universities.

Martin argues that the Bush social contract was very successful in the post-Second World War period, especially in the US, contributing to large increases in funding for science and an expansion of the number of both trained scientists and research outputs. He suggests that an alternative view of the period 1921–53 (and ever since) is that it has been mythologized as the period in which there was a 'common view' of a broad-based consensual commitment on the part of the Federal government to increased support for basic research and development.

In the 1960s the essential link between high-technology industry and universities was made in the US by Frederick Terman, renowned for making Stanford University one of the world's leading research universities. He expressed the view that universities are 'major influences in the nation's industrial life, affecting the location of industry, population groups and the character of communities' (cited in Taylor 1985, 141). In the UK, the famous letter by Prime Minister Harold Wilson of 1966 to all universities in the country exhorted them to develop their own science parks and encourage the growth of high-technology concerns. It was as a direct response to the Wilson letter that the seeds of Trinity College, Cambridge, and the Heriot-Watt science parks were sown (Taylor 1985, 137).

By the middle of the 1960s, science policy, 'the designation given to the purposeful, politically-framed activity of funding research with public money' (Edqvist 2003, 208), was constructed in a time of rapid techno-logical change associated with the beginning of the era of advances in elec-tronics and software. By the 1970s the US and other countries such as the UK were pursuing domestic co-operative technology policies designed to improve technological innovation performance downstream (Stoneman 1987) (see Allen *et al.* 1978 and Gummett and Gibbons 1978). Thus, Pavitt (2003) argues, the twentieth- and twenty-first-century phenomenon of an active role contributing to economic growth and political expectation that university-based research will be tied to broader social objectives is a return to the nineteenth-century paradigm of usefulness. More than this, universities are de facto engaged in global competition for eminence, as illustrated by the increasing number of world and European rankings of universities and national assessments of performance, which include a range of criteria which relate to scientific excellence including scientific publications and external income and also to their usefulness measured by external income (Chapter 3).

The late twentieth-century territorial role, which authors such as Wolfe, D. (2003, 99–100) would see as a natural extension of the observation that proximity is important 'in the transfer of knowledge from the institutions that generate it to those that adopt and apply it', can be seen as an exten-sion of a system in which cumulatively-superimposed layers date back to the 1940s. This progression is illustrated in Box 1.1 following Edqvist (2003) who in turn built on Ruivo (1994).

Box 1.1 Policy progression from the 1940s to the present day.

Science as a source of strategic opportunity – 1940s
Science as a problem solver – 1960s
Science as a motor of progress – 1990s

And now
Science as a driver of regional economic development – late 1990s/2000s

Sources: Adapted from Edqvist 2003

For Edqvist (page 210) the issue is not how new ideas will replace the old, but how they compete with, absorb and transform their predecessors, and he concludes that there is 'a conflict between the different layers, with different understandings of the purpose and the role of science'. So we see at the beginning of the twenty-first century internal and external debates about universities' contribution to economic development taking place within the context of a growing internationalization of markets for students, increasing dependence of technology on science and especially basic research (EC 2003b, 413) and multiple accountabilities. Universities are very much part of the 'new economy', the hallmarks of which are networks, innovation and knowledge and collaboration (Martin *et al.* 2003).

In sum, eight interconnected paradigms can be observed which collectively describe the current expectations on universities as to their contribution to innovation and economic development. First, the innovation process is increasingly integrative as firms seek inputs from a range of organizations including other firms, universities and national laboratories. Second, although there is a common agenda of university and industry interaction across Europe and the US – as there is indeed in other parts of the world – the form that it takes is extremely diverse at the national, regional/local and institutional level. Third, universities' 'quest for eminence' (Florida and Cohen 1999) has a number of utilitarian functions relating to funding and political reward. A fourth trend is a growing questioning of the role of universities and the consequences for higher education from within academia and from other analysts regarding new sets of accountability in relation to the economic development role per se as well as the territorial role. This is accompanied by a far greater public awareness of the ethics of research in areas such as stem cell research (particularly in the US) and genetically modified foods (particularly in Europe) which have profound effects on the location of scientific research and the commercialization of that research. Fifth, the life-sciences–biotechnology–pharma nexus has assumed significant importance in national innovation systems and has strong parallels with the university–defence nexus of the Cold War period. Sixth, there is a growing academic and policy-maker recognition of expanding and improving the human capital base as the key to successful technology transfer. Seventh, the entrepreneurial university has become the model for the twenty-first century. Last, related to the previous trend, increasing resources are allocated to universities and local/regional organizations for fostering the localization effects of technology transfer and translating that into economic development. This amounts to a formalization and integration of universities into local/regional systems of governance to achieve that end. These paradigms form the analytical framework for this book. Following sections expand on these and succeeding chapters review the conceptual and empirical underpinnings.

Paradigms

Within the following paradigms are implicit, normative and positive assumptions from a number of stakeholders about the position of universities in relation to innovation and economic development. These include, for example, industry; the universities and individual academics; organizations that represent both the institutions and the individuals nationally and internationally such as the Worldwide Universities Network (www.wun.ac.uk/); supra-national policy-making institutions such as the European Commission and the European Patent Agency; and national, regional and local policy-making bodies.

Paradigm 1 Innovation as a distributed and integrated process

Central to the argument that society will gain from the greater integration of university and industry research and development is the observation that the innovation process has been evolving from being less compartmentalized to being more fluid. In this paradigm, increasingly all stages and sub-processes of innovation are less likely to be conceived and implemented within one distinct enterprise and instead are likely to be 'distributed' across several enterprises or other institutions (Coombs and Metcalfe 2000, 50), so becoming a much more integrated and social process (Oinas and Malecki 2002) (see also Edquist 1997). Not only does industry now draw on a wide range of external resources, but university science and engineering are becoming cross-disciplinary (Llerena and Meyer-Krahmer 2003) and academics engage in joint scientific projects with colleagues in both academia and industry on an increasingly global scale (Archibugi and Iammarino 2002, 101). Much of this has been driven by financial incentives, for example in the European Union under its own R&D programmes such as ESPRIT (information technology) and RACE (advanced communications technology) (see Charles and Howells 1992 for a discussion). At the same time, basic research is global in application and does not necessarily relate to the region in which it takes place (Godden 2003, 23).

The blurring of boundaries is captured in Gibbons *et al.*'s (1994) distinction between Mode 1 and Mode 2 knowledge. Mode 1 knowledge is homogeneous, disciplinary and hierarchical and reflects the way that knowledge has traditionally been produced in autonomous and distinct academic disciplines. Mode 2 knowledge, in contrast, is heterarchical, transient, transdisciplinary, socially accountable and reflexive and undertaken in a context of application. The recent emergence of transdisciplinary research centres within HEIs, which engage with external research partners and increasingly rely on third-stream funding sources (developing their capability and responsiveness to the needs of business and other organizations in the wider community – www.hefce.ac.uk/reachout/news/3stream.htm), can be situated within this new mode of knowledge production (OECD 1999, 81). Pavitt (2003, 90), however, is somewhat sceptical of this divide and argues that the modes co-exist and that Mode 2 existed before Mode 1 and they are complementary. Mode 2 is seen by some as the normative model for university–industry interaction. For example, Rutten *et al.* (2003, 247) argue that universities must adopt the Mode 2 model in order to be part of the knowledge-producing sector as this is 'the only way in which HEIs can make a substantial contribution to (regional) economic development'.

The distinction between basic and applied science, and hence the nature of the relationship between these and each other and to commercial potential through transfer of technology, misrepresents the pattern of research activities (see Stokes 1997 in Hughes 2003). Stokes, amongst others, has argued that a substantial proportion of university and publicly funded research has always combined considerations both of use and of the pursuit of fundamental understanding. Stokes's diagram of Pasteur's Quadrant (Figure 1.1) illustrates the misleading dichotomous approach in the linear model. The diagram draws a distinction between research that is solely concerned with use, typified by the work of Edison; research that is solely concerned with fundamental understanding, typified by the work of Bohr; and research that involves both, typified by Pasteur, which Stokes demonstrates has a long and distinguished role in the research structure of natural sciences.

The problem for technology policy, therefore, according to Hughes, has three dimensions. The first is how to encourage the importance of Pasteur's Quadrant in scientific and policy discourse. The second is how to promote or support activity in Pasteur's Quadrant by enabling scientific recognition of society's concerns with particular areas of use as a stimulus for the pursuit of fundamental understanding in relevant areas. The third is to how to encourage communication and interaction between the quadrant communities. On this interpretation the success of the US in

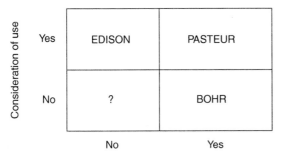

Figure 1.1 Pasteur's Quadrant (sources: Stokes 1997; Hughes 2003).

industrializing knowledge is to be understood less in terms of specific policy initiatives to transform basic into applied research than in the ability of its university system to populate all three boxes and enable inter-action across them. This, Hughes argues, has been the result of the decen-tralized, competitive and regional structure of the system and its close coupling of research and graduate education, plus diverse streams of funding and a close relationship of universities with state and regional research needs.

Evidence for the increasingly distributed innovation processes, particu-larly from the 1980s, is found in numerous studies which have documented the growth in the use of external research and technical resources by firms including collaborating or contracting out their R&D, design and engin-eering needs partly in response to the rising costs of conducting R&D (Wolfe, D. 2003, 93; see also Charles and Howells 1992; Katz and Martin 1997; Lawton Smith 2000). Estimates of the rate of return to publicly funded research range between 20 per cent and 60 per cent (Salter and Martin 2001). Returns are dependent on firms acquiring knowledge and information produced by public research organizations (PROs) (universi-ties, public research institutes and government laboratories) and success-fully applying this information to their innovative activities (Arundel and Geuna 2001, 3). The gains to universities are that inputs from industry provide scientists with information that provides a better understanding of the nature of the task, which aids in designing research programmes and conducting experiments (Stephan 2001, Poyago-Theotoky *et al.* 2002).

The many forms through which interaction takes place between univer-sities and industry are summarized below (adapted from Lawton Smith 1990). These include commercial and non-commercial activities, the inci-dence of which does not vary only by institution or by country. For example, general endowment plays a much greater role in the funding of research in the US than in the UK, while academic entrepreneurship is much less common in France and Germany than in the US and UK.

1   Transfer of non-commercial knowledge and expertise

- graduated students
- academic publications
- informal networks of contacts
- part-time secondment by academics to industry
- part-time secondment of industrialists to academia
- joint professorships in industry and academia
- industrial liaison services.

2   General research support

- speculative research paid for by industry in a university department
- general endowment

- gifts of money provided for specific purposes
- gifts of equipment (sometimes latest technology, but often out of date).

3 Co-operative research

- interaction requiring some degree of co-operative planning e.g. national joint research programmes and joint consortia
- UK KTP scheme
- collaboration in specially supported programmes
- collaborators in international programmes
- appointment of industrial fellows
- joint industry/university studentships e.g. UK CASE, France CIFRE schemes.

4 Commercial ventures by universities

- short-term contract research on a specific problem
- industrial centres and units operating on a commercial basis
- testing services e.g. carbon dating, equipment testing
- licensing of inventions
- joint industry/university ventures
- companies set up by universities/departments to exploit intellectual property
- university/colleges directly investing in local companies
- universities/colleges establishing science parks
- establishment of holding and administrative companies for university owned companies
- companies set up by universities to market university intellectual property.

5 Commercial activities by academics, technicians and students

- consultancy
- academics on boards of companies
- companies set up by academics and technicians to exploit intellectual property or to develop equipment needed by departments.

The potential benefits from R&D collaboration to industry and universities are summarized in Table 1.1. Although these have been characterized as one or the other, they are also common goods where society benefits from the gains from this process through the creation of new jobs, better products and services and raising the pool of resource income through wealth creation that can be used to benefit society as a whole. Many of these can be measured, although the process of measurement and what is actually measured are subject to much debate, not least because most long-run effects are indirect and difficult to quantify (Candell and Jaffe 1999) (Chapter 3).

Table 1.1 Gains to university–industry interaction

Gains to industry	Gains to university
Productivity gains and business innovation	Better able to conduct research and experiments with input from industry science
Enabling firms to capture knowledge spillovers	Facilitating and accelerating the transfer of research results from universities or public laboratories to industry
Reducing duplication of firms' R&D investments	Increased financial resources for research or teaching
Supporting the exploitation of scale economies in R&D	Increased contract funding for further developments into a final product
Support access of industrial firms to R&D capabilities in labs	Increasing funding for research enables larger-scale research projects
Supporting the creation of a common technological 'vision' within industry that can guide R&D and related investments by public and private entities	Funding for research that is relevant to industry and provides up-to-date teaching material
Creation and development of human capital, increased performance	Funding for students, research assistants and post-doctoral students

Sources: Goldstein and Renault 2004; Mowery 1998; Geuna and Nesta 2003.

At the same time, this is not a universal pattern. Studies have demonstrated that some industries develop without extensive engagement with universities, while others show that industrial innovation has a life cycle through which universities are important at some stage, usually the early stage (Faulkner and Senker 1995; Lawton Smith 2000; Charles and Howells 1992; Nelson 1988; Tushman *et al.* 1997; Nooteboom 1999, 2000; Glasmeier 2000).

Paradigm 2 Diversity versus uniformity and systems of governance

Common to much of the recent literature on innovation is a focus on systemic features rather than on isolated events associated with heroic scientists or engineers (Bunnell and Coe 2001; Shapira 2004a). Interest in national innovation systems lies in the systemic character of innovation and the key role given to the state as co-ordinator and last-resort decision-maker (Noisi 2003). Policies at the national and supra-national level have been based on the assumption that there is an interaction deficit within innovation systems and across national innovation systems (Geuna *et al.*

2003). Hence, the interplay at the national level of education, science and technology as well as industry and other policies constructs the rules of the game by which the commercialization function is prioritized over other activities, which in turn is how the client group(s) is/are defined at particular moments in time. This prioritization within a NIS determines the incentives (often involving funding) for the commercialization of research, for the accessibility of knowledge to industry and to wider communities, and how outcomes are evaluated.

The national innovation systems (NIS) concept, which had its roots in early work by Freeman (1987), is based on two related assumptions (David and Foray 1995). These are, first, that technical capabilities lie at the core of a country's international competitiveness and, second, that the development of such capabilities is influenced by issues of national localization and can be managed by way of proper government action. The position of universities in this framework is that the purpose of knowledge institutions is to increase take-up of technology. What makes countries differ is not only the strength of national scientific resources (Grupp 1995) but also on the distribution power of their innovation systems (David and Foray 1995; Foray 1997). This is defined as nations' capacity to ensure timely access by innovators to stocks of knowledge held in its institutions and firms. OECD (2002a, 8) reinforces the notion that it is the national system of innovation that has primacy while arguing that individual institutions are the best place to determine the practice of industry–science relations, and that it is governments which have responsibility for setting the basic rules and institutional frameworks that reflect the public interest but provide the right incentives to firms, public researchers and organisations alike.

While each country has its own specific institutional structures and national innovation systems agenda, there are two main models (OECD/IHME 1999, 28):

- the centralized model in which the national government is the main source of funding e.g. Finland, France, Hungary, Italy, Japan, New Zealand and the UK
- the decentralized model where regional authorities are the main source of funds – Australia, Canada, Germany, Spain and the US.

Recent studies have emphasized that innovation systems are constantly being reconfigured because the roles of knowledge institutions tend to change over time (Edquist 1997; Gregerson and Johnson 1999; Lundvall and Maskell 2000). In the 1980s and 1990s, Italy, France, the UK and the US among many countries introduced major legislation which changed the basis on which universities interact with industry. For example in 1999 France introduced reforms which were designed to encourage academic entrepreneurship. Llerena *et al.* (2003), however, are sceptical about

whether the reforms have in fact delivered the necessary university autonomy – the essential condition.

Other research has challenged the primacy of the national system of
innovation. This is because firms and researchers are entwined in thick
networks of international relationships that cut across national barriers
(Brusoni and Geuna forthcoming). While some of these networks are
associated with the activities of transnational corporations who collaborate
directly with universities in non-home countries and through consortia
such as EU and international programmes, in other cases small firms are
engaged in similar kinds of collaborative activity (see for example Lawton
Smith 2000). Moreover, missing in the NIS analysis is the relationship
between supra-national agencies – such as the European Union – and
international regulatory regimes. Indeed comparisons between Europe
and the US have often under estimated the importance of high levels of
public funding for basic research in conjunction with the multiplicity of
entrepreneurial funding agencies that target new lines of enquiry, and over
estimated the ability to commercialize technology (Geuna and Martin
2003). Yet another way of assessing the economic impact is to look at the
contribution to exports. For example, in Australia, the HE system is the
largest national export industry, exceeding strong sectors such as agriculture (see OECD 1999, 39).

Paradigm 3 Eminence

Lundvall (1988, 364–5) described the academic mode of behaviour in a
more innocent age: that science is produced in universities as a result of
non-pecuniary incentives and that the 'search for excellency' is a strong
motive power. Citing David (1984) he believed that 'the output of science
will be widely dispersed because the world-wide diffusion of research
results is a precondition of excellency'. He also perhaps ahead of his time
recognized the dangers of subordinating academic activities to industry:
'that the academic mode might lose one of its principal merits – the tradition for world-wide diffusion of knowledge'. Now academic eminence not
only implies distinction in scientific endeavour, it can be ranked and has a
utilitarian value.

Herbst's (2004, 17) assertion that a substantial performance gradient
separates US research universities from the rest of the world is supported
by a world ranking of universities published in 2004. (Institute of Higher
Education, Shanghai Jiao Tong University ed.sjtu.edu.cn/ranking.htm.
Universities were ranked by several indicators of academic or research
performance, including alumni and staff winning Nobel Prizes and Fields
Medals, highly cited researchers, articles published in *Nature* and *Science*,
articles in *Science Citation Index-expanded* and *Social Science Citation
Index*, and academic performance with respect to the size of an institu-
tion.) This shows that the US has the most eminent universities: eight of

the top ten are US universities and all but 15 of the top 50 universities are American. Two UK universities are in the top ten: Cambridge (fifth) and Oxford (ninth). The top non-UK EU university is the Netherlands' University of Utrecht (39th) with Paris 6 41st. A more recent ranking of the world's top 200 universities produced by the UK's *Times Higher Education Supplement* (2004), using a different set of indicators, finds the US still dominating the top places in the list, with seven in the top ten, with Oxford and Cambridge fifth and sixth. ETH Zurich is tenth, but the top non-UK European university was the Ecole Polytechnique in France (27th). An elite grouping of these leading research universities – the 'global elite 8' – including Yale and University of California, Berkeley (UCB) in the US, ETH Zurich and Tokyo University have formed a consortium designed to 'increase opportunities for global research, teaching and learning through faculty collaboration and exchange, research training cooperation, undergraduate and post-graduate student exchange, joint/double degree programmes, exchange of best practices and protocols and benchmarking' (Jobbins 2005, 6).

The European Commission (2003b) ranked top national institutions at member state level using the indicators of number of publications, number of citations, and citation impact. The last indicates whether or not a university's scientific publications in leading academic journals are cited more often (or not) than publications in those journals on average. The leading universities of each country were then ranked against each other on performance in more than 20 disciplines, ranging from clinical medicine to electrical engineering. London University came top in both the number of publications and citations, by some considerable distance. Paris 6 and Milan University were ranked second and third respectively. Cambridge University had the highest overall university impact scores. When European universities were ranked according to citation impact against the world average, 22 EU universities scored above the world average. The top two were Cambridge and Oxford, followed by Eindhoven University of Technology and Technical University of Munich. Eight countries were represented in the 22 with seven universities from the Netherlands, five from Germany and four from the UK included. The Commission Report also finds that Europe's performance is around average in 11 broad fields of science, and therefore inferior to that in the US.

In Europe, particularly in the UK, a political debate is taking place on how far the elite model should be replicated. The question is whether governments should promote a greater concentration of resources in a limited number of research centres or should make efforts to raise the qualitative level at the national level (Cesaroni and Piccaluga 2003, 2). In the UK academics and politicians have expressed serious misgivings about the 'government's drive to further concentrate research in top rated departments and universities' (Thomson and Goddard 2003). Haines (2003) asks, 'would the University of Westminster (which was given a 3b in the RAE

1996) who designed the modem for Nokia and Ericksson mobile phones have been able to do their research if their funding settlement has been dismissive of work of "attainable national excellence"?'

Eminence is also an aspect of the conditions under which universities engage in economic development and is considered to be instrumental in overcoming market failure particularly in context of markets for knowledge (Sine *et al.* 2003). These authors demonstrate that institutional prestige increases a university's licensing rate over and above the rate that is explained by the university's past licensing performance. Because licensing success positively impacts future invention production, they argue that institutional prestige leads to stratification in the creation and distribution of university-generated knowledge. Prestigious universities have a disproportionate influence on the evolution of technology not because they are necessarily superior creators of technology but because their prestige facilitates technology transfer. Moreover, if more prestigious institutions are better able to diffuse knowledge than less prestigious institutions, then inventors from high-prestige institutions will have a disproportionate effect on technological change in society. Another take on this is that the more eminent scientists are better able to maintain research output and quality. Zucker and Darby (1996), Louis *et al.* (2001) and Siegel *et al.* (1999) all found that faculty members involved in commercialization projects typically re-invest their profits in laboratory equipment and additional post-doc researchers, reinforcing their research capacity and maintaining their positions. On the other hand, Geiger (2003, 6) finds that firms seeking research assistance with product development or applied research will sacrifice prestige in research partners – which makes local partners more attractive. 'Local partners have the additional advantage of promoting closer interaction with company researchers and greater ease of hiring students'.

Paradigm 4 Defence and biotechnology

From the Second World War onwards, defence expenditure dominated national R&D expenditure and underpinned large sections of the economy. In the third quarter of the twentieth century, the biotech sector became the 'new defence industry'. A massive explosion in research funding in universities and other research institutions in the public and private sectors and their close ties with industrial customers (big-pharma, agbio companies, biotech companies) mimic patterns in the defence industry. On the other hand, while defence spending was a hidden regional policy (Boddy 1988) and the origins of successful high-tech clusters based on defence technologies tended to be suppressed for ideological reasons (Eisinger 1988 in Etzkowitz 2003), the biotech sector is identified as a key driver of economic development at national and regional levels. Moreover, unlike defence, where public concerns have been expressed about weaponry rather than the research process, controversies about the ethics of research and applications of bio-technologies are in the forefront of public debate.

The importance of university research to drug development is illustrated by the case of the three biggest pharmaceutical companies in the UK donating £4 million to medical research at universities (including Oxford) that involves animals. Animal testing is one of a number of factors which drug companies, which are major funders of university research, take into account in locating their research. For the UK, safety fears are speculated to drive research abroad, especially to the US. Other factors include prices paid for medicines by health care services and the quality of the science base – which is where the UK competes strongly (Firn 2004, 3). In the US a study of developments in medical treatments in cardiovascular-pulmonary medicine found that nearly half of the conceptual steps in the ten most important treatments came from basic researchers (NIGMS/NIH 1997).

Paradigm 5 Accountability and responsibility

Throughout the long engagement with industry, debates about ethics, problems relating to the freedom of publication and other barriers to flows of information have taken place (see Charles and Howells 1992). This is one aspect of the increasingly complex issue of to whom or what and why universities are accountable and what their responsibilities are in relation to innovation and economic development. The number of stakeholders interested in universities' performance has increased over time and now include: policy makers at national and regional levels, government and non-commercial funders of university research, the universities and their individual academics whose careers are assessed on particular criteria, students whose education may be affected by these changes, industry and society at large. Transformations in HEI systems have raised questions about accountability.

Five questions are open to debate. The first is, what is the function of universities in relation to the generation and diffusion of knowledge? The second is, how should the ownership of that knowledge be managed and how does that affect their performance? Third, how should universities' performance on both criteria be evaluated? Fourth, how can universities' greater involvement in economic development be of political benefit? Fifth, what are the consequences of changes to the first three?

For the first, in the opinion of Paul David and his colleagues (David *et al.* 1994, 19), the primary and unique function of universities is to be the 'node in the open knowledge-generating network'. Second, related to this is the question of the rights of universities to their intellectual property and the terms of trade with which they engage with industry. David and Foray (1995) identify three dimensions of knowledge affecting generation, acquisition and distribution processes: (1) degree of codification, (2) completeness of disclosure, and (3) ownership status. These are used to define a space in which various types of economically relevant science and technology can be located. They make the distinction between 'open science' which may be associated with academic research, including government-sponsored and even business-sponsored research conducted under 'university-like' organizational norms affecting the autonomy of individual researchers. In the world of 'proprietary science' research is undertaken with the intention and quasi-contractual pre-commitment of the researchers to the organizational goal of extracting economic rents from the knowledge gained, either by keeping it a secret and using it in directly productive activities that end in the sale of conventional commodities, or by converting some or all of the knowledge into assets that, as legally protected property, can be readily owned and alienated for valuable consideration. For David *et al.* (1994) the issue is not whether such involvements are mutually beneficial to the participants or the public at large. Rather they take the issue to be the terms on which such involvement can be established, and whether they allow the university's ability to function as an open knowledge-network node to be perpetuated. For Geuna and Nesta (2003, 4) the paradigm shift has gone so far that, rather than the dominant norm being that universities are mainly engaged in managing research agreements in firms, now the primary task of technology transfer is to 'assess and protect IP and make it available to industry'. They argue that positive impacts will occur only if the costs of the technology transfer operation are counterbalanced by income. Evidence from the US and Europe is that most universities do not make a profit through the technology transfer offices and/or through IPRs.

Third, the recognition of the commercial potential of university research is being matched by an increase in measures designed to evaluate the outputs of universities, public laboratories and programmes designed to improve flows of knowledge between these bodies and industry. The performance of countries, regions, institutions, departments and individuals and programmes are increasingly benchmarked (see for example OECD 2002a: *Benchmarking industry–science relationships* (IRS), Boekholt 2003 and Morgan and Nauwelaers 1999). The range of interested parties in industry–science relationships (ISR) is indicated by OECD (2002a, 7) which states that

> To benchmark ISR is to compare their relative efficiency in meeting and reconciling the needs of the main stakeholders (government, industry, public research organizations, civil society), and to relate differences in performance to observable characteristics of industry-science linkages, which are amenable to public policy. To this end, industry and science linkages should be evaluated along three dimensions: nature and relative importance of channels of interactions; their

incentive structures; and their institutional arrangements. Which leave a big hole where aspects are not amenable to public policy.

Shapira and Kuhlmann's (2003) edited book tackles the issues of the evaluation of public policy structures and initiatives designed to advance research innovation and technology. As they point out from discussion of the US case – which is generally applicable – 'science and technology evaluation is clearly influenced by broader political and societal change' (page 8 and see Cozzens same volume). Cozzens (2003, 59) argues that a sea change occurred after the Second World War in research and innovation policy which involved the claim by university-based researchers for relative autonomy within the larger political system. Since then 'US science policy has been characterized by a tension between autonomy and accountability'. Those adopting the former position want to justify Federal investments in research on the basis of general claims about the contributions of science and technology to prosperity while those who espouse the latter perspective want those benefits to be demonstrated concretely. The merits of the latter approach is implied by Kuhlmann (2003), who argues that a more deliberate effort to better integrate evaluation and science and technology assessment techniques into innovation systems, with a view to improving understanding and inform future policies through the use of 'strategic intelligence', should be adopted. He also suggests that the key concept of the new wider understanding of evaluation is 'negotiation' among participating actors, whereby decisions are made as a continuous process and evaluation results are one piece of information amongst many, and the process is participative – although not easily achieved in practice.

Fourth, the politics of why universities might see it to be in their own best interests to engage overtly in the process of economic development lie in three possible avenues to political reward (Bozeman 2000). The most common is for the laboratory to be rewarded for the appearance of active and aggressive pursuit of technology transfer and commercial success – but this might make the form of the activity being its own reward and publicity for activities being part of the game. Other less common avenues are the laboratory being rewarded with increased funding for demonstrating technology transfer and the recipient of technology transfer communicating to the policy makers the value of its interaction. Bozeman also notes there is a close connection in the US between the growth of research on technology transfer and that of policies and government activities relating to technology transfer. Kenney (1986) earlier argued that universities legitimate ideology, thus being both responsive to and for the entrepreneurial agenda.

Fifth, as well as the gains to interaction, one of the negative consequences of the closer integration is the lack of universities' ability to function as an 'open node'. Noble's (1977) corporate manipulation thesis essentially argues that corporations interfere with the normal pursuit of academic science and seek to control relevant university research for their own ends. An early version of this is reported by Florida and Cohen (1999, 593) who cited Chemistry and Engineering departments in the US at the start of the twentieth century which were host to a deep struggle between faculty who wanted to pursue applied, industry-oriented research and other faculty who wanted to study anything so long as it was basic research. This was particularly deep at MIT (Servos in Florida and Cohen 1999, 594) where departments that became dependent on industry lost eminence as prestigious faculty members moved away. One goal of postwar government funding was to counteract this negative impact of industrial support.

Others such as Paul David (see for example 2005) are sceptical about the current focus on commercialization. Van Reenan (2002, 18) for example, argues that there are risks to the public policy of encouraging universities to commercialize more of their research. There is a genuine concern that protecting of IP in universities could undermine open science that gives moral incentives for academics to do pioneering research. As long ago as 1986, Kenney highlighted the conflicts of interest in the US biotech industry 'which stem from the fact that nearly all of the biotechnology researchers have university appointments and yet work for and sometimes own substantial interests in companies that are commercialising biotechnological research' (page 113). In the UK a report published in 2003 by the Royal Society, 'Keeping Science Open', highlighted a 'most unhealthy "gold rush" mentality' originating in biotech but infecting other fields. The Royal Society (2003, v) expressed a belief 'that public funding of the UK science base should be based on quality, since high quality research is the gateway to both advances in knowledge and to wealth creation based on science'.

Coombs and Metcalfe (2000) argue that the challenge for both the universities and the policy makers is to ensure that the quality of research in the universities is not lost in the drive to align the interests of universities and business. In the US, similar problems of open science versus control and access to research findings and the loss of commitment to teaching, shifting attention away from fundamental research questions, have been found (Stephan 2001) and distrust created between adviser and students. Conflicts have been reported in Chicago, Columbia and Cornell universities (Marshall 1999 in Poyago-Theotoky *et al.* 2002).

The controversy over the potential to patent human genes is a further dimension to the issue of accountability and has a direct impact on what can be undertaken in the lab. For example, animals are patentable in the US and Japan but not in the EU. Patenting may slow down the research to innovation process. Moreover, researchers working with pharmaceutical companies realize that there is a choice of where to undertake clinical trials, but have their own moral stance and personally imposed standards on what is acceptable. Salter and Frewer (2002, 14) observe:

As one moves from pure research knowledge through its development, so there is an engagement between scientific and industrial interest in the process of standard setting. In the health arena, the state apparatus of medicines control, the CSM and the MCA, mediates that process. In this context it is interesting to note Abraham's observation that 'because the science base is so malleable, social and political factors may enter into medicines regulation *under the guise of problem solving* with relative ease, and when they do so it is of crucial importance to understand how they relate to the competing interests involved.

(Abraham 1997, 160, his stress)

Finally, it is worth considering the sources of criticism of whether university research is relevant to the needs of industry. In Europe, the debate about universities and their relevance is debated more strongly in some countries than others. Pavitt (2003) finds that while it remains the case that technologically aware companies continue to value academic researchers, critics of lack of relevance are much more vocal in the UK than in the US, Switzerland and Scandinavia. In the UK, 'Most of the criticism comes from government officials and politicians ... often based on simplistic notions of accountability'. He ascribes this to the relative weight of these officials compared to that of technologically dynamic businesses in the political system.

Paradigm 6 Massification of higher education

The teaching role of universities and contribution to the skills that are needed by industry has undergone considerable transformation since the 1960s, and is continually being revaluated in the light of the debate about universities' contribution to economic development. In line with Mason *et al.* (2004) and Bozeman (2000) it is argued that scientific and human capital is often neglected in assessments of technology transfer effectiveness, and that internal and inter-country differences in the workings of scientific and engineering labour markets are neglected. This reflects the lack of attention paid to the sub-system related to human resource development, including formal education and training and the organization of knowledge creation (Lundvall 2002, quoted in Mason *et al.* 2004). The bottom line is that promoting university commercialization is misplaced because universities are identified as a source of technology not talent (Florida 1999).

In both Europe and the US, there is, however, an increasing recognition of the importance of upgrading skills in the drive to improving economic performance. Across Europe, in the expansion of university systems in the last two decades, participation rates have risen sharply and with them there has been an emphasis on improving the performance of institutions.

The Europeanization of university teaching is part of the process of maximizing efficiency (see Chapter 4). In the US, provision of training programmes has risen in the national and regional political agenda. For example, as Walshok *et al.* (2002, 29) point out, while the research base is important for industry in San Diego, part of that story is the continual access to recent graduates and continuing education offered by research universities. Yet whether universities' prime task is to prepare students for the world of work is contentious (see Wolf, A. 2002).

Paradigm 7 The entrepreneurial university

The entrepreneurial university encompasses a third mission of economic development in addition to teaching and research (Etzkowitz *et al.* 2000, 314). This role dates back only as far as the late twentieth century. For Etzkowitz (2003, 300) 'the organizing principle of the Triple Helix is the expectation that the university will play a greater role in society as an entrepreneur'. Following Schumpeter (1949), he makes a key distinction between the entrepreneur as an individual and the individual as part of a collective system, and 'the entrepreneurial function need not be embodied in a physical person and in particular a single physical person'. He records that Schumpeter had identified the role of the US Department of Agriculture in creating an agriculture innovation system. Governments in every EU member state have implemented policy reforms to encourage innovation and entrepreneurship.

Drawing on Etzkowitz (2003), entrepreneurship is defined broadly here as those activities designed to encourage the commercial application or spin-off of university scientific and engineering research. The entrepreneurial role is defined as that activity where the intention is to put into the public-industrial domain that technology which has a commercial value. This includes patents, licences, spin-off firms and science parks. Academic entrepreneurs, as has already been suggested, are not a recent phenomenon (see for example Etzkowitz 1983, Geiger 1986 and Slaughter and Leslie 1999). Kenney (1986) records the development of professors as entrepreneurs in US universities focusing on cultural and institutional change and the associated ethical issues in the biotech sector and institutional responses. What appears to be happening is that the rate of spin-offs has been increasing since the later 1980s although the majority are formed from within the most prestigious universities such as Stanford and MIT in the US (see Shane 2004).

Indeed, not all universities are entrepreneurial or have the capacity to be so. This depends on their position with the HE hierarchy and also the models they chose to adopt for themselves. Vorley (2004) identifies three classifications of universities which are instrumental in the way IP is managed and further research identified: (1) Active Commercialization, (2) Research Internalization and (3) Science/Technology Innovators

(Capitalist and Collaborative). It is these strategies which have come to define universities, or their respective departments. The first are institutions pursuing an active commercialization management strategy and are generally those institutions which are able to generate, and are in receipt of, higher research incomes. The strategy of the second type is not immediately concerned with commercialization or with directly increasing fiscal capacity, as is the case with institutions pursuing strategies of Active Commercialization. The emphasis of Research Internalization is instead on the capacity of the university to internalize the development of science to the point of becoming commercially viable. Inevitably this means that commercial exposure to competitive market conditions comes at a much later stage and the motivations of research and development necessarily constitute part of a longer-term project. The third type of research management strategy pursued by universities may be identified as a variation of the previous two. Institutions pursuing this strategy largely focus on the earlier stages of scientific innovation and the embryonic development of technologies. This is in contrast to either spinning out the technology or pursuing development to achieve the consolidation of technology.

Science parks are included here under the entrepreneurial role rather than the territorial role because their origins lie in the entrepreneurial activities of universities rather than specifically with economic development in mind. Science parks originated in the US in the 1950s, spread to Europe in the 1960s and 1970s and have now become a worldwide phenomenon (Lindholm Dahlstrand and Lawton Smith 2003).

> A Science Park is an organisation managed by specialised professionals, whose main aim is to increase the wealth of its community by promoting the culture of innovation and the competitiveness of its associated businesses and knowledge-based institutions. To enable these goals to be met, a Science Park stimulates and manages the flow of knowledge and technology amongst universities, R&D institutions, companies and markets; it facilitates the creation and growth of innovation-based companies through incubation and spin-off processes; and provides other value-added services together with high quality space and facilities.
>
> (www.iaspworld.org/ IASP International Board, 6 February 2002)

Economic development is claimed to be an objective of the International Association of Science Parks and indeed is a popular instrument of regional development and/or technology policy, for example in France and Malaysia. Evidence suggests that, while parks have a role to play in the transfer of research-based ideas into new business ventures, many firms on parks, particularly in the UK, have little contact with the university resulting from a park location (see Massey *et al.* 1992 and Lindholm Dahlstrand and Lawton Smith 2003 for a review).

Paradigm 8 The territorial role

The last paradigm is the territorial role and the universality of engagement in local systems of governance. Here that role is defined as that which is intended and orchestrated rather than that which happens as a consequence of multiplier effects of being located within an economy such as employers, purchasers of goods and services, as ad hoc collaborators and providers of services and engaged in a variety of civic functions. The missions of universities, will of course, vary depending on size of university and of its catchment area, and the local and regional context (Glasson 2003). But for Etzkowitz and Leydesdorff (1997) the governance role is well established in the US and Europe, and they conclude that various systems which were previously considered functionally differentiated have become integrated at various levels of structure as national and regional policy have become interconnected. The extent to which system integration occurs in both continents is examined in Chapters 4 and 5 (universities in innovation systems in Europe and the US respectively).

Along with the governance role is an additional set of de facto and de jure accountabilities. These may take the form of direct reckoning where funding has been allocated for research or for outreach activities. They may be 'political' whereby the university itself – or organizations charged with bringing universities into closer contact with the customer (industry or networking organizations) – claim that the university's actions demonstrate that there has been a response to the call for greater engagement.

Conclusions

This chapter has set out to show that, although universities and territorial development are currently high on the political and academic agenda, there is a long history of engagement and parallels can be found with previous periods of history. The purpose of the eight paradigms that emerge from the brief historical overview is to provide the analytical framework for identifying how universities are positioned within economic development processes per se and within local or regional economic development in particular. Collectively they indicate that there have been changes in the organization of the innovation process, which place universities more centrally; that the degree to which this happens depends on the construction of particular systems of governance (supra-national, national and sub-national); that academic eminence has a utilitarian function; that biotechnology is the 'new defence industry'; universities are subject to multiple accountabilities; that the primary contribution of universities to economic development is through human capital development rather than technology transfer; that universities are increasingly entrepreneurial and that incentives from national and sub-national organizations to work with local industry and organizations amounts to participation in systems of governance. Above all they demonstrate a particular kind of rhetoric – that of stakeholders and agenda-setting in discourses reflecting current debates about value for money across public sector provision.

2 The regional economy and the university

Introduction

From the mid-1980s onwards, studies of geographies of innovation have established that high-tech firms cluster around universities in a way that older industries such as cars and steel did not. Now a university's presence is identified as being a key factor without which high-tech activity would have been unlikely to develop in a location and even less likely to grow: the large research university is a catalyst, whether or not it is proactively involved in that development (Doutriaux 2003 on research in Canada). This association was not always so. It was military and other public research establishments that were identified as having a significant impact on the growth of high-tech industry in some regions (see for example Breheny and McQuaid 1987 on Berkshire in the UK and Markusen *et al.* 1986 in the US). This chapter then is about why the university–territory interface has now assumed such a politically important role in regional and local economic development. It sets out the arguments that are supported or challenged by evidence in later chapters.

Distributed and integrated innovation systems and their geography

One of the driving forces behind the territorialization agenda is based on the paradigm that processes of innovation are increasingly distributed between different organizations. Theoretical approaches which address the importance of proximity to the innovation process to varying degrees highlight technological, social and economic processes. For example, Oinas and Malecki (2002) articulate the geographical and temporality of innovation processes in their concept of spatial innovation systems (SIS). The authors define SIS as consisting of 'overlapping and interlinked national, regional and sectoral innovation systems which are all manifested in different configurations through space'. Central to their approach are (1) the external relations of actors and (2) the variability of weights of different places or regions as centre points of particular technological paths in time. It is not just places that vary in importance as centres of innovation over time, the roles played by universities and national laboratories vary over time. This approach has the merit of drawing attention to the co-existence of interdependent factors operating at a particular time shaping geographies of innovation.

Technological explanations

The argument that the innovation process is more effective if it is localized is based on speed and efficiency of technology transfer in industries characterized by rapid technological change. Technical fields vary in the degree of innovative opportunities and appropriability conditions (see Carlsson 1997; Malerba and Orsenigo 1997). In general the pattern is that research is relevant primarily at the early stages of the innovation life cycle with the emergence of new technological paradigms. Therefore firms will be located close to universities only in order to gain access to the latest research findings more easily (EC 2001b) (see Swann *et al.* 1998 on the declining impact of the science base on the computing and biotech industries in the UK and the US as an illustration of this point). Moreover, the extent of the impact of proximity will be stronger where there is a close match between the scientific level of the firms' R&D personnel and scientists and engineers in universities. The better the match, the easier are processes of engagement between the two groups, particularly between personnel with doctorates (see Hicks 1995 in Mason *et al.* 2004). Hence larger firms are also more likely to have links than smaller firms (Arundel and Geuna 2001) because of their greater capacity to absorb the findings of university research, a finding supported by Veugelers and Cassiman (2003) in their study of Belgian manufacturing firms. The most obvious manifestation of the advantages of proximity determining corporate activity is the location of the research laboratories of multinational companies (MNC) near to major research universities. For example, in Cambridge, UK, Microsoft arrived in 1997 preceded by Xerox, Hitachi, Toshiba, Olivetti and Oracle, among other firms locating research facilities in Cambridge in close collaboration with university departments (Garnsey and Lawton Smith 1998).

The apparent close relationship in newer sectors is only one small part of the story of industry's engagement with universities. Numerous studies have found that older industries also have extensive links with universities although the mechanisms may different and include more short-term interaction. For example Cohen *et al.* (2002) studied several low technology sectors such as food, paper, glass and concrete. Lawton Smith (2000) compared university and industry links in a traditional industry (the flow measurement industry) with those in a high-tech industry (electronics components). Both of these studies found similar results to those found by Meyer-Krahmer and Schmoch's (1998) analysis of university–industry interaction in five fields. Their research showed that while collaborative research and informal contact overall were the most important, mechanisms differed within the different fields. In mechanical engineering the main mechanism used was contract research to solve specific technical problems, whereas in chemistry the provision of personnel and education are the most important means of technology transfer.

Social explanations

The most common explanation given why innovation works better if localized is that it is a social process. As some of the knowledge needed by firms to innovate is tacit, for knowledge transfer to occur effectively, direct, personal contact between scientists and engineers in different organizations is required. Such contact provides the basis for establishing norms and standards which form the basis of practice of interaction (Lundvall 1988). Pavitt (1998a, 797) encapsulates the thrust of the argument for geographically proximate networked relationships made by a number of others (see, for example, Antonelli 2000). Pavitt suggests that,

> the main practical benefits of academic research are not easily transmissible information, ideas and discoveries available on equal terms to anyone in the world. Instead they are various elements of problem-solving capacity, involving the transmission of often tacit (i.e. non-codifiable) knowledge through personal mobility and face-to-face contacts. The benefits therefore tend to be geographically and linguistically localized.

Thus networks, which have many different qualities and strengths, which link university research and industrial practice are embedded within particular locations linking people who are expert in different aspects of the innovation process. Granovetter's 1973 essay on the 'strength of weak ties' argued that weak ties are indispensable to individuals' opportunities, are more flexible than strong formal ties and distant contacts are particularly useful because they provide access to new flows of information. They are *channels* of the type described by Owen-Smith and Powell (2004, 5–6) as social connections that 'diffusely and imperfectly direct transfers between nodes, facilitating information spillovers' or as 'closed conduits, characterized by legal arrangements'. The context in which these networks operate is important as it matters whether 'the nodes that anchor a network pursue public or private goals' (page 17). Here the transfers of knowledge can be through informal contacts between individual academics and industrialists (weak ties), or more formally encompassing teams of people in academic departments, technology transfer organizations, venture capitalists and so on (strong ties) but where the nature of interactions are governed by the terms of trade set out in contractual arrangements.

Networks therefore can be seen as political systems that contain many competing and overlapping rationalities (Tracey and Clark 2003). Thus, in this context, pressures on academics to associate and network with people in industry, especially within the local level, may be misguided either where they overstate the importance of proximity in innovation or because individuals may be already engaged in extensive networks and the pressure to develop new ones may compete with personal professional objectives. Malmberg and Power (2004) also have their doubts about the overarching importance of local interaction. They argue that the challenge for firms is to link up with global flows of knowledge, and it is most crucial for firms to try to link up with the best universities and research institutes, whether or not they are local. Many firms and researchers are participants in thick networks of international relationships that cut across national barriers (see also Brusoni and Geuna forthcoming; Oinas and Malecki 2002).

While the importance of networks is assumed, it is difficult to prove. Arundel and Geuna (2001) point out that many available studies lack direct evidence of the knowledge flow from the producer of knowledge to the user, and that none of the research that they looked at investigated why proximity might matter. While the tacitness theme is strongly represented in the literature on universities and proximity, Arundel and Geuna (2001, 12) find that it has its limitations for explaining why innovation is more effective if it is localized, and there are two criticisms of the tacit knowledge explanation for proximity effects. First, Breschi and Lissoni (2001) comment that other factors such as the economics of knowledge codification, labour markets and appropriation strategies (for example Saviotti's 1998 model of the extent of the codification of knowledge) could explain the phenomenon of localization. They find that this argument is compelling given the paucity of direct evidence for the effect of proximity on knowledge flows. The second criticism comes from Cowan *et al.*'s (2000) theoretical evaluation of 'tacit' versus codified knowledge. They suggest that very little knowledge is intrinsically tacit in the sense that it is impossible to codify. Instead much of what is believed to be tacit could be codified if economically worthwhile, while other knowledge appears to be tacit only to the uninitiated. They argue, however, that this criticism, although raising doubts about the role of tacit knowledge per se, does not counter a need for personal contact in order to transfer knowledge effectively.

Economic explanations

Economic explanations why research-intensive firms cluster around universities fall into two main camps. The first is based on cost-reduction arising from local concentrations of industrial activity, the second is cost reduction through increasing returns to scale through urbanization economies. Of the first, Scott's (1988) transaction-costs approach assumes that the concentration of innovative firms results in the availability of agglomeration economies – that is the costs to each firm engaging with universities will be lowered by the co-presence of others undertaking the same kind of activity thus sharing the costs. The increased costs associated with increased external (as against internal) transactions will create a 'spatial pull' whereby firms will tend to agglomerate to shorten the length, and hence the cost, of external linkage. The spillover argument is that beneficial externalities accrue to organizations and individuals from co-location. Geographical spillovers are defined as flows of ideas between agents at less than original cost (Griliches 1992, in Adams 2002) and are the central theme in endogenous growth theory (Romer 1986, 1990; Grossman and Helpman 1991). In this logic, knowledge spillovers are an externality that is at least temporarily bound by geography and, as a result, confers disproportionate benefits on nearby firms. This is not a general pattern as not all types of industrial structures can promote knowledge spillovers equally; they are not constant over time, and affect mature and young industries differently, being more important at the early stages of an industry's life (Acs and Armington 2004). Antonelli and Quere (2002, 1058) favour the positive effects of the reduction transaction and communication costs of geographical proximity in explaining how innovation systems work. For them, 'geographical space acts as the basic governance mechanism' in reducing such costs and makes interaction easier. A different kind of economic explanation is that dense concentrations of firms in metropolitan or urban environments benefit from economies of urbanization i.e. production costs of firms fall because of the total increase in activity in an area – increases that contribute to innovation (Simmie and Sennett 1999). Acs and Armington (2004) also find that city-based economic areas are more suitable as units of analysis than states or nations because they are more homogeneous.

Evidence of R&D spillover networks (spillovers) associated with university research has been found by Jaffe (1989) to cause a large gap between social and private rates of return (a difference amounting to between 50 and 100 per cent). A high social rate of return is, however, not sufficient to justify a state's or a region's investment in research or a Federal agency's decision to fund R&D in a specific region. The reason for this is that these benefits may be only temporary. Fogarty and Sinha (1999, 474) argue that, 'At best, geographic proximity confers only a temporary advantage to a region and its industries. Capturing spillover benefits hinges on speedy diffusion of knowledge within local R&D networks'. They argue that a region's performance of R&D by itself is not sufficient for producing stronger economic performance in the long run. If university research is to raise a particular region's productivity growth via technology, it must connect with local industry performance. Eventually local gain requires new technology to be commercialized and take the form of investment in local facilities – start-ups, attraction of new industry – or raising the region's educational level. Therefore geographic limits create the possibility of policy intervention as growth depends on aspects of region building that exceed the decision-making abilities of individual firms and industries (Adams 2002).

Yet the evidence suggests that the proximity effect of inducing or catalysing economic development is not universal even in high-tech sectors. Studies which have contrasted 'old' with 'new' economies have highlighted general transformations in economies with high-tech or 'knowledge-based' sectors of growing importance in the economy, especially in knowledge-intensive services (KIS) (see for example Martin *et al.* 2003). Laafia (2002) in examining Eurostat data shows that over the period 1995–2000 while employment in high-tech and medium-tech was stable, accounting for 7.6 per cent of employment in the EU15, employment in KIS was rising and accounted for a third (32.3 per cent) of all jobs. Both national and regional differences are highlighted. For example, whereas Sweden is the most specialized in KIS, German regions specialized most in high-tech and medium-tech manufacturing, which represented ten out of the 15 leading regions, with the Italian Piedmont and Lombardy regions, Alsace in France, Antwerp in Belgium and the West Midlands in the UK making up the rest. These are largely not the ten 'islands of innovation' identified by the EC (1994) which contain 80 per cent of the research laboratories and enterprises that participate in transnational R&D and have a strong presence of university research and industrial research (South East England; Paris/Ile de France; Frankfurt; Stuttgart; Munich; Turin; Milan; Lyon/Grenoble; Rotterdam/Amsterdam; Rhein-Ruhr (EC 1994, 203)).

A rather different picture emerges in the services sector, where the more densely populated regions had the highest percentages of service sector employment. Inner London had the highest percentage, followed by Stockholm, outer London, Noord-Holland, Berkshire, Buckinghamshire and Oxfordshire and Ile de France. In the US, areas with the highest high-tech locational quotients are on the west and east coasts for example in San Francisco Washington–Baltimore, Boston, Raleigh Durham, in the South at Austin–San Marcos, in the Mid-West in Denver–Boulder and in the North in Minneapolis–St Paul (Baxter and Tyler 2004). These patterns suggest further support for the argument that it is urbanization rather than localization economies that are important in fostering innovative behaviour, although the two are not mutually exclusive.

Diversity versus uniformity, systems of governance and localized interaction

An extensive literature on national innovation systems dating back to the 1980s has illustrated national differences in the relative research strengths of universities, national laboratories and in industrial sectors and in the degree of integration of the many components within national or sectoral systems (see for example Freeman 1987, Nelson and Rosenberg 1993, Metcalfe 1997). Riccaboni *et al.* (2003), like Brusoni and Geuna (forthcoming) and Geuna *et al.* (2003), highlight how the combination of actors which are integrated into innovation processes and the extent to which that combination is effective comprising the necessary complementary expertise is a result of the construction of the national innovation system and of sub-national innovation systems as the characteristics of a region.

Brusoni and Geuna (forthcoming, 4) suggest that it is the national system that underpins local patterns. They argue that a country's knowledge base may have a strong science base but lack the engineering capabilities to embody scientific results in profitable products. On the other hand it can have strong development capabilities that are not supported by robust science. These authors find that national specializations tend to be relatively stable, hence patterns of interaction will be so – although this might not be the situation desired by policy makers seeking to increase the uptake of knowledge. Moreover, they argue that analysis should focus on whether a country's sectoral specialization cuts across different types of research (knowledge integration). A sectoral knowledge base with high knowledge integration would have similar specialization by field across different typologies of research. These authors found that in the chemistry field (the underlying science for the pharmaceuticals industry) the US has a much higher integration than the EU while within the EU there was considerable variety of specializations in particular combinations of chemistry fields and in research typologies. For Europe as a whole they found that it was not that EU firms would not be capable of exploiting an efficient research system because of a lack of 'development' capabilities, but that what is missing is the basic research bit. The result of this is that EU pharmaceuticals firms have to source research results from the US (pages 26–7).

Brusoni and Geuna find distinct differences between the US and Europe in the case of biomedical–biotech–pharma innovation system. They conclude that the US system is much more diverse than that in Europe, having public research organizations that are more generalist and integrative. This combined with a highly mobile labour force and a host of regulatory policy initiatives has promoted widespread commercialization of academically originated research, especially through the formation of small biotech firms, whereas in Europe universities have developed competencies in molecular biology much less quickly. Hence, geographical outcomes of research are as a consequence qualitatively different in each continent. Local centres of excellence around universities and other research institutes in the US tend to be generalist, integrating innovation and development work. This sets in train cumulative effects of attracting talented researchers, high-quality students and increasing shares of R&D funding as well as the in-migration and establishment of new firms. While some of these effects are observable in Europe, funding sources may be national rather than European and have served to deepen already narrow competences rather than enabling broad exploration. Moreover, the dominance of the pharmaceutical companies in funding university research 'may also have militated against the broadening of regional scientific and organisational competences' (page 190). They recommend that policy efforts should be made to generate integration between basic research and clinical development (as is now happening in the UK, see DTI 2003) and greater linkages between the various actors in the industry.

The justification for the focus on regional scale for policy intervention comes from Cooke (2002). He argues that the region is the scale at which the most important knowledge and exploitation capabilities concentrate, and secondary ones, attracted by increasing returns to knowledge, including local knowledge spillovers are found in secondary nodes or even more diffused networks knowledge spillovers can be captured. This view is supported by Oughton *et al.* (2002) who not only cite Lundvall (1999), who calls for a greater integration between technology and industrial policy, but also argue that the regional dimension of both is central and that regional government 'can play the role of catalyst to strengthen government–industry–university links and regional learning' (page 104). Yet this is not that simple. A number of possible models of regional innovation systems (RIS) exist depending on state form (degree of regional autonomy and type of activity within a region). Cooke's (1998, 24–5) typology of three types of RIS (grassroots, network and dirigiste) illustrates different levels and degrees of institutionalization (system of governance) within which local or regional government and knowledge institutions, firms and other local organizations could co-ordinate university and industry interaction to foster economic development. Moreover, Howells (1999) and Gertler (1997) both argue that the role of nation state institutions is underestimated in respect of both incentive structures and the long-term effects of cycles of investment on regional specializations. To reiterate the earlier point, what appears to be a local phenomenon may not have local causes (Massey 1995).

Eminence

The eminence of particular universities translates into the geography of innovation in a number of respects because by definition top universities and their 'star' scientists are few in number (Zucker and Darby 1996; Feldman 2001, 380–1). This scarcity has at least four effects. First, the more eminent the university, the more research funding it can attract from a variety of sources, a greater store of potential technological applications. Second, the higher the calibre of the staff attracted to those institutions, the more likely they are to act as growth poles which attract eminent scientists and engineers and graduate students to particular locations

(Florida 1999). Third, the knock-on effect of high-quality basic scientific research connected to international science by these top researchers is a key means by which localities are linked to global research systems. Learning transferred into new firms formed within scientific environments influences paths of development of firms providing the means of identifying and developing market opportunities but also shaping their technological profiles, hence the region's scientific profile (see Rickne 2000; Saviotti 1998). Fourth, the combination of both makes them more likely to spin-off new firms than those less research-intensive universities as star scientists are the most likely group of academics to spin-off new companies (Di Gregorio and Shane 2003). Zucker *et al.* (1998b) find in their study of start-ups in 183 US regions that it is the top university researchers in a region who contribute to firm formation (see also Swann and Prevezer 1996). In this reasoning, the impact of the 'best' universities will be felt more strongly in some rather than other places.

Defence and biotechnology

In the 1980s, much of the literature on the location and development of high-tech industries focused on concentrations of activity around government research establishments (mainly defence) rather than on universities. The rise of the defence–industry nexus of activity can be seen for example in the UK in the Reading–Newbury–Oxford triangle (see Hall *et al.* 1987; Breheny and McQuaid 1987; Lovering 1991) and in the US on the west and east coasts (Markusen *et al.* 1986, Saxenian 1994). Markusen *et al.* (1986) concluded that the US academic–industry linkages can be clearly recognized only in those regions receiving Federal funding for defence-related research. An emerging pattern that parallels the defence–university nexus of the 1920s to the 1950s is the big investment in university pharmaceuticals and biosciences (Hart 1988).

In the 30 years since the first biotech firm was formed in the US (Genetech in 1976) and the 25 years since the first UK company was established (Celltech 1980), life sciences research and biotech have assumed an equivalence of defence in the national research agenda. By the 1990s in the biotech industry a similar literature on dynamics of the clustering of biotech firms around universities developed (see for example Kenney 1986).

Geographically, the industry concentrates in a small number of locations, some of which are emerging as megacentres. This concept, according to Cooke (2002, 2004), captures the *knowledge value chain* from *exploration*, through *examination* to *exploitation* knowledge. Thus megacentres are science-driven, public and privately funded institutional complexes that in biosciences have as their ultimate goal the production of patient healthcare. They are hierarchical networks that include: industrial hierarchy expressed in the ever-concentrating ownership structure of 'big

pharma', government hierarchy regarding basic research funding and regulation of bioscience, and research hierarchy, most of it concentrated in
medical schools, hospitals and universities. Their importance lies in the
contribution the healthcare, pharmaceuticals and biosciences sector makes
to national GDP, probably under-estimated as at least one-sixth for the
US and 25 per cent for the UK (Sainsbury 1999). Cooke finds megacentre
candidates based on sheer scale of activity to be Boston, California, Montreal and Toronto in North America, Cambridge (and possibly Oxford),
Munich and Stockholm in Europe. He finds that concentrations of firms in
the US in the other five states – New York, Washington, North Carolina,
Pennsylvania, Maryland – are not in the same order of magnitude of activity as California (San Franscisco and San Diego) (see Cortright and Mayer
2002, 3). In Europe, other concentrations of firms are in central Scotland
(Sainsbury 1999), in France in the Grenoble/Lyon region and in Germany
in Munich (see Cooke 2004).

The evidence on the causal relationship with university science is
mixed. On the east coast, the presence of biotechnology firms in the
Boston–Cambridge area can be directly attributed to the proactive role of
the Massachusetts Institute of Technology in fostering entrepreneurship in
new technologies. Yet, in other places, it is not the universities that have
been the catalyst for the growth in the number of firms. In downstate New
York, New Jersey and Maryland (including Washington DC and Philadelphia), substantial concentrations of biotechnology activity are a function
of the historical presence of the nation's largest pharmaceutical manufacturers and their R&D activity (Feldman and Schreuder 1996). The emergence of San Diego, Seattle, and Raleigh-Durham as biotechnology
clusters is built upon well-funded medical research establishments (see
Walcott 2001 and 2002 on San Diego and Haugh 1995 on Seattle). Yet, in
the UK, the pattern is that, while biotech firms might be concentrated near
universities, the research units of pharmaceutical companies tend to be
located near their company HQs and not near universities (see Howells
1985).

Other studies have cast doubt on the direct relationship between proximity and university–industry linkages and the performance of individual
firms, hence the nature of the life–science–university nexus. For example
Liebeskind *et al.* (1996) concluded on the basis of case studies of two successful California-based biotechnology firms and their linkages with scientists external to the firm that the presence of long-distance relationships
reduces the strength of the argument that biotechnology collaborations
are locally embedded. Zucker *et al.* (1998b, 66) found on the basis of case
studies and interviews with Californian biotech firms that what appear to
be geographically localized external economies located near university
stars turn out to exist only for that much smaller set of enterprises that are
linked to particular star professors by contract or ownership – in fact by
market exchange. Moreover, it is these firms that perform best in terms of

industry growth. Also in the US, Audretsch and Stephan (1996) used data on initial public offerings (IPOs) of biotechnology firms between March 1990 and November 1992 to examine the functions of scientists linked with these firms. They find that most often the founders of firms and the chairs of scientific advisory boards (SABs) are likely to have local linkages, whereas members of SABs are less likely to have local linkages.

In Europe, Lawton Smith (2005), reporting on a survey in the UK of 75 Oxfordshire biotech firms, found that being close to universities was not the top locational advantage of Oxfordshire. Neither were universities the prime source of information. They were ranked ninth along with local sector networks, national trade associations, technology transfer departments and independent research organizations. Firms generally did not view proximity to Oxford University and the local research base as an important factor in the development of interactions, other than those of an informal nature. The evidence from this industry supports Malecki's (1997, 127) suggestion that universities are an overstated ingredient in accounting for the location of R&D and high-technology industry.

Accountability and responsibility

Changing forms of accountability are being driven by the increasing complexity of policy interventions, incentives and necessity of responding to audits. Within Europe, universities are increasingly subject to common national policy measures designed to increase their contribution to wealth creation. At the same time, institutional differences which determine particular accountabilities have major impacts on that relationship. In particular, accessibility and efficiency are related to pre-existing rules or new rules which govern ownership of intellectual property and the autonomy of institutions to set their own guidelines for technology transfer. Indeed, coming back to the point made by Owen-Smith and Powell (2004), Castells and Hall (1994) argue that universities can play a successful innovative role only if they remain fundamentally autonomous institutions, setting up their own research agendas, and establishing their own criteria for scientific quality and career promotion. While they suggest that the more generally academic a university is, the less likely it is that it will contribute to technopole development, an idea supported by Adams (2002). This argument runs counter to that made above and the evidence with regard to spin-offs (see below) and from Stanford and MIT in the US, but until recently has been the case with Princeton (Chapter 8) and Oxford (Chapter 7).

Incentives to work on industry-related research in the form of funding of research and/or technology transfer activities are important in the territorial role of universities. In the US to varying degrees (Chapter 5) scientific research is funded at the regional or state level. Thus scientists are accountable and will be judged according to the funding criteria. At the same time, researchers are also enabled or constrained by national frameworks in which there are ethical considerations on the kinds of research that can be undertaken and which might lead to commerical possibilities and their realization, for example in both biomedical and agbio biotechnology.

Massification of higher education, teaching and graduate recruitment

Central to the understanding the effectiveness and quality of networks at the territorial level is the identification of the impact on the quality of human capital and mobility between university and industry. Bozeman and Gaughan (2000) argue that it was human capital generated by governments – for example in the US in basic R&D – which led to developments in the biotech industry and hence to economic wealth. The government was making investments in scientific capacity generation rather than financial investments. In their view, public R&D evaluation should centre on this growth in capacity by developing and nurturing 'the ability of groups to create new knowledge uses, not simply develop discrete bits of knowledge or technology'. They make the argument that human capital is not just that held by the individual as its value lies in the personal skills and know-how with which individuals engage with others. Hence these authors suggest that much human science and technology capital is embedded in social and professional networks which 'integrate and shape scientific work, providing knowledge of scientists' and engineers' work activity, helping with job opportunity and mobility, and providing indications about possible applications for scientific and technical work products' (page 8).

Evidence on the way that networks facilitate transfers of knowledge through the migration of individuals between organizations seeking career advancement comes from Zucker et al. (2002). These authors examined two different sources of labour mobility among scientists. The first is the classic pattern labour mobility of changing employer from a university or research institute to a firm, which they define as 'affiliated scientists'. The second, and empirically more common, is when academic or research institute scientists collaborate on joint research projects or patenting within a firm or through other activities such as membership of scientific advisory boards ('linked scientists'). They found that the quality of the researcher (as measured by scientific citations), the commercial potential of inventions, moving costs, reservation wage and social networks are significant determinants for involvement in commercial applications of biotechnology as employees or as entrepreneurs. Reservation costs are determined by scientists' quality, moving costs, trial frequency, interfering academic offers and productivity of stars already in firms. In group-duration analysis for biotechnology, stars were found to move to firms faster as their quality increased; local firms and productivity of local stars in firms increase; but as the number of top local universities grows larger the probability of a star being tied to a firm decreases. Productivity was also assessed in terms of quality rather than quantity of output. Moreover, the extent to which the inventor's knowledge is embedded in economically valuable inventions is positively related to the interest of outside firms in the person's work. Hence the more specialized the know-how inside the firm, the higher the interest is of a firm hiring an inventor. It is a particularly attractive proposition for the firm to hire an inventor if the inventor's work is independent of other colleagues and can be acquired without necessitating the recruitment of other researchers. They found that university scientists who work with firm scientists have a strong positive effect on products in development, products on the market and employment growth. In the US, owing to these sources of value, the labour of star scientists has strongly moved to firms, but, because of the scarcity of star scientists and their concentration in relatively few institutions, they have done so in very concentrated, localized areas and are the strongest anchor firms to those locations (Gertler and Wolfe 2002).

The recognition of universities' key role in shaping the quality and quantity of human capital is demonstrated by the expansion of university systems worldwide. Chapter 3 will show that the number of students attending university in Europe and the US has increased over the last decade and that a radical change has taken place in the kinds of courses offered to people in work, in the form of part-time degrees, continuing professional development and extension courses.

The largest cohort in most universities, that of undergraduate students, is considered to be the primary contribution of universities to technological innovation through the human capital it produces (see for example, Branscomb *et al.* 1999; Rosenberg and Nelson 1994; Feller 1999; Etzkowitz 1999; Antonelli 2000). At the local level, graduated students and other university personnel are a means of enlarging and diversifying the local talent pool for science-based companies and providing bridges between the university, faculty and science-based companies (Lee and Walshok 2003), transferring knowledge directly to companies and indirectly – through knowledge spillovers, and an increasing match of employer and employee skills (see for example Scott 1988; Angel 1991; Saxenian 1994; Henry and Pinch 2000; Scott and Storper 1987).

Post-graduate students offer a different kind of human capital. Mason *et al.* (2004) argue that the incidence of enterprise research linkages with universities and other public or non-profit laboratories (e.g. charities) in a given country will be positively related to the orientation of the national higher education system towards the production of PhDs and other postgraduates in engineering and science subjects. Thus post-doctoral training programmes, executive programmes and continuing professional development also 'ensure the continuous dissemination and integration of the newest knowledge and most advanced forms of practice to employees in globally traded clusters of a region' (Lee and Walshok 2003, iv).

Whether students of both kinds stay in the region following graduation depends largely on characteristics of those localities (McCann and Shepherd 2001). Florida's (2002) view of the geography of uneven development is that talented individuals with high levels of human capital are likely to locate in places which give added strength or support to their productivity and which contain other talented people with whom they can interact and learn from, thereby building on existing knowledge and/or generating new knowledge (see also Dicken and Malmberg 2001; Black and Henderson 1997). In other words, students are more likely to stay not only because of the number of jobs, but also because of the quality of the people with whom they will be working. Geographical variations in mobility between countries and within countries are demonstrated in Chapter 6.

Productivity and efficiency relating to the ability of higher education infrastructure to increase the stock of capital within the local labour market will depend on the region's attractiveness to appropriate labour and whether people will stay. Rates of attraction and retention vary regionally. Where rates are very high and local agglomerative forces are at work, the growth in human capital fostered by HEIs may engender further local growth in both public and private investments. Once a pool of skilled labour is established, stocks of human capital – the knowledge and competences embodied in people – give rise to localized capacities (Dicken and Malmberg 2001, 357).

Returning to Florida's point, although the location of talented individuals is central to explaining why a city such as San Diego has produced a biotech cluster whereas equally ambitious neighbours such as Orange County and Los Angeles have not, the importance of individuals in shaping those environments should not be overlooked (Walcott 2002). This importance, Walcott argues, relates to the quality of the networks that develop through the actions of key players. Regional attributes alone overlook the networks that individuals construct through their associations with institutions or by virtue of personal leadership. In San Diego, the nexus of key individuals was based in the university and a group of serial entrepreneurs played a crucial role in transforming the city from another Sunbelt site to a 'Bioscience best practice' model. Walshok (1994 in Collinson 2000), also on San Diego, described the critical role of 'influencers' who acted as 'visionaries and champions' in interactions between academic/research communities and the business community in the support for the evolution of Silicon Valley enterprises.

The entrepreneurial university

The entrepreneurial university (Etzkowitz *et al.* 2000) of the last 20 years is defined by the activities it takes to encourage the commercial application or spin-off of university scientific and engineering research. This idea encompasses the entrepreneur as an individual and the individual as part of a collective system, which includes formal procedures to 'sell' or otherwise commodify and market intellectual property arising from university research. Governments are increasingly providing incentives for universities to establish technology transfer offices (TTOs) to facilitate this process.

In the US following the Bayh-Dole Act of 1980, the number of universities with TTOs grew rapidly. Although this growth has been ascribed to the influence of the Act the pattern was rather of the Act giving a boost to a trend that was already under way (see Chapter 5). In Europe, a great variety of arrangements results from decisions made within each member state and by individual universities (see Chapter 4). Critical organizational factors which encourage academic entrepreneurial activity are faculty reward systems, technology transfer offices, staffing/compensation practices and cultural barriers between universities and firms (Siegel *et al.* 2003) (see also Coombs and Metcalfe 2000). In Europe too, legislation and policy are only one part of the task environment. For example, in commenting on the efforts of Chalmers University in Sweden to transform itself into an entrepreneurial university, Jacob *et al.* (2003, 15) commented that it 'may be seen not as a policy outcome but an internally driven process that may be better explained by the culture of the engineering school than responses to top down steering'. The shift in research policy at the national level created a climate which legitimized what had been taking place at Chalmers for nearly two decades.

With the expectation that universities will be enterprising, so evidence of their performance including patents, licences and spin-offs and publications is increasingly collected at the national level. Spin-offs, which are overwhelmingly located in the vacinity of the incubating university, are the most obvious contribution to local economic development. In the US this information has been collected nationally since the formation in 1975 of the Association of University Technology Managers (AUTM), membership of which has increased as a growing number of universities have allocated resources for smoothing the process by providing expert services, patent protection, venture capital and so on. The entrepreneurial university is not necessarily a territorial model. The prime responsibility of university technology transfer offices is to capitalize on the university's intellectual property and not to create local jobs or in other ways to support economic development. De facto the impact of some of these activities is local. For example the majority of university spin-off firms stay within the locality of the university.

Yet while the stimulation of university spin-offs has become one of the main foci of public policy with Stanford University in Silicon Valley and MIT as models for others to emulate (Saxenian 1994), such universities are the exceptions rather than the rule. Research from the US finds that what makes some universities better at spin-outs are intellectual eminence, the policies of making equity investments in start-ups and maintaining a low inventor's share of royalties. They found no effect of local venture capital activity and only limited support for an effect of the commercial orientation of university research (Di Gregorio and Shane 2003). Jacob *et al.* (2003) draw similar conclusions from evidence in Europe, arguing that not all universities have the potential to become entrepreneurial, where the propensity for universities to spin off varies considerably as it does in the US.

The early science parks, such as those at Stanford (1957) and Cambridge, UK (1970) predated the explicitly territorial role. They are both part of the entrepreneurial activities of universities and increasingly part of the governance structures of local innovation systems. Massey *et al.* (1992) comment that the popular conception of science parks is in two parts: the definition of what a science park is and a set of postulated causal relationships, effects which will happen as a result of these characteristics. On page 21 the authors identify 26 different science-park objectives ranging from the obvious one of stimulating the formation of start-up new-technology-based firms to improving the performance of the local economy to improving the image of the academic institution in the eyes of government. Numerous studies of science parks have variously examined combinations of these aims (see Lindholm Dahlstrand and Lawton Smith 2003 for a review).

The majority of the currently existing science and technology parks in the world were created during the 1990s. Data from the International Association of Science Parks (ISAP) shows that, by the end of 2000, a third of science and technology parks (STPS) (worldwide) were located inside a university campus, or on land owned by a university and adjacent to the campus itself. Although this proportion is quite low, almost 70 per cent of the 'parks' share services with their university. A similar percentage of STPs host university researchers in their facilities. Almost half of STPs share scientific infrastructures with the university. On the other hand, 33 per cent of the universities find that it is convenient to have their technology transfer office (or industrial liaison department) in a STP, thus being closer to their customers (Survey methodology: on-line questionnaire. Universe: 250 Science/Technology Parks (IASP members). Sample: 94 Science/Technology Parks).

The territorial role

The book is predicated on the premise that universities and policy makers now generally accept that universities do have a territorial role to play, an assumption that draws on statements in policy statements and reviews of the evidence from such organizations as the OECD and the EC. The 1999 OECD report, for example, finds that universities can play a role in regional networking and in institutional capacity building. They can act as regional animateurs through representation on outside bodies and as intermediaries in providing commentary and analysis for the media. The Report concludes that universities have much to gain from adapting to modern realities of the regional economy.

Goldstein *et al.* (1995) suggest that, in addition to the range of financial and technological inputs on economic development, at the regional level, universities can deliver regional leadership, co-production of the know-ledge infrastructure and co-production of a particular type of regional milieu. This instrumentalist role, like that of science parks, has placed universities explicitly within the system of governance of regions though their engagement in regionally-based initiatives in partnership with local authorities, business and other stakeholders, to assist in the development of commercialization and business interaction services (Charles 2003, 13). Indeed Etzkowitz and Leydesdorff (1997, 4) observe 'the spread of technology policy to virtually all regions (which naturally includes universities), irrespective of whether they are research or industrially-intensive'.

Yet the success of the regional role depends on the matching of HEIs and the region, the university's own missions and the policy mechanisms which exist to build on existing complementarities. OECD (1999, 15) argues that in establishing the capacity of a university to respond to regional needs there are a number of important dimensions, not least the university's own strategy. In problematizing territoriality, which they identify as an extremely complex and problematic concept for HEIs, they raise a number of questions: What would the HEI define as its territorial unit; what management structures would need to be in place to manage the portfolio of territorial roles; how can HEIs expand national and international activity whilst meeting regional needs; do mechanisms exist to embed a belief that the institution can, and should, operate within different territorial levels for the benefit of the region?

In considering what might influence the success and direction of strategy and how universities will respond to regional needs, OECD (1999, 31) focuses on organizational features and local agendas, raising a number of questions which are central to what the response might be. These are: What are the characteristics of the region in terms of its economic base, cultural activity, employment structure and levels of entrepreneurial activity and civic networks; what are the characteristics of the regional institutional networks and what lead or regulatory agencies exist; and what expectations do regional stakeholders voice to HEIs?

To illustrate how these characteristics might be understood, the report cities Davies's (1997) typology of four regional types within which the university system can fulfil a different role: Low income, stagnant region; Low income, growth region; High income, stagnant region; High income, growth region. Further, the Association of European Universities (CRE) created a three-region typology to identify different contexts for university–region dialogues. These included regions of concentration (high levels of economic development and educational development), regions of economic revival and peripheral regions. The Report argues that it is also important to understand the number and character of stakeholders in the region and points out that stakeholders or organizations involved in promoting regional economic development, unlike universities, function within explicitly defined areas. Hence it is clear that enormous expectations are being placed on universities whether or not they have the resources and competences to engage in addressing the challenges associated with these agendas.

The involvement of the university in regional economic agendas also depends on the role that the university chooses for itself – within legal and political constraints (Goldstein and Renault 2004). The impact could be simply mercantile, through primary income generation effects which benefit the local economy, as opposed to the technologically pro-active model where universities attempt to promote technology transfer to influence the trajectory of local economic development (Lanza and Piccaluga 1995). In this model, Lazzeroni and Piccaluga (2003) describe universities' role in very instrumentalist terms as four kinds of factory: knowledge, human capital, technology transfer and territorial. Within these organized roles, other and perhaps hidden individual engagement exists (Kenney 1986, 34).

An issue for policy makers internal and eternal to the university in designing their responses is that mapping university research on to local clusters (Peck and McGuinness 2003) is not always straightforward. A recent survey conducted by Charles and Conway (2001, 6) in the UK suggests that only 19 per cent of business research contracts currently secured by HEIs were from within the same region as the HEI. This implies that combining regional HEI expertise with RDA cluster priorities may prove to be problematic, with competition between regions for sectors and a duplication of facilities.

For example, Peck and McGuinness argue that on the basis of present industrial structures (DTI 2001), all three regions in the North could be argued to possess cluster potential around selected firms based in chemicals, food processing, metal industries and furniture manufacture. There are also some potential overlaps between pairs of regions in electronics, automotive assembly and leisure software. At present, there are relatively few instances of cluster development that involve inter-regional collaboration. Hence, not only might the local industries be the ones which traditionally have not worked with universities, it is not necessarily the most efficient strategy to target sunrise industries. Co-location does not necessarily imply functional interdependence – even in the biotechnology industry in the US (see Cortright and Mayer 2002). One of the major limitations of the regional innovation systems literature is therefore that it is inward-looking and implicitly reinforces the prioritization of the largely self-sufficient and autonomous region.

Conclusions

The literature reviewed here demonstrates that universities have been brought into the general discussion which has long exercised the mind of geographers and economists – that of why proximity matters in the co-location of economic activities. Universities as economic actors have joined firms in this form of analysis. Arguments have been based on analyses of technological, social and economic factors of why geographically concentrated knowledge flows (knowledge spillovers) contribute to the effectiveness of the innovation process.

The chapter also highlights that proximity may be more important at the early stages of the emergence of a new technology and its associated industry, that university–industry networks might be sector-specific and that proximity effects might fade over time. Larger firms are more likely to be able to take advantage of proximity when a field is established. Size of place also appears to be significant in the growth of high-tech sectors, especially with KIS, rather than a causal relationship with the source of knowledge flows but this might vary. Other caveats include the over-importance of tacit knowledge as a concept within social processes, the assumption that all networks are good, that institutional regimes are significant in the kinds of networks their members can participate in (Owen-Smith and Powell 2004) and that networks' potential for delivery of knowledge flows is difficult to prove.

National and regional innovation systems literatures highlight the varying degrees to which elements within the innovation processes are integrated within different countries and regions or localities. The eminence of a university is also associated with geographically variable impacts. Both of these points relate to Owen-Smith and Powell's point about the effects of distinctive institutional rules on the importance of universities in the engagement in the innovation process.

Close parallels between the defence–university nexus and the university–pharmaceuticals–biosciences are also highly significant in shaping geographical patterns of economic and innovation activity. The chapter has also suggested that there are close parallels between the defence–university and the university–pharmaceuticals–biosciences nexuses – both being highly significant – shaping geographical patterns of economic and innovation activity.

Underpinning all of the discussion about networks and innovation is the relationship between universities and human capital formation, development and recruitment. This is with regard not only to the quality of the localized pool of labour but also to the quality of 'influencers' who catalyse developments in particular locations. The theme of institutional autonomy re-emerges in the discussion of how and why universities become entrepreneurial. Finally, the realities of the territorial role appear as politically determined assumptions about the university's engagement in governance systems whether or not the expectations of the success of that role are realistic.

3   Measuring the impact

Introduction

The possibility of measuring the impact of universities on innovation and economic development, specifically on their local/regional economies, is central to confirming the validity of the dominant paradigm that capitalizing on university research equals innovation equals economic development. This chapter's focus is on what is being measured, the criteria by which 'effectiveness' of that contribution is evaluated, the magnitude of any effects and at what scale the effects are felt, and over what period. It considers the limitations to measurement methods and hence to information about the contribution of universities to economic development in general and their territorial role in particular. This discussion is relevant to the current political trend of evaluation – both of policy designed to enhance the environment for innovation and technology transfer and of the increasing practice of assessment of university output (Hughes 2003).

Distributed innovation systems

Studies on university–industry interaction point to a number of caveats to the assumption of the pervasiveness of research and technology externalization, collaboration and networking (Coombs and Metcalfe 2000). Most surveys show that universities and public research institutes are not the main sources of firms' external knowledge and that sector is one of the most important factors in the incidence of links and whether they are primarily within or outside of the national system of innovation.

First, universities are ranked well below customers and suppliers as direct sources of new technological knowledge for innovation in innovating firms in every study of external innovation and technology transfer (see for example Keeble *et al.* 1997; Lawton Smith 2000; Charles and Howells 1992; Cosh and Hughes 2001; Lawton Smith 2005; Baxter and Tyler 2004; Mansfield 1991, 1998; Beise and Stahl 1999; Arundel and Steinmuller 1998; Monjon and Waelbroek 2003). The Third CEC Community Innovation Survey (2004) shows that only 5 per cent of innovating firms indicated that universities were highly important for innovation (3 per cent for government or private non-profit research institutes) compared to 28 per cent from clients or customers (the highest external source). Arundel and Geuna (2004) cite a number of case studies and surveys that find that fewer than 10 per cent of innovations in the United States and 5 per cent of new product sales in Germany depended in some way on public science. Similarly Hall *et al.* (2000) report that, in the US, the vast majority of research partnerships registered under the National Cooperative Research Act (1984) and the National Cooperative Research and Production Act (NCRPA) of 1993 do not include a university. Yet Frenz *et al.* (2005) find evidence of a positive and significant effect on firm–university co-operation on innovation using CIS data for 8,172 UK firms for the periods 1998–2000 which suggest that, for the UK at least, universities are under-resourced.

Second, university research is highly relevant to some industries, not necessarily high-tech, and not others and while manufacturing firms are more likely to have close ties, service sector industries also have strong links. In the case of manufacturing, Salter and Martin (2001) as Pavitt (1984) and Nelson (1993) had done earlier, found that the contribution of academic research is very high in some industries such as computers and pharmaceuticals and low in industries such as rubber and plastic products and paper. Similarly, Klevorick *et al.* (1995) conducted a survey of 128 industries and found that, where its relevance was high, the most relevant discipline was usually either an engineering or an applied science discipline rather than a basic science discipline – except in the case of biological sciences (see also Nelson 1993, Lawton Smith 2000, Faulkner and Senker 1995). This pattern is likely to persist as applied subjects such as engineering geology continue to account for more than half of academic research in leading OECD countries (Pavitt 2003).

Arundel and Geuna (2004) use the results of the *Policies, appropriation and competitiveness of Europe* (PACE) survey of Europe's largest industrial firms to evaluate both the importance of public science to innovation and the role of distance in accessing public science outputs at the national level and international level. Proximity is defined by the importance firms give to knowledge obtained from domestic versus foreign sources. They argue that this survey has two advantages for addressing these issues compared to other European surveys such as CIS or comparable surveys in the US. First, PACE asks firms about the importance of public science results from four main regions (their own country, other Europe, the United States and Japan). Second, PACE includes a series of questions about the methods that firms use to learn about public science results. Research on the localization of knowledge is largely framed in physical distance but a NIS approach suggests that distance is related to more than absolute measures.

The authors found that public science is one of the six most important external knowledge sources for the innovative activities of Europe's largest industrial firms – second only to knowledge sourced from affiliated firms. Contrary to expectations, it is most important for firms in low-technology sectors, followed by firms in high-technology sectors and lastly by firms in medium-technology sectors. These results differ considerably from aggregate results using CIS surveys, where public science is one of the least important sources of technological knowledge. Much of the difference, however, vanishes once CIS results are weighted to account for a proxy of innovation output (R&D expenditures) and limited to large firms that perform most of the R&D in Europe, and which access public science in North America because it offers unique advantages. They also found evidence that rather than firms using informal contacts to access domestic sources of knowledge, they use their contacts to access knowledge outside the firm's domestic country. While their results do not support the hypothesis that tacit knowledge is a cause of proximity effects, they do not refute it either. The authors propose that there is a possible connection with EU supra-national collaborations that have led to the development of network proximity.

It should not be overlooked that university research is relevant to the service sector. Grossman *et al.* (2001) have found industry challenges in service industries such as financial services and transportation and logistics to be an important stimulus to both basic and applied research in the US.

National diversity in spend on research in universities

The level and sources of income for academic research in different countries is one of a number of explanatory factors for patterns of university–industry interactions. The following sections examine each of the following variables which are implicated in what is being measured and how the results are interpreted.

- the sources, level and stability of overall academic funding and changes in their relative importance
- the distribution of funding among the different R&D activities (basic research, applied research, and development)
- the distribution of funding among S&E broad and detailed fields and national sectoral specializations and their relative strengths
- the distribution of funding among the various performers of academic R&D and the extent of their participation
- the state of the physical infrastructure (research facilities and equipment)
- the role of the national government as a supporter of academic R&D and the particular roles of the major national agencies funding the academic sector
- the regulatory system which determines accountability and includes

scrutiny of the kinds of research and development undertaken in institutions including that of public opinion, hence the commercial potential of different kinds of research
*   the extent to which funding for research is at the regional level.

(adapted from NSF 2004)

Academic R&D

Variations in the extent to which academic research is a component of national R&D and to which academic R&D is funded by industry in selected OECD countries are illustrated in Table 3.1. In advanced industrialized countries such as the Netherlands, Canada and Italy, academic research comprises a much greater share of national R&D than in the US,

Table 3.1 Academic R&D share of total R&D performance, by selected countries: 2000 or 2001 (%)

Country	Academic R&D
All OECD	17.2
Australia	27.1
Canada	32.7
Czech Republic	15.7
Finland	17.9
France	18.5
Germany	15.8
Hungary	24.0
Iceland	15.5
Italy	31.0
Japan	14.5
Netherlands	28.8
Poland	32.7
Slovakia	9.0
South Korea	11.3
Spain	29.4
Switzerland	22.9
Turkey	60.4
United Kingdom	20.8
United States	14.9
Non-OECD	
Argentina	35.0
China	8.6
Israel	18.4
Romania	11.3
Russia	5.2
Singapore	23.6
Slovenia	16.6
Taiwan	12.2

Source: OECD (2002c).

Japan and Germany, where a higher share of R&D is conducted by other organizations, including industry. Overall, government and industry together account for roughly 80 per cent or more of the R&D funding in each of the G-8 countries.

The extent to which the balance of funding between government and industry has been changing over the past two decades is illustrated in Table 3.2. The pattern is that the government's share, including both direct government support for academic R&D and the R&D component of block grants to universities, has fallen by 8 percentage points or more in five of the G-7 countries since 1981 (France and Italy have had lower

Table 3.2 Academic R&D expenditures, by country and source of funds: 1981, 1990 and 2000 (%)

Country and source of funds	1981	1990	2000
Canada			
Government	78.8	75.0	59.9
Other	17.1	20.0	31.2
Industry	4.1	5.0	8.9
France			
Government	97.7	92.9	91.5
Other	1.0	2.	5.8
Industry	1.3	4.9	2.7
Germany			
Government	98.2	92.1	85.9
Other	0.0	0.0	2.5
Industry	1.8	7.9	11.6
Italy[1]			
Government	96.2	96.7	94.4
Other	1.1	0.9	0.8
Industry	2.7	2.4	4.8
Japan			
Government	57.8	51.2	50.2
Other	41.2	46.5	47.3
Industry	1.0	2.3	2.5
United Kingdom			
Government	81.3	73.5	64.7
Other	15.9	18.9	28.2
Industry	2.8	7.6	7.1
United States			
Government	74.1	66.9	65.0
Other	21.5	26.2	27.9
Industry	4.4	6.9	7.1

Sources: Organisation for Economic Co-operation and Development, Science and Technology Statistics database, 2003; and National Science Foundation, Division of Science Resources Statistics, *National Patterns of R&D Resources* (Arlington, VA, annual series). From NSF 2004.

Note
1 Italian data are for 1999.

percentage falls). The greatest shift was in Canada where government funding fell by a fifth, indicating a substantial reorganization of the Canadian national innovation system. The degree of integration of industry and university research is most developed in Germany which has the highest percentage of university research funded by industry (more than 11 per cent, 2000). This is considerably higher than in the US, where such funding in 2000 amounted to 7.1 per cent, up from 2.6 per cent in 1970. Much of the increase took place in the 1980s as a result of the new university–industry R&D centers (Bozeman 2000).

The apparent causal link between economic performance and university spend, however, can be misunderstood (Jacobsson 2002). NSF (2004) and Jacobsson and Rickne (2003) point out that different accounting conventions among countries may account for some of the differences in amounts of university research funding reported, hence the measurement of outputs. For instance, the national totals for academic R&D for Europe and Canada include the research components of general university funds (GUF) provided as block grants to the academic sector by all levels of government. Therefore, at least conceptually, the totals include academia's separately budgeted research and research undertaken as part of university departmental research activities. In the US, the Federal government generally does not provide research support through a GUF equivalent, preferring instead to support specific, separately budgeted R&D projects. Universities generally do not maintain data on departmental research, which is considered an integral part of instruction programmes. US totals thus may be underestimated relative to the academic R&D efforts reported for other countries. Other accounting differences include the inclusion or exclusion of R&D in the social sciences and humanities, the inclusion or exclusion of defence R&D, treatment of capital expenditures, and the level of government funding included.

Moreover, the organization of scientific work conducted outside of industry varies greatly between countries. For example, private non-profit organizations are of some importance in a few countries and therefore need to be included in the analysis. In particular, this is the case in US, Israel and Japan with a share of 8–17.5 per cent. The average for the EU is 2.5 per cent, while it is 8.9 per cent for the OECD. The Swedish share is low, less than one per cent, along with countries such as New Zealand, Canada and Ireland. Figures are also a misleading guide to value added, as rapidly growing smaller countries are spending more per head than the US, but that conceals regional spend. For example, the state of California spends almost four times as much as the UK on business R&D and would be ranked 39th (1995) (see Salter *et al.* 2000, 20).

Does the balance of government versus industry-funded share of academic R&D have negative effects on academic R&D? This has not been proved, Crespi and Geuna (2004, 42) developed an approach to analyse the phenomenon of crowding in (or crowding out). They find, with a number of caveats, that the total impact of a given increase in government investment in HE research will be determined mainly by the importance of other sources of funds in total research expenditure.

Eminence

The complexity of what is actually being measured is illustrated by evidence on the impact of individual and institutional eminence on inputs and outputs to and from academic research. The eminence of academics has been found to have a direct impact on the levels and kinds of commercialization of university research such as patenting and licensing through a series of Matthew effects (Owen-Smith and Powell 2001). The Matthew effect is a social psychology effect identified by Merton in 1968 which means that, the more renowned scientists are, the more honour they receive, while unknown scientists are not acknowledged (Zhou *et al.* 2004). Hence, for the same quality of scientific research, more prestigious scientists receive more citations than less prestigious scientists (Sine *et al.* 2003, citing Merton 1968). Carayol (2003) explains that this occurs because some academics choose research collaborations on the basis of the potential returns to their own research collaborations – those that are not supported by industry. Then their reputation enables them to benefit much more from such collaborations than ones with departments that accept industrial support in order to maintain or increase their funding. On the other hand, some laboratories can use accepting industrial funds as a means of achieving a critical size that would allow them enough funds for funding fundamental lines of research.

A variation of this effect is that researchers decide to patent because of the perceived positive personal and professional outcomes. Propensity to patent is influenced by the faculty to which they belong. Patenting is more likely to occur in a supportive environment and where there is ascription of academic status to commercial success – both of which contribute to institutional environment in which basic and applied research are likely to be undertaken simultaneously. This form of Matthew effect has a reinforcing effect when the better universities are able to reinvest in research and repeat the cycle (Geuna and Nesta 2003).

Sine *et al.* (2003) investigated a possible Mathew effect of universities' institutional prestige on their ability to license innovations. Their analysis of 102 US universities examined in the period 1991–8 found that institutional prestige increases a university's licensing rate over and above the rate that is explained by the university's past licensing performance. This prestige effect occurs after controlling for the amount of technology produced by the university, the source of research funding, the presence or absence of a medical school, the geographical location of the university and the resources of the technology licensing office. They argue that institutional prestige leads to stratification in the creation and distribution of university-generated knowledge and that the most prestigious universities will have a disproportionate influence on the evolution of technology and industry. If a local effect of this prestige is found – as proximity is argued to be a causal factor in the technology transfer process – then this also has a direct link to the uneven geography of technology transfer.

Defence and biotech

The rapid expansion in inputs into biomedical research and the correspondingly high level of outputs such as patents, licences and publications has tended to take the focus away from defence, as the major sponsor of university research, on the ramifications for academic freedom and indeed on the civil benefits of defence-funded university research. Military involvement with science, engineering and technology (SET) is concentrated in a fairly small number of countries, with the US dominating: its defence R&D is more than four times that of the EU and 75 per cent of the OECD-area budget for defence R&D (OECD 2003). In the EU, the UK, France, Spain and Germany account for 97 per cent of total government military SET (Langley 2005).

In the 1980s, defence research spending was a major component of total R&D in the US, in France and in Germany, with much of that budget being spent in the universities as well as the public sector research laboratories (Charles and Howells 1992; see Evans *et al.* 1991 on the UK case). From when Mikhail Gorbachev came to power in early 1985, which marked the beginning of the end of the Cold War period, defence R&D accounted for a massive share of the US's spend. That year the US Department of Defense (DoD) spent $30,332.4 billion on research. In the same year, the UK's Ministry of Defence (MoD) was the world's second largest single institutional funder with $4,106.8 million. The MoD spent more than any private sector organization and more than the total spend on R&D in Spain, Portugal, Greece, Denmark and Ireland added together. The next largest organizational spenders in Europe were the Ministries of Research and Technology in France and Germany, both at around $3 billion.

At the end of the decade, in 1989 the UK spent 45.5 per cent of its R&D budget allocation on defence, France 37 per cent and then a big drop to Spain 19.1 per cent and Germany 12.8 per cent. In the 1990s in the UK, defence spending fell by 25 per cent in the 1990s from the peak in 1985–6 (www.york.ac.uk/depts/econ/research/documents/rusi.pdf). Since 2001, the 'War on terror' has reversed the drop in military expenditure that followed the end of the Cold War (Langley 2005). UK defence spending also remains high. It is the world's second largest funder of military SET. In 2003–4 the military spent approximately £2.7 billion on UK R&D. £2.6 billion came from the MoD – 30 per cent of the total public R&D budget – and more than 40 per cent of government R&D personnel are employed by the MoD (Langley 2005). Historically, most of this research was undertaken by the Defence Evaluation and Research Agency (DERA) on a non-competitive basis, with DERA sub-contracting about a quarter of the work outside the MoD. In 1999, the MoD initiated a pilot scheme whereby a small percentage of the research programme was opened up to competition. Competition is now firmly established as a route for the procurement of research programmes. Following the creation of QinetiQ (the part-privatized commercial arm) and the Defence Science and Technology Laboratory (DSTL) in 2001, the MoD plans to increase the volume of work competed for, year on year, so that, by 2007, over 50 per cent of the research programme will be procured via direct competition (www.mod.uk/business/excel/competition_in_mod_s_research_programme.htm). The routes to funding university research are therefore complicated and constantly changing.

In the US, the DoD provides about 8 per cent of the university research budget. In the UK in 2000–1 official figures from the DTI are that the MoD spend in HEIs was £16.9 million, compared with £1,650.6 million spent in private industry/public corporations. The MoD funds R&D in universities both directly (through the Joint Grants Scheme) and through contracts. In 2003, funding provided by the Joint Grants Scheme amounted to £5.6 million but no information is held centrally about the number of sub-contracts. These amounts are a considerable underestimate of the total defence spending in UK universities.

While defence spending on R&D has declined, funding for research in biosciences has escalated rapidly in Europe and in the US where massive investments have been made in universities and other research institutes. In the US life sciences (plus engineering and the computer sciences) are receiving an increasing share of national R&D funding. In 1999, the overwhelming share of academic R&D expenditures went to the life sciences, which accounted for 57 per cent of total academic R&D expenditures, 56 per cent of Federal academic R&D expenditures, and 58 per cent of non-Federal academic R&D expenditures. Within the life sciences, the medical sciences accounted for 29 per cent of total academic R&D expenditures and the biological sciences for 18 per cent (www.nsf.gov/statistics/seind02/c5/c5s1.htm#c5s116). An additional 12 per cent of national funding was provided by NSF, 4 per cent by the National Aeronautics and Space Administration (NASA); 3 per cent by the Department of Energy (DOE); and 2.5 per cent by the Department of Agriculture (USDA). NSF and NASA experienced the next highest rates of growth: 3.8 and 3.4 per cent, respectively. In 2002, the NIH budget was $23.6 billion and projected to be $28.7 billion in 2005, a 2.8 per cent increase on 2004. The rate of increase in spend is set to slow down. After enjoying double-digit budget increases from FY 1998 to FY 2003, in FY 2004 the budget increase was only 2.8 per cent, and for the FY 2005 another minimal increase was recommended (www.the-aps.org/pa/action/fy2005/FY05Budget.htm). National charities such as the US Heart Foundation, and the Leukemia charity are also source of major funds for research. Figure 3.1 shows the faster growth of Federal funding for life sciences than for other disciplines. Moreover, in both the US and the UK there has been a growing convergence between defence and biotech as biomedical research is increasingly militarized (see Langley 2005).

In the UK, five main sources of national funding exist for biotech-related university research: the research councils, medical charities, the Higher Education Funding Councils (for England, Scotland, Wales and Northern Ireland), the pharmaceutical industry and the EU. No funds for university research are available at the regional or local level. The Medical Research Council (MRC), like the NIH, has its own research centres (40 centres account for about half the annual budget and employ 3,700 staff compared to 3,000 staff, and 1,000 students in the universities). The Biotechnology and Biological Sciences Research Council (BBSRC) (non-medical research) funds research in universities and recently in some government laboratories. (These are the MRC, the Natural Environment Research Council (NERC) and the Biotechnology and Biological sciences Research Council (BBRC). BBRC awards £200 million per year to scientists working in universities and eight sponsored research institutes (e.g. Roslin in Scotland and Babraham in Cambridge) and funds seven thousand scientists, post-graduate students and support staff.) Spending on research in biological sciences is increasing (www.ost.gov.uk/research/ forwardlook03/tables/index.htm gives detailed breakdowns of spending). In 2001 the MRC spent £175.7 million of its £346.5 million budget in universities, ten times larger than the MoD direct spend in universities. The MRC's budget rose from £415 million (2002–3) to £500 million (2005–6). The MRC's budget is 36 times smaller than the NIH budget but per capita NIH is still six times greater than the MRC. The MRC's programmes on

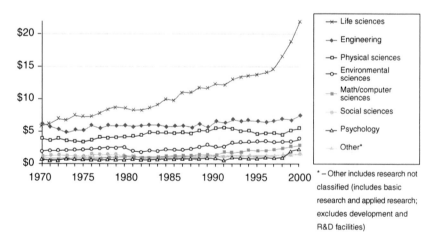

Figure 3.1 Federal R&D by discipline (AAAS), FY 1970–2001 (obligations in billions of constant FY 2002 dollars) (source: Shapira 2004a).

genomics and proteomics, 'e-science', basic technology, stem cells, and brain science are being taken forward in co-operation with other Research Councils and key stakeholders, including the health departments and National Health Service (NHS) and medical research charities. In 2001–2 BBSRC provided £2.13 million of funding per year to scientists working in universities and in its eight research institutes. Of that, £130.3 million went into universities. Collectively, according to the 2003–4 HESA Finance Returns, the amount of income for research grants and contracts for the biosciences cost centre equals £397,533,000: this is 14.6 per cent of the total income for research grants and contracts in universities. In addition, the budget for the Higher Education Funding Council for England (HEFCE) for research for biological sciences in 2005–6 was £91.3 million.

Medical charities such as the Wellcome Trust and Cancer UK also pump millions of pounds into university research each year. For example, the Wellcome Trust spent £1.2 billion on research grants between 2000 and 2003, declining from a peak of £480 million in 2000 to £393 million in 2003. Its commercialization department, Technology Transfer, works in partnership with academia, business and investors to promote the translation of research innovations into healthcare benefits through advice, support and the administration of tailor-made awards for early-stage research and development. Cancer Research UK is the largest volunteer-supported cancer research organization in the world. The budget for research grants and activities for 2003–4 was £184.28 million – over half to programmes activities including clinical units and chairs (£50.23 million) and institutes (£51.17 million), with £10.5 million funding clinical trials. Academics in the UK also have access to European Commission Funds under successive Framework Programmes that are the financial instrument of the European Research Area. The budget for FP6 in the Thematic Priority Life Sciences, genomics and biotechnology for health is €2,514 million, of which €1,209 million is allocated for advanced genomics, €1,209 for applications for health, and €1,305 for combating major diseases. Most of this money goes to the universities and other public sector research centres. Much larger than all of these sources of funding is the amount invested by big-pharma. The UK pharmaceutical industry spends some £3.3bn a year in R&D – six times as much as the Department of Health, five times as much as medical charities, and eight times as much as the MRC (House of Commons Health Committee 2005).

Yet while in both the US and the UK there has been a massive increase in government funding for biomedical science, Nightingale and Martin (2004, 565) found there was an explosion of patents and licences in therapeutically active compounds – 'low hanging fruit' – and they also found a decline in R&D productivity in the US as measured by the number of patents per dollar of R&D expenditure. They conclude that 'any qualitative productivity increases that biotechnology has brought to R&D has not kept pace with the increased complexity of the problems that the pharmaceutical industry and its regulators are now addressing'. Moreover, the peak in the mid-1990s needs to be interpreted within the context of shifting regulator goal posts, following the Prescription Drug User Free Act 1992 and the FDA Modernisation Act (1997) which allowed accelerated approval and fast-track registration. In addition, on the basis of the very small number of biopharmaceuticals evaluated between 1986 and 2004, they find no support for the notion that there has been a biotechnology revolution. They find this pessimism reflected in the 2004 FDA White Paper *Innovation or stagnation?* which emphasizes the need for translation and critical path research focused on the clinical assessment of novel products. Similarly, Langley (2005) finds that the civilian benefits from military SET are overstated, and have a negative effect on openness in SET.

Accountability and ownership

The growing trend of multiple accountabilities is indicated by the enactment of policies which determine ownership of intellectual property – the terms of trade and the criteria by which the commercial performance of university research and that of technology transfer offices are evaluated. Such articulated institutionalization of accountability has implicit assumptions about what scientific research is for, the merits of the closeness of the relationship between industry and universities and the forms that those should take.

Ownership of IP and publication issues

Geuna and Nesta (2003) find that the increasing number of patents and licences held by universities has been accompanied by legal changes in the reward or incentive structure within universities. In a number of EU countries, researchers may now receive a proportion of the royalties derived from their patented discoveries even though the patent legally belongs to the institution. Rules vary by country. Table 3.3 shows the rules on ownership of intellectual property in universities in selected OECD countries. Hence outcomes in terms of numbers of patents and their ownership will vary not only by the content of the rules but also by the means by which those rules are implemented. This is illustrated by OECD's 2001 survey of member countries' technology transfer offices which examined national laws and regulations. It was found that in countries that enacted legislation, awareness of and support for technology transfer increased among the major stakeholders even though relatively little growth in patenting, licensing, or spin-offs occurred. In addition, most licensing of technology from universities and public research organizations is based on non-patentable inventions.

While the universal trend is for universities to find ways of increasing their income through the sale of intellectual property, there is considerable concern, not only from within academia, that this is in conflict with

Table 3.3 Ownership of academic intellectual property in OECD countries: 2003

Country	Owner of invention			Status/recent initiatives
	University	Faculty	Government	
Australia	X	na	na	
Austria	X	na	na	
Belgium	X	na	na	
Canada[1]	X	X	na	
Denmark	X	na	na	
Finland	na	X	na	Consideration of legislation in 2003 to restrict faculty's right to retain ownership of publicly funded research.
France	X	na	na	
Germany	X	na	na	Debate during 2001 over awarding ownership to universities.
Iceland	na	X	na	
Ireland	X	na	na	
Italy	na	X	na	Legislation passed in 2001 to give ownership rights to researchers. Legislation introduced in 2002 to grant ownership to universities and create technology transfer offices. Private technology transfer offices authorized in 1998.
Japan[2]	na	X	0	
Mexico	X	na	na	
Netherlands	X	na	na	
Norway	na	X	na	Legislation passed in 2003 to allow universities to retain ownership of publicly funded research.
Poland	X	na	na	
South Korea	X	na	na	
Sweden	na	X	na	Recent debate and consideration of legislation to allow universities to retain ownership of publicly funded research.
United Kingdom	X	0	na	Universities, rather than government, given rights to faculty inventions in 1985.
United States[3]	X	0	0	

Sources: OECD 2002d; Mowery and Sampat 2002; *NSF Science & Engineering Indicators – 2004.*

Notes

X legal basis or most common practice.

0 allowed by law/rule but less common.

na not applicable.

1 Ownership of intellectual property funded by institutional funds varies, but publicly funded intellectual property belongs to institution performing research.

2 President of the national university or interuniversity institution determines right to ownership of invention by faculty member, based on discussions by invention committee.

3 Universities have first right to elect title to inventions resulting from federally funded research. Federal Government may claim title if university does not. In certain cases, inventor may retain rights with agreement of university/Federal partner and Government.

the scientific norm of publicizing research results. Specific potential dangers of an increase in academic patenting and licensing are summarized below (NSF (2004) and Geuna and Nesta (2003)).

- emphasis or diversion of resources toward research areas with commercial potential which may harm or slow progress in these non-commercial areas and may erode the widely held precept that universities promote knowledge for knowledge's sake
- clauses in licensing agreements often restrict or delay publication of research results or require researchers to obtain approval or pay costs for using their technology in upstream applications
- increased cost of accessing research material or tools etc.
- costs of setting up, maintaining, and administering technology transfer activities outweigh potential profits on these activities
- exclusive licensing agreements result in higher costs to consumers, a slower pace of innovation and adoption of the technology
- substitution effects between publishing and patenting
- diverting research resources from the exploitation of long-term research questions that tend not be suited to the development IPRs
- threat to future scientific investigation from IPR on previous research
- threat to teaching quality.

These potential dangers are recognized in both the US and Europe. In the US, guidelines were issued by the National Institutes of Health in December 1999 for universities in receipt of Federal funding. These were designed to *discourage* patenting unless patent protection was necessary to attract investment needed for full development. The guidelines urged that tools be licences with as few encumbrances as possible, and argued against reach-through royalties – a practice in which the owner of a research tool seeks royalties on any product that might be developed through its use. Tool developers, such as emerging biotechnology firms, argue that reach-through royalties are an alternative to charging high up-front user fees or restricting access (Business Higher Education Forum 2001, 14). The Committee's conclusions were published just as the US House of Representatives made a similar recommendation that research funded by the NIH should be freely available. In the UK in 2004, the House of Commons Science & Technology Committee Report on scientific publishing recommended that UK research funding bodies mandate free access to all their research findings. The Report recommends that all UK HE institutions should establish institutional repositories on which their published output can be stored and from which it can be read, free of charge, online. It also recommends that Research Councils and other government funders mandate their funded researchers to deposit a copy of all of their articles in this way. The role of defence in funding university research should also be more transparent. Langley (2005) argues that professional bodies, scientific and engineering institutions and publishers should require that all academic papers and reports based on work funded by the military publicly acknowledge this funding and scale.

Yet, while these issues will continue to be debated, most authors find that no evidence one way or the other to show that the increase in technology transfer activities is to the detriment of research activity or that research directions have been changed as a consequence (Hughes 2003; Geuna and Nesta 2003). Stephan *et al.* (2002) found no evidence of a substitution effect of patents for publications and in scientific disciplines such as life sciences, physical sciences and to a lesser extent engineering they found that there is a positive effect and they are complementary activities. Zucker and Darby (2001) found that star scientists working on commercial problems are not any less productive. On the other hand, Louis *et al.* (2001) and Blumenthal *et al.* (1996) report greater secrecy and less disclosure over research findings amongst industry-funded researchers. Poyago-Theotoky *et al.* (2003) and Geuna and Nesta (2003) also sound a note of caution. In analysing university patenting and its effects on academic research they find that data collection and interpretation are far from clear-cut and can be misleading.

Evaluation

As the pressure on universities to commercialize their research has increased, so has the institutionalization of that pressure in the form of evaluation of their performance. University research evaluation and allocations of government funding are increasingly related, reflecting global demands for efficiency and accountability (see Geuna and Martin 2003, Campbell 2003). Two forms of evaluation are discussed here. The first is that which evaluates the quality and impact of university research and the second that which evaluates the commercial value of university technology and technology transfer.

Geuna and Martin (2003) find that the first kind of evaluation can be either ex-ante or ex-post but there is no agreement as to which measurements work best and their objectives tend to be defined by the agency that conducts it. The main virtue of performance-based approaches is said to be that they increase efficiency in the short term and may provide greater accountability through being meritocratic, rewarding success and improving quality. On the other hand they suggest that there will always be reasons for opposing this approach, not least because the process is costly, it engenders competition, widens the gap between teaching and research, discourages risky and longer-term research and leads to an excess of government influence (pages 16–17).

Evaluations of university research, as in the Netherlands, the UK and Australia, are characterized by Campbell (2003) as being systemic, nationally promoted and institutionally orientated, with the use of explicit grading and ranking systems. (The RAE conducted every five years ranks units of assessment (subject groups) according to criteria such as quality of publications and esteem indicators.) Until recently, unlike in the UK which has the most advanced system, in the Netherlands this was not linked to research funding. University evaluation in Germany and Austria is targeted more towards the individual. The German system is based on a series of metrics rather than peer group review. Widespread adoption of the UK or Netherlands model is uncertain given what Campbell finds as the ambiguity and apprehension about the effectiveness of such exercises. The numerous methods for evaluating the impact of university research that exist (see Georghiou and Roessner 2000; Jacobsson 2002, 23; Arundel and Geuna 2001) have the basic problem that they do not fully capture the non-economic benefits from research or those benefits that are not easily translated into monetized forms. Moreover, they are likely to suffer from a variation of the uncertainty principle in physics, Goodhart's Law, which states that the instant a measure is used as a target, it loses all value as a measure because all effort goes into meeting the target and loses sight of what the object of the exercise is for (Caulkin 2004).

The second kind of evaluations falls into two basic categories: production function analyses and studies seeking social rates of return (Georghiou and Roessner 2000). Production function studies assume that a formal relationship exists between R&D expenditures and productivity. Aggregate social rate of return studies attempt to estimate the social benefits that accrue from changes in technology and relate the value of those benefits to the cost of investments in research that produced both changes. The authors find that both tend to show that the aggregate rate of return is positive and make a number of other critiques of methods deployed. A major problem, however, is that it is not possible to measure indirect effects accurately. Berens and Gray (2001) suggest that the 7 per cent of US academic research funded by industry may lead, because of leverage effects, to a share of approximately 20–25 per cent of academic research being directly funded by industrial funding.

Bozeman (2000, 628) summarizes the 'Continent Effectiveness Model' of technology transfer. This model considers a number of determinants of effectiveness, including various characteristics of the technology, transfer agent and the technology recipient. The most important point of the model is that technology transfer can have several meanings including market impacts, political impacts, impacts on personnel involved and impacts on resources available for other purposes and other scientific and technical objectives. It is based on the assumption that parties to technology transfer have multiple goals and effectiveness criteria. The model includes five dimensions of effectiveness: (1) the characteristics of the technology transfer agent, (2) characteristics of the transfer media, (3) characteristics of the transfer object, (4) the demand environment, and (5) characteristics of the demand recipient. It is assumed that no single notion of effectiveness makes sense and the model lists six technology effectiveness criteria, their focus and relation to research and practice. They range from 'out-of-the-door', which is common in practice but uncommon as an evaluation measure, to scientific and human capital which is a concern among practitioners but rarely examined in research. He finds that the out-of-the-door criterion for evaluation is likely to become more important as a result of the increased concern for quantitative demonstration of results in the US (page 646). The Government Performance and Results Act (GPRA) passed by the US Congress 1993 has contributed in part to the 'metric mania' gripping the US 'Federal bureaucracy'. Bozeman suggests that the public policy argument of the out-of-the-door criterion is that it is the university's (or government laboratory's) job to create technologies or applied research attractive to industry, but it is industry's job to make them work in the marketplace. In the wake of GPRA, this argument may no longer be sustainable. Likewise Geoghiou and Roessner (2000) find that the short-term and aggregate perspective of performance reviews conflicts with the longer-term, programme-level yet context-dependent perspective of technology programmes evaluations.

The entrepreneurial role

Looking specifically at the entrepreneurial role, measurement of activities such as patents, licences, collaborations, joint university–industry scientific publications and university spin-offs have been the subject of many studies. Each activity, however, has merits and demerits as indicators of the strength and quality of the impact of university research on research undertaken in industry. Moreover, implicit and explicit in the increase in the number of technology transfer organizations designed to aid these entrepreneurial activities is the notion that there are barriers or boundaries to be overcome.

Patents

Geuna and Nesta (2003, 8) define university-invented patents as 'patents with a member of university faculty amongst the inventors, whether or not the university is the assignee of the patent'. The merits of examining patent citations and scientific publications are fourfold. (1) They are a means of measuring the cognitive distance between universities and industry by measuring the impact on innovations in industry and differences in the relevance of different research fields (Balconi *et al.* 2004). The web of science and technology linkages allows for the observation of certain governance shifts in certain S&T areas. (2) They measure the intensity of science and technology interaction. (3) They track potential knowledge flows between certain scientific and technological fields. (4) They provide an indication of the closeness of a relationship between scientific and industrial laboratories.

Evidence shows that entrepreneurial activity in the form of academic patents in the US and Europe has increased dramatically over the past three decades. In the US, the number of patents increased rapidly following the Bayh-Dole Act. In the 1970s patents issued to US universities were fewer than 250 per year, increasing to more than 3,200 in 2001. Over the period 1991–2000 patents granted rose by 160 per cent. The share of academic patents has also risen significantly, even as growth in all US patents increased rapidly during this period. US academic institutions accounted for more than 4 per cent of patents granted to the US private and non-profit sectors in 2001, compared with less than 1.5 per cent in 1981. The share, however, was down slightly from a peak of almost 5 per cent during 1997–9. During this period, the number of academic institutions receiving patents increased rapidly, nearly doubling in the 1980s to more than 150 institutions and continuing to grow to reach 190 institutions in 2001 (see Siegel *et al.* 2003).

NSF (2004) report that, in the 1990s, some 75 per cent of references to scientific publications in US patent applications originated in publicly funded science. The number of US scientific papers cited in US patent applications rose more than sixfold between 1985 and 1998. The number of new patent applications more than quadrupled between FYs 1991 and 2001, indicating the growing effort and increasing success of universities obtaining patent protection for their technology. Despite the increase in institutions receiving patents, the distribution of patenting activity has remained highly concentrated among a few major research universities and in a few sectors. The top 25 recipients accounted for more than 50 per cent of all academic patents in 2001, a share that has remained constant for two decades. These institutions also account for a disproportionate share (40 per cent in 2001) of all R&D expenditures by academic patenting institutions. Including the next 75 largest recipients increases the share to more than 90 per cent of patents granted to all institutions in 2001 and much of the 1990s. Many smaller universities and colleges began to receive patents in the 1980s, which pushed the large institutions' share as low as 82 per cent, but the trend reversed in the 1990s. In 1999, 14 patents were produced for every 1,000 S&E doctorate holders employed in academia, which was almost double the number in 1993. The rise in this indicator suggests that states and their universities may be focusing on academic patenting more than in the past. States vary widely in academic patenting, which ranges from 0 to 27 patents per 1,000 S&E doctorate holders employed in academia.

Although the number of patents from universities in Europe is measurably greater in the last two decades, the European Commission's European Innovation Scoreboard (EIS) found in 2003 a specific European weakness in patenting. In fact, the US is patenting more actively in Europe than Europe itself, particularly for high-tech patents. The report argues that the future implementation of the EU patent will facilitate patenting in Europe and there is justification for a concerted EU effort to boost patenting. In France, Belgium, Finland, Germany and Italy, there has been a decline in university patents owing to the practice of researchers or professors leaving ownership of the patent to be assigned to the firms that financed the research project. Other studies have shown that the number of university invented patents is much higher than the number of patents owned by universities, e.g. Balconi *et al.* (2004) for Italy, Meyer (2002) for Finland and OECD (2002c) for Germany. Other studies have found similar patterns in Belgium and France (see Geuna and Nesta 2003). Geuna and Nesta (2003, 10) find that the US has been much more aggressive than Europe in enforcing and exploiting IPRs on the research carried out by their researchers. Between the late 1980s and the end of the 1990s the number of USPTO patents granted to US academic institutions more than tripled and by 2002 numbered nearly 3,300. This rapid growth was accompanied by the development of specialized management or administrative organization within universities and by the creation in the science curricula of specialist training in patent law, and the development of a code of conduct designed to cope with conflicts of interest.

The relative balance of university versus other PROs in the research-to-innovation system is illustrated by a study by Cesaroni and Piccaluga (2002). They constructed a database of comparable data for France, Italy and Spain on PRO internationally granted patents from the European Office (EPO) and the US Patent Office (USPTO) during the period 1982–2002. They found that PROs in these countries were granted respectively 911, 723 and 127. The Centre National de la Recherche Scientifique (CNRS) (France), Consiglio Nazionale delle Ricerche (CNR) (Italy) and Consejo Superior de Investigaciones Científicas (CSIC) (Spain) are the three PROs with the highest number of patents. In France and Italy only about 10 per cent of granted patents are owned by universities, while in Spain universities own nearly 50 per cent. The study also highlights the high level of co-patenting activity, with between 20 per cent and 30 per cent of the patents having more than one assignee (more than 50 per cent of which are with firms).

A number of provisos on both the pattern of patenting and the reliability of the data are identified in the literature. First, sector and institutional status are key variables explaining the overall trend of increasing university patenting activity. The growth in academic patents has occurred primarily in the life sciences and biotechnology in both Europe and the US (OECD 2002a; Geuna and Nesta 2003). Patents in two technology areas or 'utility classes', both with presumed biomedical relevance, accounted for 39 per cent of the academic total in 2001, up from fewer than a quarter in the early 1980s. The class that experienced the fastest growth – chemistry, molecular biology and microbiology – increased its share from 8 per cent to 21 per cent during this period. By the mid-1990s, some 60 per cent of US university licences result from a biomedical invention (Pressman 2001), such as hepatitis-B vaccine at the University of California, San Franscisco, and Taxol at Florida State University, while in 1998 41 per cent of USPTO patents were in three areas of biomedicine, indicating a strong focus on developments in the life sciences and biotechnology fields. About half the total royalties were related to life sciences. While the number of patents is increasing, net income generally is very low and net losses can occur. Payoff is mostly associated with one or two big hits, the choice of which may be the result of luck rather than judgement (Mowery and Sampat 2001, Powers 2003). The 1999 AUTM survey found that about half of universities' royalties were concentrated in technology related to the life sciences. Licensing income is also highly concentrated among a small number of universities and blockbuster patents. For example, the 2000 AUTM survey found that fewer than 1 per cent of active licenses gener-ated more than $1 million in income in FY 2000, a figure that includes licences held by US universities and hospitals, Canadian institutions and patent management firms.

Second, Geuna and Nesta (2003) found considerable variation in the propensity for UK universities to patent, with most patents emanating from the most eminent universities. They reported on a survey (University Companies Association (UNICO)) conducted in 2002 which found that the 77 universities that responded (which account for 85 per cent of research spending in universities in 2001) accounted for 1,402 invention dis-closures, 745 patent applications and 276 patents granted. The majority of universities (56 per cent), however, had not had any patents granted, 60 per cent earned less than £50,000 a year from licences, while 40 per cent had no income at all from licences; for two-thirds expenditure on IP management was less than £50,000 but only 14 per cent had no expenditure for this item. Compared with the US and Canada, the UK is behind in income from licensing, in the number of licences executed and number of patents issued.

Third, recent attention has been focused on the significance of regula-tory change in stimulating patenting activity. In both the US and Europe, legislation has established a common ground for university patenting. Yet academic analysis suggests that the impact of legislation has been minimal. In both locations, patenting is not a new phenomenon and specific policy incentives were not needed for it to develop (Geuna and Nesta 2003).

Fourth, Meyer (2003) argues that university-owned patents are only a partial indicator of useful research outputs of universy research. This is because patents are of limited value as measures of innovation as many patents are not put to use and the distribution of value among those that are is highly skewed. This problem is also exacerbated by incomplete data collection, hence its unreliability (OECD 2003; Geuna and Nesta 2003); and because measuring patents and patent citations underestimates the value of public science as many innovations are not patented (see Arundel and Kabla 1998). Balconi *et al.* (2004) also highlight methodological limitations. In particular, re-classifying patents by inventor rather than by applicant could lead to a more positive evaluation of university–industry links in Europe, an evaluation which takes into account the relative inexperience of European universities in handling IPR.

Finally, the usefulness of the measure itself is in doubt. Cohen *et al.* (1998), in line with other studies such as Agrawal and Henderson (2002), argue that patenting ranks well below graduate recruitment, consultancy and publication in importance as a means of technology transfer.

Licensing

Licensing has been on the increase in the US and Europe since the early 1990s. Annual AUTM surveys show how invention disclosures, patenting and licensing of patented technologies has increased and has created thousands of jobs. Income to universities from patenting and licences has grown substantially over the decade 1991–2000, reaching more than $850 million in FY 2001 – more than half as much again as the FY 1996 level. Licensing income, however, is only a small fraction of overall academic research spending, amounting to less than 4 per cent in the FY 2001.

Yet licensing data has its limitations as an indication of how universities fit into processes of technological change. A recent NSF (2004) report argues that obtaining patent protection does not always precede negotiation of a licensing agreement, underscoring the embryonic nature of university-developed technology. It reports that, according to a recent survey of more than 60 major research universities by Thursby *et al.* (2001), 76 per cent of respondents reported that they 'rarely' or 'sometimes' had patent or copyright protection at the time of negotiating the licensing agreement, whereas 25 per cent responded 'often' or 'almost always'. In addition, most inventions were at a very early stage of development when the licensing agreement was negotiated, and nearly half the respondents characterized their inventions as a proof of concept rather than a prototype. The majority of licences and options (66 per cent) are conducted with small companies (existing companies or start-ups). Indeed it is the Bayh-Dole Act's mandate that universities give preference to small businesses. In cases of unproven or very risky technology, universities often opt to make an arrangement with a start-up company because existing companies may be unwilling to take on the risk. Faculty involvement in start-ups may also play a key role in this form of alliance. The majority of licences granted to small companies and start-ups are exclusive, that is, they do not allow the technology to be commercialized by other companies.

In contrast with this extensive information in the US and Canada, European data on licences is almost non-existent (Geuna and Nesta 2003, 27). In the UK, the number of IP licences granted to UK-based companies based on Higher Education Institute's IP increased by 38 per cent from 382 in 1999–2000 to 527 in 2000–1, while total new (initial) patents filed rose by 26 per cent from 725 to 913 over the same period. The majority of these are concentrated in the top few universities (see HEFCE 2003). This compares with 4,672 new licences and options in the US in the FY 2001–3 (AUTM 2004a).

Publications

The absolute and relative number of scientific publications and the level of citations are indicative of the strength of the science base by country and of the synergies between universities and industry by sector. First, the United States had the largest single share of articles in the world in 2001, accounting for approximately one-third of all articles (Table 3.4). When the shares of Japan, Germany, the United Kingdom and France are added to the US, these five countries account for nearly 60 per cent of all articles published in 2001, with the US accounting for 31 per cent (NSF 2004). However, Europe's EIS study showed that Western Europe's article output grew by about two-thirds from 1988 to 2001 and surpassed that of the US in 1997. Output gains were substantial across most countries, especially many of the smaller and/or newer members of the EU. This growth may reflect, at least in part, EU and regional programmes to strengthen the S&T base, as well as these nations' individual efforts.

But, in terms of the citation frequency, the US's papers dominate, suggesting that US research is rated more highly than that in Europe within and outside academia. Moreover, citations from the US are much more likely to be to publications outside the US whereas in some European countries and Canada the proportion of own-country citations is higher, suggesting a greater integration of the US than Europe into geographically extensive systems. Of the top 30 citations on all patents only three were non-US (UK, France and Japan) with Harvard, Scripps Clinical & Research Foundation and National Cancer Institution some way ahead in combatorial synthesis. For all countries the number of citations to their own country's papers is higher than for all countries taken together, suggesting a geographical localization effect at the national scale. For the US this difference is small while for EU countries the difference is much more significant. In the cases of France, Germany Japan and the UK the 'own-country' citations are three to four times higher than for all countries combined. For Italy and Canada, the most extreme, more than 50 per cent of citations originate in the author's own country (Malo and Geuna 2000, 317).

The field distribution of scientific articles changed little between 1988 and 2001. The life sciences dominated the portfolio of the OECD countries, including the US, and of Central and South America and sub-Saharan Africa (NSF 2004).

Table 3.4 Number of published scientific articles for all types of organizations in a number of rich countries, 1999, in relation to GDP (million US dollars, purchasing power parity) (ranking within parentheses)

Country	Number of articles in all fields of science per GDP, 1999	Number of articles in natural science, engineering and medicine, 1999 per GDP
Israel	42.9 (1)	39.3 (1)
Sweden	38.6 (2)	36.7 (2)
Switzerland	34.0 (3)	33.1 (3)
Finland	33.4 (4)	31.5 (4)
New Zealand	32.3 (5)	28.1 (5)
United Kingdom	28.6	25.4
Denmark	28.2	27.0
Australia	25.8	23.0
Netherlands	24.9	22.8
Canada	24.3	21.6
Singapore	20.6	19.4
France	19.7	19.1
Norway	19.5	17.8
Belgium	19.4	18.5
Germany	18.4	17.8
United States	17.7	15.5
Austria	17.2	16.6
Spain	16.3	15.9
Iceland	15.3	13.7
Japan	15.1	15.0
Ireland	12.7	11.8
Italy	12.4	12.2
South Korea	10.4	10.3
Luxembourg	1.5	1.2

Sources: NSF (2002): Science and Engineering Indicators, National Science Foundation, US, and OECD (2003), Main Science and Technology Indicators, 2003:1 for data on GDP; Jacobsson and Rickne (2003).

Note
Natural sciences, engineering and medicine includes the following categories: clinical medicine, biomedical research, biology, chemistry, physics, earth and space, engineering and technology, mathematics.

Herbst (2004) examined the comparative performance of Europe versus the US in scientific publications using data from the EC (1997) and CEST. His study shows significant variations between countries and institutions. He finds that the former shows that between 1981 and 1995 Switzerland had the highest number of publications per inhabitant, ahead of Sweden, Canada, the US and the UK, and also scores highest on the relative impact of publications, ahead of the US, Sweden, the UK and the Netherlands. Herbst explains that averaged data conceal internal variations of significance: individual US states or German Länder, for example, may perform better than some of the smaller nations listed. To overcome this, CEST focused on 1,000 institutions worldwide on the basis of biblio-metric selection criteria. This found that US universities were heavily over-represented among 100 best rated institutions. When this is broken down by sub-field (academic discipline), US universities performed strongly, and in the vast majority of academic disciplines or fields US uni-versities were over-represented. In fact in more than two-fifths of all sub-fields assessed, the corresponding relative share of US institutions amounted to at least 70 per cent. A similar pattern is observable for Nobel laureates in physics, physiology or medicine, and economics, but not in chemistry, where Europe has a long tradition and industrial strength. Zucker *et al.* (1998b) found that, for an average firm involved in biology, two genetic sequence articles co-authored by an academic star scientist and a firm's scientists result in about one more product in development, one more product on the market and 344 employees; for five articles these numbers were five, 3.5 and 860 respectively.

Moreover, the assessment of the impact of scientific publications also has a time factor. Crespi and Geuna (2004) found that the full effect of an increase in HE research and development spending on publications takes six years to occur, and on citations seven years, with no significant return on investment for at least two years. They also found evidence of decreas-ing returns for publications and citations to the domestic component of HE research and development but slightly increasing returns at the inter-national level. Ranking publications, they found considerable stability over time, with the US first, UK second, followed by Germany, France and Canada. The pattern of citations was similar but with the notable excep-tion of Canada falling behind to 13th place in 2002, compared to third place in 1987. In making comparison of scientific productivity overall (defined as how far the scientific system is from the best way of producing science output), they showed that the US and the UK scientific systems are the most technologically efficient (the best organizational set up and highest productivity). At the same time, the US and the UK, like Australia and Canada, do not have positive productivity growth rates. The knock-on effect is catch-up: all countries are converging to the efficient frontier represented by the US, the convergence of the UK with the US is mainly due to a deterioration in US productivity. While that of the UK has declined it has been at a slower rate, and 11 of the other 12 countries studied are catching up with the UK.

The centrality of Canadian universities' position in industrial research is illustrated by a study of publications by Godin and Gingras (2000). They found that, in 1995, the Canadian university sector was present in 81.9 per cent of the 25,666 papers in the *Science Citation Index* (CSI) containing at least one university address (up from 75 per cent in 1980). Government sectors were present in 16.5 per cent followed by the hospital sector (12.8 per cent) and industry (4.6 per cent). The authors conclude that the real effect of diversification has been to stimulate university research further through collaboration and not to diminish universities' presence in collaborations. Therefore, rather than receding from central places as suggested by Gibbons *et al.* (1994), universities – at least in Canada – have been able to stay at the centre of knowledge production systems as research collaborators. Moreover, since their data show a growing presence of industries among knowledge producers, there is evidence of stronger relationships between the components of the innovation system rather than marginalization of any one of the actors. Balconi *et al.* (2004) came to similar conclusions about the role academic inventors played in chemical technologies and that they have contributed significantly to innovation in electronics, instruments and industrial engineering in Italy.

Spin-offs

University spin-offs have symbolic value as indicators of how entrepreneurial universities are. They are credited with a number of benefits to society through their employment generation and generating significant economic value, thus promoting and encouraging economic development; linking science to markets and inducing investment in university technologies and stimulating innovation; helping universities with their mission, supporting additional research, attracting and retaining faculty, and training students (OECD 2001b; Shane 2004). Yet the potential for measurement of their performance and inter-institutional and inter-country comparison is limited because no common definition of what counts as a public-sector spin-off firm has emerged from the technology policy literature. The term is used rather loosely and refers generally to any new, small, high-technology or knowledge-intensive company whose intellectual capital somehow has origins in a university or public research institution (OECD 2001b). (OECD surveyed 19 countries on their spin-offs activity, asking for number of spin-offs and definitions used to define them.)

Current problems of defining what spin-offs are and measuring their performance is the equivalent of the 1980s vexed question of how to define 'high-tech'. At the broadest level, a university spin-off is deemed to be a company founded by members or former members (i.e. existing academics, research staff, technicians, undergraduates, graduates and postgraduates). This definition can lead to an extensive range of firms included, especially when there is no commonly agreed cut-off point of the time lag between the founder being a member of the institute and the actual creation of the organization (if the time lag is long, the factors leading to the formation of the organization may be only associated remotely with the original institution). Some countries, such as the US, chose very broad definitions, while the Italy, Hungary and UK definitions are narrowly focused on single factors: obtaining licences, faculty and staff foundations, and firms with equity investments, respectively (OECD

2001b). There is also the problem of including ownership of university IP in a definition if universities do not own academic IP – as in Sweden.

However defined, the patterns are that spin-off activity is increasing. It is more common in some countries than others. Spin-offs tend to be formed more often by the more research-intensive universities. The net number of spin-offs is small and their size, growth rates, revenues, and product generation are modest, at least in the first decade of their existence, and most do not grow into large firms. Spin-offs are mainly in the biomedical and the information technology fields, and most stay within the same geographical area as the institution from which they came. Those in Europe do not tend to grow as fast as in the US and the number of public spin-offs is small as compared to total new firm creation and corporate spin-offs (OECD 2001b). Table 3.5 shows a comparison of the rate of spin-off formation across the OECD.

The explanation for high figures for Germany given by the OECD is that in the ATHENE study commissioned by the BMBF in 1998 the organizations counted include non-university research institutions, which receive some public funding, include the Hermann von Helmholtz National Research Centres, the Frauenhofer-Gesellschaft, the Max Planck Institute, and various regional and national research laboratories. Over the course of the early to mid-1990s, an average of 58 spin-offs per year had affiliations to these laboratories. With university and *Hochschule* spin-off foundations totalling several hundred per year, Germany appears

Table 3.5 Comparison of spin-off formation across the OECD

	Institutions	*Cumulative number*	*Period*	*Per year*	*Period*	*Reference*
Australia	All	138	1971–99	10	1991–9	Thorburn
Belgium	All	66	1979–99	4	1990–9	Clarysse and Degoof
Canada	Universities	746	1962–99	47	1990–8	Cooper
France	All	387	1984–98	14	1992–8	Mustar
Finland	Public labs	66	1985–99	4.5	1990–9	VTT data
Germany	Public labs	462	1990–7	58	1990–7	ATHENE
Germany	Universities	2,800	1990–5	467	1990–5	ATHENE
Norway	Public labs	122	1996–8	41	1996–8	Research Council of Norway
United Kingdom	Universities	171	1984–98	15	1990–7	PREST
AUTM[1]	Universities	1,995	1980–98	281	1994–7	AUTM

1.   AUTM includes universities and research hospitals. Cumulative totals are for the United States alone, the per-year figures are for US and Canadian institutions. Sweden is excluded from the OECD data because it includes students.

Source: OECD 2001b.

to be one of the best-performing public entrepreneurs among the countries for which the OECD has received data. The ATHENE definition is very broad, including firms founded by recent university graduates, public employees, and employees from mid-sized or large firms who have an advanced academic degree. The ATHENE study also estimated that about half of all firms in technology and science parks could be considered spin-offs given the affiliations of their founders to academic and public institutions. In 1996, about 1,200 new firms were established in science parks, so they estimate that close to 600 could be academic spin-offs (some of which may be double-counted with the university and other research institutes).

More recent data for the UK and for the US would suggest that the formation rate in these countries at least is much higher. In the UK the formation rate has settled to around 200 per year. The third annual Higher Education Business Interaction Survey (HEBI) shows the rapid increase in the number of spin-off companies at the end of the twentieth century. From around 70 a year on average on the previous five years, 203 were formed in 1999–2000, 248 in 2000–1 and 213 in 2001–2. (The rate in 2003 slowed as a consequence of legislation contained in Section 22 of the Finance Act. This had an unintended consequence for university spin-offs. 'The intention of the law was to stop up a loop hole that was allowing companies to avoid paying tax when rewarding employees. But an unintended consequence has completely killed off our business – which was going incredibly well until then' (Tim Cook, *Oxford Times*, April 16 2003, 20).) This is about half the number (450) formed in the same year in the US and Canada (AUTM 2004a). Thus the rate of UK spin-off performance is better than that in the US when adjusted for the relative number of universities. Moreover, the spin-off process is more efficient in the UK on the basis of research expenditure per spin-off. On average one spin-off firm is formed for every £15 million of research expenditure in the UK, compared with one for every £44 million in the US (HERO/DTI 2004). On the other hand, employment generation and turnover in UK spin-offs are low: only around 12,000 people are employed in spin-off companies and combined turnover amounts to less than £300 million. The contribution to regional development varies by year. The majority of spin-offs are in England, but the pattern of formation fluctuates. In 2001–2 London had the highest (38) followed by the North West (27) but in the previous year Yorkshire and Humberside in the North of England had the most (29) followed by London (27) and the North West.

The impact of spin-offs on regional economies in other European countries has been much later than in the UK and the US. In the mid-1990s, in many European regions the university spin-off process had barely started. Lawton Smith and De Bernardy (2000) reported on the findings of a FP4 Network which showed that in Munich, Milan, Barcelona and Utrecht relatively few SMEs had been generated by universities. In Milan, the growth of the high-technology SME sector has been largely independent of the university. In the Munich region, only 6 per cent of high-technology SMEs were founded by graduates from Ludwig Maximilian University and the existing technology transfer was nowhere near fully utilized.

On the other hand, in France and Sweden some institutions had very high rates of spin-offs. For example in France, Sophia Antipolis developed many spin-offs particularly from INRIA. The most prolific period of public sector spin-off formation was the late 1980s to early 1990s, which saw an average of 37 firms formed per year, although the trend in the mid-to-late 1990s seems to be towards less public sector entrepreneurialism (OECD 2001b). Gothenburg in Sweden has one of the highest levels of spin-offs in Europe. By 1995, Gothenburg's universities had spun-out 350 firms, of which 250 came from Chalmers University of Technology (Lindholm Dahlstrand 1997). She explains that, in Gothenburg, the high rate of university spin-off combined with its official encouragement has had the effect of reinforcing the process because of continuing links between the new firms and the institutional origins of their founders.

While other studies have monitored the rate of spin-offs formation and factors responsible they have generally failed to discuss how to evaluate their performance of spin-offs other than through employment growth (see for example Shane 2004) or to consider the significance of sector or business models (Druilhe and Garnsey 2004). Of those that consider the rate of spin-off and the growth of firms, Di Gregorio and Shane (2003) found that spin-off activity is negatively related to the share of inventor royalties compared to industry licensees, and positively related to total industry spend on university-based research. The EC (2003b, 77) argued that creating professional patent and licensing agencies on a regional basis (thus commercializing innovations for several universities) would strengthen commercialization. Similarly Hsu and Bernstein (1997) emphasized the necessity of clearly articulated and well-understood policy on licensing and IPR. Geuna and Nesta (2003) find that in Europe there is a considerable lack of expertise in TTOs at the local level. While TTOs have an important organizational and political role, their precise contribution is difficult to measure (see Siegel *et al.* 2003). While variables such as the university's royalty and equity distribution formula can be obtained, a significant contribution may be 'boundary spanning' between customers (entrepreneurs or firms) and suppliers (scientists) increasing communication.

Focusing particularly on the impact of location on spin-off activity, Clarysse *et al.* (in OECD 2001b) used results from a Belgian study of the early-growth phase of new technology-based firms to explain why European new technology-based firms fail to grow like their US counterparts. They conclude that 'structural deficiencies' such as the financial, fiscal or regulatory climate cannot explain this slow growth. Rather, the entrepreneurial climate of the firm's region and its experiences and opportunities for knowledge acquisition are determinative. Regions that are not supportive of spin-off early-growth needs – before the first infusion of venture capital – have a lower incidence of high-growth ventures. The challenge for Europe, they conclude, is to create an environment that allows spin-offs to learn how to translate research into a product tailored to market demand and to develop an appropriate business model in which intermediary institutions and incubation centres will play a key role.

Few studies have considered the financial rewards for the individual. Stephan and Everhart (1998) studied the payback received by US university scientists affiliated with biotech companies making an IPO in the early 1990s. They found that 420 university scientists were affiliated with 52 university-based firms they studied and 37 of these had sufficient holdings and close enough ties with the company to warrant disclosure at the time of the initial public offering. Three others were classed as insiders by the Securities and Exchange Commission. This means that 10 per cent of university-based scientists could be classed as insiders. Over half were founders (55 per cent). Of these 14 exercised options and then made a sale and realised a profit during the time of the study. The maximum profit realized was $11,760,000 in one day, while the mean was $1,237,598. Universities of course vary in the proportion of profits that academics are allowed to keep (see Chapter 8 for the example of Oxford University).

The immediate economic benefits are only one criterion for evaluating the contribution of spin-offs to society. OECD argues that spin-off firms fill a special niche between public research and the private sector – they are mediators or intermediaries that sell their knowledge as consultants or contract researchers. In other words, the importance of public sector spin-offs lies in their role as rapid conduits of commercially relevant ideas, rather than in their employment generation or direct contribution to wealth creation. Morever, other forms of technology transfer and commercialization compete with spin-offs for being the best route into the marketplace. For example, the licensing of commercially relevant technologies to industry has the advantage of being less time-intensive for research personnel. The training of highly qualified scientists and technologists is of far greater significance than the spin-off process (Hughes 2003; see also Branscomb *et al.* 1999 and OECD 2001b for similar criticisms).

The massification role and human capital formation

The interpretation of measurable effects of human capital impacts on a region, like other forms of measurement, necessarily has to take account of temporal, geographical, political and historical factors. As in other indictors of universities on economic development at the national and at the regional level, the measurement evidence is far from conclusive.

Studies which have used econometrics to test for what factors influence technological change at the national level have found a close relationship with technological change and employment of highly skilled workers (see for example Berman *et al.* 1994, for the US, and Betts 1997 for Canada). Crespi and Geuna (2004) found that the impact of the science budget on the 'production' of PhD students is connected with a significant rise in the number of graduates in a country. They find benefits to this trend, that there are constant or slightly increasing domestic returns to scale. Countries which have experienced more rapid growth tend to have more highly educated workforces (Bils and Klenow 2000). On the other hand, education is only one explanation for economic growth. Betts and Lee (2005) suggest that levels of education can explain only about one-third of the variation between countries. They find that although studies which compare cross-country performances do indicate the importance of levels of education in explaining variations in economic performance, they can be limited by unobserved differences between countries.

The problem of assessing the outcomes of even applied industry-related training programmes is illustrated by Brighton's (2004) review of the UK's Knowledge Transfer Partnership (KTP) scheme (previously the Teaching Company Scheme, TCS) (2001–2). Since it was established in 1975 it has assisted over 1,500 companies. The rationale for the TCS scheme was that firms have difficulties exploiting technology outside established capabilities, that they make insufficient use of knowledge base and that there are deficiencies in graduate skills and employers' reluctance to employ graduates. The basis of the scheme is a business-defined project undertaken by an 'Associate' who is normally based in the business and who is jointly supervised by a 'knowledge-based partner' and business. The projects normally run for two years. This was initially a large company scheme, but by 2001 90 per cent of businesses were SMEs.

Brighton found a range of outcomes, from the negative – that significant numbers did not meet technical or commercial objectives – to the positive – smaller companies do better: prior collaboration improves technical success, and eminence (defined as RAE grade) had no relation to commercial success. He found that, while the impacts of the programme to the companies rating over 50 per cent include increases in sales (59 per cent) and increases in value (57 per cent), the top benefits were less measurable impacts, particularly increase in technological knowledge or skills (99 per cent), networking (78 per cent) and increase in R&D (77 per cent). For the associates, over half were recruited by the company and were paid above-average salaries. He concludes that the programme compares poorly with some other programmes on the basis of ratio of grant to increased turnover – 1:0.83–1:0.87 – but that, of programmes recently completed, many are aimed at process improvements so that turnover and employment may be poor measures, the continued added value by associates may not be captured and wider (and longer-term) benefits may not be valued.

The link between the supply of university graduates and rates of innovation at the regional level has been the subject of numerous studies (see for example Goldstein and Luger 1992; Felsenstein 1994). When Beeson and Montgomery (1993) estimated the amount of university-induced migration to a region that would not otherwise have occurred, a study similar to that of Felsenstein, they found very little evidence of any measurable effects. Their study of 218 SMAs using census data found that area employment growth and percentage of the workforce employed as scientists and engineers are positively related and significantly related to measures of university quality such as university R&D funding, top-ranking science and engineering programmes, number of bachelor's degrees awarded and bachelor's degrees in science and engineering. Their results indicated that university activity differentially affects the demand for workers with specific skills, and is consistent with the finding of other researchers that a firm's ability to implement new technologies is dependent on workers' skills. However, their data could not reject the hypothesis that university quality has no significant effect on area income, the employment rate, net migration rates, or even the share of employment in high-tech industries.

Likewise, Betts and Lee (2005) point out that none of the evidence does in fact establish that a thick network of universities is either necessary or sufficient for a country to experience rapid innovation of productivity growth and that some countries might obtain skilled labour through immigration. They cite De Fontenay and Carmel (2004), who contend that the immigration of Russian scientists has done much to foster high-tech clusters in that country, as in Silicon Valley (Saxenian 1999), and that Israel's military is an important source of well-trained technicians. They suggest that there is a need to be sceptical about claims that a region with a weak supply of university graduates can never succeed at innovation. The quality of schools matters, as does the propensity of the private sector to import graduates.

For Walshok and the CONNECT Programme in San Diego (see Walshok *et al.* 2002), the importance of universities and research centres in creating San Diego as one of the most innovative regions in the USA lies in three hooks. These are the store of intellectual capital in a region; the breadth and depth of advanced skills and knowledge of human capital; and, connecting these two, the character and extent of catalytic business and financial networks. Lee and Walshok (2003) developed a series of indicators of the role of University of California San Diego in workforce training. In addition to enrolment and graduation statistics they looked at extension programmes such as non-credit post-baccalaureate education, non-credit workforce training programmes, students' motivations for pursuing training, and who paid for the training. They found that these represented greater flexibility than degree programmes and gave rise to a far greater degree of impact of each campus on its region than their traditional degree programme enrolments would suggest.

The territorial role

The emphasis on the territorial role is predicated on the assumption that proximity, improved innovation and economic performance of firms are linked. Studies have focused on proximity effects in two main ways: either looking at the impact of individual institutions on their local economies through case studies or by modelling knowledge production and spillovers and identifying the degrees to which the impacts are localized.

Of the first, direct economic impacts as indicated by multiplier values and employment impact have been undertaken using a regional input–output model. Several have been undertaken in the UK and show that the former are in the order of 1.2 per cent to 1.5 per cent (see for example Glasson (2003) for a review and case studies of Oxford Brookes and Sunderland University). The impact can be much larger, however. A recent study (GLA 2004) showed employment multiplier effect for London HE institutions of 1.98 per cent and a contribution of 2.5 to 3 per cent of total London output.

Case studies based on surveys of businesses and other organizations which have asked the importance of the university to locational decisions, productivity and competitiveness, innovation, and output levels of respondent organizations (Goldstein and Renault 2004) also fall into this category. These authors cite Thanki (1999), who finds that these methods have not captured many of the potential ways that universities contribute to economic development either because of methological limitations or because of a failure to understand how regional development occurs, and also comments that indirect effects are very hard to measure.

A variant of the case study approach is those that focus on activity within specific regions and which include universities in their focus on particular sectors such as biotech (see Bagchi-Sen *et al.* 2004; Lawton Smith 2005). Such studies show that universities are only one of a range of sources of technology and are usually not the most important. Even when they are important, it is not necessarily the closest university that has the greatest impact. For example Bagchi-Sen *et al.* (2004) found that, although collaboration with universities was an important factor in explaining business performance in both samples of biotech firms in California and Massachusetts, physical proximity to collaborators was only somewhat important. In Britain Athreye and Keeble (2000) found a significant statistical relationship between SME product innovativeness and local (county-level) university and government R&D expenditure, using a multivariate model incorporating other influential variables.

Of the second kind (modelling knowledge production and spillovers), studies show that knowledge flows from universities to industry decline with geographical distance but have the limitation that they do not model or trace knowledge flows (Arundel and Geuna 2001) or explain why distance matters (Arundel and Geuna 2004). Jaffe (1989), using a production function analysis based on a model developed by Griliches (1979) that uses registered patent inventions registered by the US patent office as the dependent variable, shows that the diffusion of knowledge from the university to industry is localized through a positive relationship between corporate patent activity and university research spending at the state level, but the effect fades with patent age and with the diffusion of ideas. Anselin *et al.* (1997) using the Griliches–Jaffe model identified a consistent spatial range of interaction between universities and industry. They found that spillovers of university research on innovation extended over a range of 75 miles from the innovating Metropolitan Statistical Area (MSA), and over a range of 50 miles with respect to private R&D. More recently Anselin *et al.* (2000) in their analysis of data for MSAs found differences in the mix of applied local knowledge inputs in general, and in the role of university research in particular sectors. University spillovers seem to be specific to certain sectors, being particularly strong in electronics and instruments, and absent in others – for example drugs and chemicals and machinery. In the case of the latter, spillovers extend beyond the boundary of the MSA within a 75-mile range from the central city.

Adams (2002, 274) looked at spillovers from academic and industrial research. He found that academic spillovers are more localized than industrial spillovers. He argues that open science makes it possible for firms to go to local universities to obtain information that is reasonably current and not proprietary – normal science. This increases the localization of academic spillovers. However, when quality of the school and the science is taken into account, there is a difference in geographical patterns. Laboratories that work with top private universities search over longer distances, not merely with top institutions but also with other universities. Top private universities concentrate more than others on basic research, and spillovers from these institutions are not necessarily localized. Adams makes the point that public universities are constrained by policies that are conducive to localization. Similarly Mansfield and Lee's (1996) study of R&D expenditure by firms in universities found that firms prefer to work with local university researchers, formalized at a distance within 100 miles of the firm's R&D laboratories. This fadeout in firm support of universities is less for basic research than for applied research. Firms also support applied research of less distinguished faculties nearly as much as faculties in top schools, though basic research supported by firms takes place mostly at top schools (in Adams 2002). On the other hand, a study of 2,300 German firms by Beise and Stahl (1999) found that firms located near universities or polytechnics do not have a higher probability of using the results of publicly funded research. They, like Martin and Sunley (2003) in their criticism of Porter, recognize that a central issue is the geographical unit of analysis i.e. how near counts as proximity.

Howells (2002) cites a study by Feldman (1999) which finds that codified knowledge in the form of patents may be localized but fades rapidly (i.e. after the first year following the patent). Even in this relatively short period of time the competitive edge given by localization in some key sectors is important. Yet, maturity of the technology does not necessarily mean a cessation of research links, as the portfolio of links can expand through the establishment of sets of norms of behaviour involving formal and informal contact, creating and transforming established relationships and having an indirect effect (Smith 1997).

Goldstein and Renault (2004) set out to estimate the magnitude of the contribution to changes in regional economic well-being, and to separate out the regional development impacts of different functions of universities. They studied all 312 MSAs in the US over the period 1969 to 1998 but in two time periods, 1969 to 1986 and 1986 to 1998, using a quasi-experimental approach which examined which university-based activities, e.g. teaching, basic research, extension and public service, technology transfer, technology development and businesses spinning off from university research, are the most responsible for any net regional development impacts from the presence of universities. Average annual earnings per worker was used as the measure of regional economic development.

They found that research and technlogy functions generate significant knowledge spillovers that result in enhanced economic development that would not otherwise have occurred. Yet, they also found that the magnitude of the effects was small compared with other factors but also varied. In the earlier period they found that, rather than the presence or activities of universities, important factors included general regional economic conditions, agglomeration economies and aspects of industry structure. In the later period, total university R&D activity was significant, but there was no evidence to support the hypothesis that human capital creation was important. While university patenting was non-significant, local factors such as the presence of an airport and the size of the business services sector were important. The authors explain the difference by saying that before 1986 economic development was not part of universities activities, but since then the match has been increasing, with the trend for economies to become generally more 'knowledge-based'.

Conclusions

This chapter has set out the many different ways of measuring impacts of universities on economic development, internationally, nationally and regionally, and raises a number of questions about what is being measured. The review has found that the importance of universities to innovation and economic development is overstated and that methods and targets chosen vary and the practice of measurement is undertaken for different reasons to show different outcomes. Moreover, the use of data can be selective to support argument; any data set also at best shows a partial picture when it is total links that matter (Lee and Walshok 2003). Not all contacts are measured, of course as Betts and Lee (2005) point out, the focus on innovations directly linked to universities, such as patents, seriously undercounts the impact of university scientists and engineers. For example, faculty consulting is not tracked by formal university means. Data are often not comparable because of differences in national industrial structures and national and regional innovation systems and not least because of the differing definition of regions, the difficulties in demonstrating both direct and indirect impacts, and measuring the variety of different forms of engagement. Hence, the causal link between universities and economic development has not been proved by current methods.

This chapter has indicated that measurement of inputs and outputs has to take account of considerable variations in the position of universities within national systems of evidence, the propensity of different sectors to assimilate and stimulate university research and the fact that this will vary by country and by region. It has also highlighted the multi-dimensional features of multiple accountabilities of universities that are implicit in the agenda of evaluations of performance. For example, as a result of a combination of historical, psychological and economic factors, some academics and institutions will have more impact than others. It has also been argued that any measurement of universities' contribution to economic development must take account of the still pervasive level of defence R&D funding in the core group of countries that dominate global defence activity. In the UK, as in the US and France, a deeply embedded relationship exists between universities and the MoD, which 'pervades research, development, teaching and science communication, and extends across disciplines from engineering and the physical sciences, through life sciences and the social sciences' (Langley 2005, 73).

The chapter has also pointed out the necessity of considering the timeframe of effects and the unpredictability of longer-term trends. If the role of universities in the formation of new innovation systems is to be understood, then this involves mapping processes which span over decades and where mechanisms involved are many and difficult to trace.

4   Europe

The knowledge society depends for its growth on the production of new knowledge, its transmission through education and training, its dissemination through information and communication technologies and on its use through new industrial processes or services. Universities take part in all three processes and are at the heart of the Europe of Knowledge.

(EC 2003a, 4)

Introduction

This statement from the European Commission's *Third European report on S&T indicators 2003: towards a knowledge-based economy* demonstrates that universities are central to European Union economic and social policy. European science, along with regional policies, is designed to address the European paradox which is that Europe has a strong science base but poor performance in terms of technological and industrial competitiveness compared to the US (EC 1996; EC 2003a). The creation of a 'Europe of Knowledge' has been a prime objective for the European Union since the Lisbon European Council of March 2000 and the 'European Higher Education Area' set out in the Bologna Agreement in 1999. These new systems of governance in which the EU and national governments will work together are designed to combat the unnecessary fragmentation and compartmentalization of university research and teaching policies to overcome that paradox (EC 2003a). The accession of ten new states to the EU in 2004 further complicated efforts to bring about a unified system of teaching and research.

The Lisbon Agenda recommends raising national expenditures on R&D. By 2010, investment on research should account for 3 per cent of GNP (EC 2003b, 20–1). The co-existing plan for the European Research Area (ERA) is intended to remove remaining obstacles to researchers' mobility, will institute a system of benchmarking of R&D policies of member states and will establish a Community patent (EC 2003b, 21). This strategy, it has been argued, is long overdue. Noll (1998, 10–11), for example, finds that Europe has not made as great an investment as the US in its university systems, commenting particularly on Germany, where spending has been stagnant since the 1970s; on France, where only the *grandes écoles* have fared reasonably well in the budgetary process; and the UK, where 'only universities at the top of the system are equipped to provide world-class education, and universities are starved of resources in comparison with those in the United States and the rest of Europe'.

Possible explanations for Europe's poor showing in world rankings are that, since the mid-1990s, the EU has lagged behind the US in terms of the absolute volume of R&D, in the rate of growth of R&D activities and R&D intensity and that the US has the advantage of a much greater match and integration between the different elements within innovation systems. The EC (2003b, 55) finds that one of the distinctive features of R&D expenditure in the EU in comparison with Japan and the US is the ratio between the public sector (including government and the higher education sector) and the private sector. In the EU, public research accounts for a much larger share than in either Japan or the US, likewise the business share of total R&D funding is lower, although this is changing and there has been an expansion of competitive research funds relative to core funds, particularly from industry.

Moreover, not only may the supply of cutting-edge scientific research be inadequate, the EU may also be losing out because of the unattractiveness of the European environment to US research: too little US research is done in Europe. These problems could be addressed through higher levels of research funding but also through higher degrees of pluralism in funding sources and a higher integration of research with teaching, clinical research and medical practice (Pammolli *et al.* 2001, v). Walshok (2002) argues that key to the San Diego region's economic success was interdisciplinary research in its universities and research laboratories. Therefore integrating different elements within the research and innovation process has important effects at the regional as well as national level.

Against this background, this chapter sets out to consider what factors will mediate both EU policies towards the EU higher education system and the potential impact on economic development across Europe and its regions. This is illustrated by examples from some of the EU15 countries. The chapter discusses whether the evidence is more compelling that universities will contribute more to economic development in some of those countries than in others. It does this by assessing which of the eight paradigms are dominant and what the implications of this are for Europe as a whole.

Distributed innovation systems

In the move towards a coherent system of governance across Europe, Georghiou and Kuhlmann (2002) find a shift in the rationale for EU innovation policy, which between the 1960s and the 1990s was based on market failure arguments, to the now structuralist-evolutionist approach based on the systems of innovation approach. In the ascendancy are strategies to develop bridging institutions, networks and the means of overcoming firms' resistance to adopt new technologies. This has meant a radical change of direction for the EC's research policies, the moving away from the programmes of collaborative research under the Framework Programmes and work in the Commission's own laboratories which account for only 5 per cent of public funding to an approach which involves mobilizing the 'entire research resource of Europe'. The Commission's proposed new measures for 2007–11 further embrace the concept of an integrative approach to innovation – which will be at the forefront of policy. They include incentives for cross-border collaboration and the use of structural funds for innovation (Mason *et al.* 2004).

Europe has traditionally relied on the internationalization of scientific networks to improve the research and development activities of member states, through the Framework Programmes. These programmes are highly selective, and success is influenced by eminence and reinforced by participation (Geuna 1998, 686). This author finds that science research productivity influences both the probability of joining an EU-funded R&D co-operative project and the number of times an institution has participated in EU projects.

The first four Framework Programmes focused on building research communities, with growing emphasis on technology transfer and human capital and mobility. The Fourth Framework Programme (FP4) had a budget of ECU 13,100 million, and covered all the research and technological development (RTD) activities which were funded by the European Commission during the period 1994–8. With a budget of €14,960 million, the Fifth RTD Framework Programme (1998–2002) was intended to help solve problems and to respond to major socio-economic challenges facing Europe. 'To maximise its impact, it focuses on a limited number of research areas combining technological, industrial, economic, social and cultural aspects' (europa.eu.int/comm/research/fp5/fp5-intro_en.html).

The drive towards a stronger and more unified European scientific and technological research effort, underpinned by understanding from the social sciences, is explicit in the EU's Framework Programme for Research and Technological Development, a major tool to support the creation of the ERA. Framework 6 covers the period 2002–6. It includes social science research themes which address such issues as the relationship between public and scientific communities, for example public trust in decisions made on genetically modified organisms (GMOs) and stem cell research. While a growing share of European universities' income is generated through EU programmes, under Framework 6 they will still account only for 5.4 per cent of total public research effort (see www.iserd.org.il/what.htm).

Illustrating the emphasis placed on greater co-ordination between the different actors in the innovation process within the European Union, Georghiou and Kuhlmann (2002) report that the new policy instruments for the ERA include:

- networks of Excellence, designed to reinforce European scientific and technological excellence through integrating research capabilities across Europe
- integrated projects which are expected to cover innovation and the dissemination, transfer and exploitation of knowledge
- Article 169, which opens the possibilities of participation in member states' national programmes by organizations from outside the home country.

Diversity and uniformity in national innovation systems

The scale of the task of overcoming fragmentation and moving towards greater integration in Europe is considerable given the number of universities and increasing heterogeneity within member-state innovation systems as universities move away from the Humboldt model (EC 2003b, 5). The post-2004 European Union plus the other countries of Western Europe has approximately 4,000 universities. This equals the number of HE establishments in the US (EC 2003b).

The relative importance of universities in national innovation systems varies by country. In Greece, Portugal and Italy they are core components but not in Germany (where research institutions such as the Max Planck Institute dominate), France, Finland and Denmark. Most countries operate a dual support system in which core separate institutions allocate university funding and funding for research projects – as in Germany, the UK and the US. France, the main exception to the dual support model, operates a mixed system. Core funding of about 25–30 per cent comes from the MRET while the rest comes from a multiplicity of sources.

Across Europe systems of HE are changing in diverse ways. In some countries, broadening the range of institutions within the ambit of higher education has increased the points of potential contact with industry. Some more than others have adapted to the prevailing philosophy of becoming knowledge-based economies (OECD 1999, 26). A further example of systemic changes is that in some countries higher education systems have begun to absorb non-university public research organizations (such as research institutes e.g. CNRS in France, CSIC in Spain, etc.) (Geuna and Nesta 2003, 3) (although in the UK, the drive to privatize government laboratories in the mid-1990s led to a reverse trend – Lawton Smith 2000). EC (2003a, 24), using composite indicators of investment in the knowledge-based economy (which includes educational spending and human capital growth – new PhDs and researchers), finds that the Nordic countries Finland, Sweden and Denmark are the 'best prepared and are rapidly turning their economies into knowledge-based economies, while another six, Austria, Belgium, France, Germany, the Netherlands and the UK have a level of growth much closer to the European average'. It is also the Nordic countries that have the most competitive economies – Finland (1), Sweden (3), Denmark (5) and Norway (6) (World Economic Forum 2004) – which suggests that there is some connection between the two.

While these changes are profound, as compared to even the early 1990s, structural differences between the US and Europe remain. Whereas Europe has been more proactive in promoting university–industry interactions, the US has a deeper structure of interactions between university and industry, with tighter networks linking leading firms and universities (Geuna *et al.* 2003). These authors suggest that in the US it is the need for knowledge that generates network formation rather than the policy actions of governments (although this is qualified by experiences in the US). On the other hand, policy in Europe has created networks that are in search of demand. One of the explanations for the lack of demand was the decline in European R&D expenditure in the 1990s, for example in Germany, France and the UK, thus reducing the demand for university research. Moreover, there can be decreasing returns to networking, and only a few permanent long-distance links result in the socially optimal production of knowledge (citing Cowan and Jonard 2003 in the same volume).

Next, six countries illustrate the diversity in national innovation systems, and the degrees to which there has been a realignment of national and institutional policies towards a greater engagement with industry, hence the economic development agenda. The discussion highlights the increasing degree of integration within the UK, Netherlands and Swedish *university* systems, whereas it is shown that in Italy, France and Germany other research institutions have traditionally had much closer relations with industry than the universities have.

The UK

The UK has perhaps the most advanced and coherent stated agenda of harnessing universities to wealth creation and at the regional scale. While this represents a recent and evolving policy agenda which dates back to the post-1979 Conservative governments, it has many similarities with the position which universities played in the economy in the nineteenth century and that of the former polytechnics, most of which became 'new' and now 'modern' universities in 1992 (Charles and Howells 1992).

The 1979–97 Conservative governments prioritized the commercial role at the expense of the research role of universities. In 1981, the UK's total spending on R&D as a proportion of its GNP was higher than that of any other member of the G7, with the exception of Germany, but slumped under successive Conservative governments, as did the number of Nobel laureates, which fell dramatically after 1980 (SBS 2003). The rationale contained in the 1988 DTI White Paper *DTI – the department for enterprise* and reinforced in the 1993 White Paper *Realising our potential: a strategy for science, technology and engineering* was that there should be a greater emphasis on enterprise, greater value for money and exploitation. Following the election of Labour governments in 1997 and 2001, this pattern has been reversed with increasing amounts awarded to science and universities under successive Comprehensive Spending Reviews. The rhetoric, however, has strong similarities to that under the Conservatives, emphasizing building bridges between science, business and government in order to increase national wealth and quality of life. What is different is the regional role. That appeared in 1998 in the White Paper *Our competitive future: building the knowledge-driven economy.*

Significant systemic changes in the structure of the higher education system are under way which affect the economic development agenda. Four changes are illustrated. The first is the mergers between universities, intended to provide greater opportunities for providing a more integrated and coherent set of opportunities for industry–university collaboration. The biggest is the merger of Manchester University and the University of Manchester Institute of Science and Technology in 2004. It is now the UK's largest university with an estimated 34,000 students. Although the 2002 proposed merger between the two top London colleges, UCL and Imperial, did not go ahead, others are predicted.

Second is the impact of evaluation of research and the resulting competition for eminence between universities. The RAE which takes place every five years, the sixth being in 2008, provides quality profiles for research across all disciplines. For 2008, submissions from institutions will be assessed by experts in some 70 units of assessment (www.rae.ac.uk/) on a variety of criteria. The key one is the publication of four journal articles in top-quality journals by individual academics. Currently the RAE does not take account of the more applied, industry-related research which does not immediately translate into 'academic' output. This can act as a disincentive to academics whose careers depend on undertaking research that can be published and in other ways counted to taking on industry-related projects.

The third is the changing distribution of research in the academic base as some scientific fields are declining, particularly chemistry and physics, while others, notably biosciences, are increasing. Chemists fear that there could be as few as six university chemistry departments left in ten years' time. Recent high-profile closures of chemistry departments include that of King's College, University of London, which is credited as having developed crucial techniques which led to the discovery of DNA. Currently there are between 35 and 40 departments but the Royal Society of Chemistry has predicted that at best 20 will survive and at worst only six (those at Durham, Cambridge, Imperial, UCL, Bristol and Oxford) will remain in 2014 (Curtis 2004). As with physics, there will be regions not served by a locally focused university department (SBS 2003).

The fourth is the greater financial and political incentives for universities to work with industry. The 2003 White Paper *The future of higher education* announced the expansion of the Higher Education Innovation Fund (HEIF), with funding from the Office of Science and Technology (OST) to stimulate enterprise from research across the regions (DfES, 2003). This expanded HEIF, on which OST and HEFCE will be working together, will have two main aims: first, to build on the success to which all universities have contributed in knowledge transfer; second, to further broaden the reach of these activities particularly through support for 'less research-intensive' university departments. The White Paper proposes to create a network of around 20 Knowledge Exchanges as a new strand of HEIF, which will be exemplars of good practice in interactions between 'less research-intensive institutions and business and underline the distinctive mission of these' (DfES 2003, 39).

Such is the drive towards university–industry interaction in the UK that Richard Lambert, the author of the Lambert Report on business and higher education links, has been asked by the DTI to chair a committee that will draw up standard paperwork for the commercial exploitation of academic ideas, producing model contracts. This is intended to overcome the problems of lack of clarity over IP rights such as the ownership of patents or designs as well as the increased time and costs in negotiations that have prevented some deals from being completed. The Report recommended a new stream of public funding for 'business-relevant research' and a greater role for business in influencing courses and curricula (Hill 2004, 60).

In changes to the economic relationship between universities and industry, universities have received large increases in 'third party' (i.e. other than government) research funding which now accounts for well over 40 per cent of university research funding compared to less than a quarter in 1988–9. The result has been a significant short-term increase in the apparent productivity of the research base but one which puts its sustainability at risk. Therefore OST is proposing that universities recover the full economic costs for the totality of research they undertake. From 2005–6 the research councils will be given additional resources of £120 million per year to pay a larger proportion of the cost of research they are supporting (SBS 2003, 6). This will dramatically increase the cost of research and may act as a disincentive to industry which studies have shown matters more in some, mainly traditional industries, than in others (see Lawton Smith 2000). A policy statement put out by the Engineering and Physical Sciences Research Council is highly instructive on what it sees as the balance between basic and applied research. Currently, 35 per cent of its grants involve partnerships with industry. It aims to ratchet that up to 50 per cent and to exercise a tighter grip over where the money goes, targeting a third of grants on priority areas. Hailing the 500 spin-outs it has helped fund in the last decade, the statement devotes 20 per cent of its length to areas such as 'Working for Wealth' and 'Industry sectors', but less than 5 per cent to 'Fundamental Research'.

In the UK, universities are given incentives to perform better at outreach while it is also recognized that industry needs to raise its game (see for example HM Treasury 2003) and that regional offices of state agencies such as patent office could do more to raise awareness of potential for using technology. Many universities have responded to signals within the local economy and, working with industry, have established degree courses dedicated to providing specialist skills. The Oxford Brookes Motorsport degree developed in conjunction with the motorsport industry is one example (see Lawton Smith *et al.* 2003).

In a drive to create a nexus of teaching, research and business that bears a similarity with the Grenoble model (Chapter 8), in 2005 the UK government established the 'science city' initiative. Newcastle is one of six universities that are intended to be world-class centres for science and innovation. Newcastle is working in partnership with the city council and the regional development agency One NorthEast and is looking for Treasury support to create 250 new technology-based businesses over the next decade and 5,000 science-based jobs by 2010 (Baty 2005).

The Netherlands

The Netherlands, like the UK, has a holistic approach to innovation policy with policies aimed at individuals and attitudes as well as at companies and organizations in the public and private sectors (Hughes 2003, 2). Yet Hughes finds a number of paradoxes, with the country performing well on some indices and below the EU average on others. The Netherlands' economy scores well against other EU economies on measures such as relatively high levels of R&D expenditure, patenting, scientific output, and relatively positive nascent entrepreneurs' attitudes to failure, as well as relatively high levels of equity and venture capital, of innovative output. It scores well in the Global Entrepreneurship Monitor survey (GEM). While the Netherlands has a lower level of university spin-offs than other EU countries owing to the now well-recognized pattern of constraints in relation to university–industry interaction, policies to overcome these problems are in place. For example Kreijen and van der Laag (2003) outline a new streamlined techno-partnership strategy designed to raise the quality rather than the quantity of spin-offs and a number of complementary measures aimed at facilitating spin-offs. In line with both the GEM survey and the conclusions of these authors, others such as Waasdorp (2002) and Stevenson (2002) argue that many of the conditions that are thought to be necessary for high levels of innovation entrepreneurship based on technology transfer are now in place.

On the other hand, there are significant weaknesses in the scientific labour market. The proportion of new science and engineering graduates per 1,000 of the population is half the EU average and employment in high-tech and medium-tech manufacturing and high-tech services is about average compared to the EU (EC 2001a). Moreover, Muizer (2003) found considerable weaknesses in the technology transfer processes, which is also consistent with the GEM programme analysis which suggested that there were doubts about the effectiveness of measures introduced to transfer technology from universities and public research centres to new and growing firms.

Sweden

Since the 1990s, Sweden has sought to emulate US models of strategic research, carried out in the university system but linked to long-term industrial and social interests. The new paradigm brought into the Swedish system a Mode 2 knowledge-production model rather than the Mode 1 which occurred after the Second World War and became the dominant framework of science and science policy (Edqvist 2003, 215, 281). Edqvist reports that new institutions – Foundations, established in 1994 – have brought about fundamental changes which have amounted to a restructuring of the university research system. The new Foundations have been allocated larger resources and were intended to become sites of dialogues between different interests – researchers and the politicians and industrialists who served on their boards. In addition, in 2001, three new research councils and a new agency for research and development were established to replace a number of research councils and other bodies. The aim of the new organizational structure was to promote concerted action in key scientific fields, strengthen researcher control, promote collaboration between different research fields and improve the dissemination of information about research and its findings. Further, the new structure aims to stimulate interdisciplinary and multidisciplinary research and provide outstanding scientists with adequate support to allow them to develop their own independent innovate research (www.sweden.se/templates/cs/BasicFactsheet____3925.aspx).

Italy

In contrast, although since the 1980s Italy has introduced new laws allowing universities the right to obtain private funding, introduced measures to increase their autonomy and changed the law regarding ownership of intellectual property, Italian universities are still not active in pursuing technology transfer strategies. Until 2001, ownership of IPR was regulated by Italian patent law which dated back to 1939. A recent amendment shifted all IPR over academic research output to individual researchers

(Balconi *et al.* 2004, 133). The problems lie in that not only do universities still lack managerial knowledge necessary to organize a for-profit range of activities (Etzkowitz *et al.* 2000), but it is only recently that they have started moving away from a passive attitude towards IPR-related technology transfer (Balconi *et al.* 2004, 133). One of the driving forces for change was the financial crisis resulting from severe cutbacks in public funding which challenged the conservatism of classical teaching (Etzkowitz *et al.* 2000). Balconi *et al.* argue that

> despite being regarded by the law as the natural owners of all IPRs concerning their employees' inventions, Italian universities have traditionally made no effort to take advantage of this, and left patenting entirely to individual professors' initiative. IPRs over inventions derived from sponsored research programmes were left entirely to the sponsors, either private (such as many chemical and pharmaceutical companies, or ST Microelectronics, the largest European semiconductor company) or public ones (the most important being the National Research Council (CNR) and the National Agency for Energy and the Environment (ENEA)).

Inventions stemming from generic funds from the Ministry of University and Research (MUIR) were often left with no IPR protection, unless individual professors took the initiative and even then often found resistance in their administrative offices.

At the regional level, industry has taken a proactive role in stimulating university–industry links. For example, the *confindustria*, the industrial association of Lombardy, has had a major influence in shaping the university course system covering the natural sciences. Yet, such changes are said to be 'modest since the percentage of industrial research remains low and universities have not been accepted as partners in the innovation process' (Etzkowitz *et al.* 2000). These authors find that the polytechnics, on the other hand, have been more successful in finding industrial partners. The most famous ones, located in Milan and Turin, were originally set up by Olivetti and Fiat respectively to secure the recruitment of engineers for these firms.

France

Like Italy, France has introduced new reforms to its public research systems designed to 'increase its socio-economic relevance' (Llerena *et al.* 2003). These authors assess the changes that were made in the late 1990s, focusing particularly on the 1999 Innovation Law (Allegre's Law) that at last allowed academics to participate in the development of spin-offs (Llerena *et al.* 2003). It also instituted a call for tenders to fund the establishment of public and regional incubators (Lanciano-Morandat and

Nohara 2002b). The new policies are intended to address the French weakness which is its failure of public research, which dominates French R&D, to interact with industry, limiting the country's capacity for economic growth. Llerena *et al.* (2003) conclude that the incentives to encourage academics to become entrepreneurs and the institutions to support this activity are missing or too weak. Senker (2005) finds that, in the case of the biotech innovation system, France underperforms largely as a result of the highly fragmented research system, block grant funding which attempts to co-ordinate research and the tenure held by academics that discourages competition between research institutions.

Germany

Germany has also recently adopted an integrated policy framework. Georghiou and Kuhlmann (2002, 204) report that the German 'Futur' initiative, a new kind of foresight programme, is illustrative of the new, systemically orientated RTD and innovation policy instruments in Europe. The programme is run on behalf of the Federal Ministry of Education and Research (BMBF) as a means of priority setting for future innovation-oriented research policies. The process, which is designed to identify future funded research programmes or projects, started with workshops in 2001. The German system, however, has a number of institutional rigidities which will need to be overcome. These, according to Etzkowitz *et al.* (2000), include the prevalence of the traditional central European view of natural science as a value by itself, tensions between federal and state responsibility for education and research and the inertia of public institutions.

German universities are financed and operated by the 16 German states. The Federal government determines only general guidelines laid down in the Framework Act for Higher Education (Hochschulrahmengesetz) (HRG). Each state has its own legal regulations, the Higher Education Acts (Hochschulgesetze). Each state develops HRG regulations, and develops its own education legislation which differs from state to state. Leifner *et al.* (2004) describe how the German university system is undergoing drastic reform, but cultural differences prevent the effective application in German universities of funding mechanisms and incentives developed elsewhere. In particular they point to its inflexibility, the lack of or unattractive job opportunities for young and promising academics, a lack of competition between universities and between a university's departments for financial resources. Very few incentives for outstanding research performance are available. The low degree of differentiation (range of courses, quality standards in teaching and study fees) is in part responsible for the cultural stasis. They remark that 'in contrast to universities in the US, these differentiation mechanisms are barely visible or non-existent' (page 24).

In 2005, it was announced that Germany was going to revive its stagnating university system by creating elite universities to rival Oxbridge. The Chancellor of Germany, Gerhard Schroeder, and the 16 regional prime ministers signed a €1.9 billion agreement for the Excellence Initiative which will provide additional support for institutions competing to form a German Ivy League of about ten universities and finance the development of about 30 research clusters and 40 graduate schools between 2006 and 2011. Three-quarters of funding will come from the national government and the remaining quarter from the states (Chapman 2005).

Eminence

The link between universities and economic performance is related in part to the quality of universities as demonstrated by their ability to attract the most external funding and the quality of their research staff and students. The 2003 EIS finds evidence of strong regional variations in performance in Europe, which is in part linked to the presence of universities. It finds a positive relationship between regional innovation and GDP. The most innovative regions in the EU are in Sweden (Stockholm and Sydsverige), Finland (Uusimaa) – these have the best-educated workforces – and the Netherlands (Noord-Brabant) and Germany (Stuttgart and Oberbayern) which have the best patent performance.

The assessment of quality or eminence and associated rankings is increasingly becoming the indicator of the strength of Europe's scientific and technological reputation. Evaluation is being built into the process of development of the European Research Area (Georghiou and Kuhlmann 2002). They predict that it is likely that such rankings based on other entrepreneurial indicators such as patenting, industry income and spin-offs will appear in the near future.

Defence and biotech

Within Europe, two parallel trends can be observed. The first is the growing increase in funding for life sciences research and a decrease in defence funding, the two major areas of government and industry spending on science and technology. In both cases a small number of countries have dominated European activity (see Chapter 3). The second is a concentration of activity in particular locations, what Cooke (2004) calls 'the rise of bioscience megacentres', a pattern which is well established in the US. In defence, the US, France and Sweden experienced the strongest decline in the 1990s.

In the UK the megacentre pattern in defence relationship is evolving through new and expanding collaborations being set up between universities, government bodies and defence corporations. There are three main initiatives. The first is the Defence Technology Centres (DTCs), which are now the main route for defence funding. These are located at Bristol, Cambridge, Cardiff, Cranfield, De Montfont, Imperial College, Southampton and Surrey. The second is the Towers of Excellence which 'aim to produce world-beating projects'. They are co-operative groupings, led by the Ministry of Defence, which bring together key players in the UK defence industry sector and leading UK academic establishments. Their main characteristics are that Towers are generally created at the level of major sub-systems technology and that the location of Towers must be selected in partnership with defence equipment suppliers, since the ultimate objective is to give them the capacity to supply world-class equipment (see www.mod.uk/toe/#dtcs). They include programmes at Cranfield and Imperial College. The third is the Defence and Aerospace research partnerships (DARPs) including one in High Integrity Real Time Systems (HIRTS). The purpose of the DARPs is to carry out work, which is of value to the defence and aerospace community as a whole, and thus is best undertaken in an open partnership, not as a company-specific activity. Members of the HIRTS DARP are BAE Systems, Rolls-Royce plc, QinetiQ and the University of York (www.cs.york.ac.uk/hise/darp.php).

While the MoD provides information about programmes which involve university research, Langley, however, found it impossible 'to obtain details of the extent and levels of funding by the military sector in UK universities'. He cited a written response in Hansard (2003) given by the Parliamentary Under Secretary of State for Defence which reported that the MoD had placed contracts over the period 1999–2003 worth over £3 million. The universities involved were likely to be those involved with the Defence Technology Centres and Towers of Excellence.

The pattern of a concentration of defence-related activity is replicated in the bioscience sector. Efforts are being made to concentrate activity in a few locations with universities spearheading these developlments (Cooke 2004). Two examples of this are (1) the tri-national Biotech cluster known as 'BioValley' covering the Alsace in France, the north-west of Switzerland and the region of South Baden in Germany with one of the world's highest density of life science industry and (2) London University in the UK.

London University is bidding to launch itself as a leading centre for bioscience in a bid to overtake Oxford and Cambridge, thus hindering efforts to increase integration of Europe's activities. Between 2003 and 2007, the London Development Agency (LDA) plans to build two bioincubators and revive the Enfield science park. Yet, in line with so many developments at the regional level in the UK, it pledged to bridge the funding gap and improve access to business angels – but not to spend any money. The intention is to lever funds out of industry (Davis 2003).

Box 4.1 The BioValley

The BioValley was created in 1996, with the prospect of a trinational region becoming an European Centre of biotechnology. After the merger of Ciba and Sandoz into Novartis in 1996 Dr Georg H. Endress and Hans Briner had the vision of a Silicon Valley dedicated to biotechnology and chemical technologies in the Upper Rhine region. They implemented the BioValley concept into a concrete initiative. In 1997 the former BioValley Promotion Team and the former General Manager Beat Löffler acquired an Interreg II European programme with a budget of €2.2 million. Many of the projects and activities described below were started and created during the Interreg II period between 1997 and 2001. In July 2002 a new budget of nearly €2.4 million, funded by Interreg III and co-financers in the three countries, started. It is scheduled to end by mid-2005. BioValley ranks among the top three European bioregions, including 15,000 scientists in life sciences, 70,000 students, over 150 academic or public institutions and more than 400 research groups. There are high-quality higher education and research establishments at the universities of Strasbourg, Freiburg, Basel and the universities of applied science in Mulhouse and Offenburg. Five Nobel Prizes for research in chemistry and medicine have been awarded to scientists working in BioValley over the past 15 years.

Source: www.biovalley.com

Accountability

New expectations on universities to contribute to society are far wider than at any other time in history (OECD 2003, 8–9). In addition to their traditional teaching and research roles, they are being remade as the focal point of transformations in the economy and society more generally. For example, they must cater for new needs in education and training which arise from the knowledge-based economy, become more engaged in community life. And, 'given that they live thanks to substantial public and private funding, and that the knowledge they produce and transmit has a major impact on the economy and society, universities are also accountable for the way they operate and manage activities and budgets to their sponsors and to the public. This leads to increasing pressure to incorporate representatives of the non-academic world within universities' management and governance structures.' This is a significant paradigm shift from the Humboldt and Vannevar Bush models of the past, realigning the status, function and accountability of universities and challenging their autonomy, which academics have argued is crucial to their broader contribution to society.

Within the EU, the prospects of a common pattern of accountability are limited because of national differences in the stance taken on the ethical and moral issues for particular kinds of research, for example on defence and bioscience. In the case of the latter, in 2003 it was argued that the prospects for a European policy on stem cell research within a European Research Area are limited because the ethical and scientific decisions on acceptability of stem cell science are left to member states. This makes it clear that there are some fights that even the EU knows that it cannot win (*THES* 2003b, 14).

Massification

After the Second World War, higher education expanded rapidly in Europe (Geuna 2001, 609). Within that broader trend, there are substantial variations in recruitment in general and in the proportions of students in science and engineering subjects, the numbers of researchers and in patterns of mobility. As with national differences, substantial differences exist between Europe as a whole and the US in recruitment patterns, although the size of the graduate population is similar.

In 2000, the EU produced a total of 2.14 million graduates compared to 2.07 from the US. Five member states accounted for almost 80 per cent of EU graduates. The UK contributed the most (504,000), followed by France (500,000) and Germany (300,000). In the 1960s, only 3 per cent of the UK's population went to universities, now some 43 per cent are in higher education while in Finland the figure is 60 per cent. Spain has also rapidly expanded its university system with the number of institutions rising from 46 to 66 in the 1990s as state universities were set up in national capitals and private universities appeared in big cities. The country is now, however, like Italy, facing problems of under-recruitment. In October 1994, 305,000 new students entered Spanish universities but this level was not maintained and the number had declined to 250,000 by October 2000 (Bompard 2003, 10, 11).

The number of graduates in science and engineering (S&E) varies both by discipline and by country. In the EU15, just over a quarter of the 555,647 graduates were in S&E with more engineering than science graduates (14 and 12 per cent). Ireland, the UK and France account for most of the S&E graduates, with the highest proportions found in Ireland, Sweden, France, Austria and Finland (EC 2003b, 186). Countries such as Denmark and Belgium have very low shares of very highly qualified people in their younger populations, and a general problem of an ageing population of S&E researchers.

Career opportunities for researchers in Europe vary considerably within the EU. In 1999, approximately 920,000 people were working in the EU as research scientists and engineers (RSE). Researchers in universities account for a third of all Europe's researchers and 80 per cent of fundamental research in Europe (EC 2003b, 5). The total is about 300,000 less than the total number of researchers in the US. The countries with the largest number of researchers are Germany, the UK and France, which combined host over 60 per cent of all of the researchers in EU member states. Italy and Spain have the next most RSE but each with less than half the number in France. Although during the 1990s the number of researchers increased by 24 per cent, this was slightly below the 26 per cent increase in the US (EC 2003b, 180). On the basis of these figures, the EC concludes that the US creates greater opportunities for researchers than Europe (page 253). Moreover, as in the UK as discussed in Chapter 3, all is not well in France. In March 2004, directors of more than 2,000 French laboratories and research centres, dissatisfied with decreases in the country's research budget, submitted resignations of their administrative functions to the science ministry. Funds had been frozen even at the national medical research centre, Inserm (Henley 2004). The mass resignation was largely symbolic, however, as scientists will continue to carry out their scientific duties and receive full pay. To address the concerns, a new budget of €3 billion by 2007 in scientific research was announced by the Prime Minister (http://english.people.com.cn/200403/10/eng20040310_137075.shtml).

One of the major problems for Europe as a whole is the limited influx of individuals from other continents, the argument being that in-migrants are likely to be among the most talented. Young and Brown (2002) propose that talent attraction of star academics, researchers, highly skilled knowledge workers is increasingly replacing inward investment attraction as a key role for regional development agencies. Bachtler (2004) supports this with the example of Quebec, where the government is offering five-year income tax holidays to attract foreign academics in IT, engineering, health science and finance to take employment in the region's universities. In Finland, Nokia invests in the cultural adaptation of foreign IT workers as a way to improve productivity but also to help to retain this 'talent' (OECD 2004). But compared to the US, European universities are attracting fewer students and in particular fewer researchers, from other countries.

Entrepreneurial universities

Chapter 3 showed that the increasing rate of patenting, licensing and spin-offs in Europe have been accompanied by changes in the laws in many countries concerning government ownership of intellectual property and the terms and conditions under which organizations can move towards the entrepreneurial model. Many countries have adopted new policies to encourage entrepreneurial activity. Italy, for example, has altered its technology transfer regulations to benefit SMEs whilst there are new funds and emergence of incubators to fuel high-technology innovative activities in France (Hague and Oakley 2000).

Not only do countries vary in the degree to which the entrepreneurial model has become articulated in national policy discourse, but some universities are further along that path than others. Clark (1998) considers

Twente (Netherlands), Warwick, Strathclyde (both UK), Chalmers (Sweden) and Joensuu (Finland) to be paradigmatic of the entrepreneurial response to the new challenges now faced by higher education. Changes in organizational structure undertaken by these universities have involved adopting a reinforced management core, improvement in their peripheral development, diversification of their funding bases, stimulation of the academic sphere and integration of the entrepreneurial culture into the organization.

One of the earliest to do this was the University of Twente, which positioned itself in the 1980s as the 'entrepreneurial university'. This was enshrined in the establishment of the University of Twente Entrepreneurship Centre (UTEC) which brings together activities in the field of entrepreneurship from across the university (OECD 1999, 43). It has also established UT-Extra, which acts as a private foundation to encourage entrepreneurial activity. This was necessary as Dutch law inhibits universities from being involved in excessive forms of entrepreneurial activity (Hague and Oakley 2000, 46).

The territorial role

The territorial role is ascendant in the European Union because of the application of the subsidiarity principle, *that the development of research must be co-ordinated to promote projects for the development of research which are as close as possible to the citizen* (EC 2001a, 4). This report stresses that regions are expected to have an important bridging role between the European and the local level, 'including strengthening international cooperation by mobilising the potential of local universities together with regional and local authorities'. Universities are encouraged to be entrepreneurial and to spin off new firms, to engage more closely with firms in their immediate hinterland and to take on social responsibilities (see EC 2003a).

Regionalization, hence the territorial role, varies by character and degree across member states of the EU, including the extent to which the financing and management of HEIs occurs at a regional level. Germany's Länder are the strongest sub-national units, while Spain's autonomous regions vary in degrees of power. In France, while regions have only limited power, regional authorities on average fund a third of final expenditure on higher education (although this varies considerably). The EC report concludes that less clear impulses towards regionalization occur in Denmark, Finland, Greece, Ireland, Luxembourg, the Netherlands, Portugal and Sweden. The diversity in the extent to which the territorial role has been adopted is illustrated by the examples of the UK, Italy, Spain, Germany and France.

The UK

The potential contribution that universities can make to regional development was recognized in the National Committee of Inquiry into Higher Education (1997) (The Dearing Report), which included the chapter 'The local and regional role of higher education'. The Report identified one of the four main purposes of higher education as being 'to serve the needs of an adaptable, sustainable, knowledge-based economy at local, regional and national levels' (paragraph 5.11). This position was expanded in the White Paper *Our Competitive Future* (DTI 1998, chapter 5), in the Sainsbury Report on Biotechnology (1999), the 2000 White Paper on science and innovation policy and in the 2003 *Lambert Review of Business–University Collaboration*. The role of the university as regional economic growth protagonist was confirmed in practice as a policy objective since the formation in 1999 of the nine English Regional Development Agencies (RDAs). An ambiguity in UK policy is that at the national level policy objectives both of the Department for Education and Science (which has overall policy for universities) and of the Higher Education Funding Council for England, HEFCE (which has responsibility for funding universities in England) state that to be really successful universities must be free to take responsibility for their own strategic and financial future. (Similar funding agencies exist for Wales and Scotland, which have their own, more powerful regional development agencies which predate those in England.) At the same time, the policy announced in the 2003 White Paper that the RDAs were to be given a stronger role in steering the Higher Education Innovation Fund, which will amount to £90 million in 2005–6, will remove some of this autonomy by devolving powers to the RDAs whose missions do not include the support of scholarship, do not want to take on responsibilities for funding basic research but are charged with stimulating economic development. And, as exemplified by the LDA's response to the Lambert Review (www.hm-treasury.gov.uk/consultations_and_legislation/lambert/consult_lambert_al_universities.cfm), they do want a role in co-ordination across regions to avoid duplication and competition. Against this background, the majority of universities now are in favour of developing a territorial role, which is hardly surprising given the financial incentives.

A recent study of UK universities (Charles and Conway 2001) found an increasing alignment between the geographical unit considered of greatest priority in the institutional mission and the Government Office or Regional Development Agency region. This was almost 43 per cent, an increase from 25.30 per cent in 1997, whereas the locality had decreased from 15.66 per cent in 1997 to 8.70 per cent in 2001. Also the percentage of universities which said that the regional or local area was not of any significance to the mission had decreased from 8.43 per cent to 4.30 per cent, although, as Charles (2003, 13–14) points out, there are philosophical and methodological problems in defining a university's 'local' community (see Goddard *et al.* 1994). New or modern universities, possibly reflecting their history of LEA funding, gave economic development a higher priority than the old universities (86 per cent: 44 per cent). Indications are that there will be a polarization within the university system as the newer universities opt out of the RAE system and focus their efforts on winning third-stream funding – encouraged by funding proposals in *The future of higher education* for less research-intensive universities for funding for skills development and technology transfer through the establishment of 20 knowledge exchanges (page 36). The main post-1997 financial incentives for the funding of research, which implicitly might have commercial applications, encouraging the adoption of the entrepreneurial model and the territorial role, are shown in Table 4.1.

The majority of regions (defined as RDA regions) have established Regional Science Councils. For example, The Science and Industry Council of the North East of England (submission of the Science and Industry Council of North East England to the Lambert Review) was established in December 2001 at the instigation of One NorthEast with the

Table 4.1 UK incentives to university–industry engagement

Department	Initiative
DfEE, DTI, HEfCE	Higher Education Reach-Out to Business and the Community (HEROBC) scheme 1999. Universities can apply for special funding for activities to increase their capability to respond to the needs of business, including companies of all sizes and the wider community, where this will lead to wealth creation • includes the promotion of spin-out companies
DTI/OST/ Engineering and Physical Sciences Council (EPSRC)	Science Enterprise Challenge Fund, 1999 financed Enterprise Centres and the Foresight Directorate • encourages regional-level activity Faraday Partnerships 2000 • joint university–industry initiatives Biotechnology Challenge Fund
OST/HEFCE	Joint Infrastructure Fund (JIF) (1998) Science Research Investment Fund (SRIF) (2001)
OST/Treasury/Wellcome Trust and Gatsby Foundation	University Challenge Fund (UCF) • provides seed funding to help selected universities make the most of research funding through support for early stages of commercial exploitation of new products and processes
HEFCE	Higher Education Innovation Fund (2001) • £140 million over three years to encourage academic spin-off

Source: Author's survey.

objective of maximizing the contribution of the North East of England's scientific research base. It both enables 'high-level communication between universities, industry and the public sector' and 'champions the role of science and technology in the region'. The strategy for success is developing five centres of excellence to act as focal points for commercialization of science in the region and is based on five technologies that reflect the universities' research strengths.

Other initiatives are organized by the universities in collaboration with others to provide a regional focus on RDAs. Examples include Knowledge House established by Newcastle University. This is co-ordinated between all the universities in the North East and provides an entry point for SMEs which want to access the universities' expertise. Another mechanism involving Newcastle is the Regional Centre for Innovation in Engineering Design (RCID) which is a collaborative venture with two other regional universities and offers engineering design and services to around 15 of the region's innovative SMEs. The RCID works on a cluster basis.

Italy

In Italy, universities' territorial role is not very advanced and neither are universities in general engaged in locally or regionally focused systems of governance. Viale and Ghiglione (undated, 3) argue that universities are relatively strong within Italy but not very strong within Europe or within the world, and links with industry are relatively underdeveloped. While companies tend to establish links directly with universities rather than through regional technology transfer agencies, universities and research centres in Lombardy rarely play the role of setting up hybrid agents of innovation such as science parks. They find that the only successful example is the Photonic Research Centre at the Politecnico di Milano funded by Pirelli, which implies spontaneous convergence of industry and academia with approval and incentives from local government. These authors conclude that 'the Lombardy universities are far from the university actor in the technology market. Technology policy concentrates on the national level and only three regional laws for innovation finance have been introduced. They have partially failed as a result of the lack of a serious technology foresight study'.

Spain

In Spain, the extent to which a territorial role is adopted by individual universities depends variously on the region and the city. Spain has, within a spectrum of regional governments, a sub-group of strong autonomous regions based on separatist claims, such as Catalonia and the Basque country which have significant amount of power and resemble the German Länder (OECD 1999, 34). In Catalonia, for example, universities have

been targeted as the means by which economic development will be stimu-
lated. Public and private spending on S&T, human resources and infrastructure have all been increased in recent years. As yet, OECD finds that
more finance has been allocated to technology programmes than to incentives for spontaneous industry–university interaction.

The Barcelona science park, located close to research activity in the University of Barcelona, Catalonia Polytechnique University (CPU) and CSIS
institutes, is argued by the OECD (1999) to represent a more dynamic
model. Trilaterial relationships have developed: the University provided
the site, Catalonia autonomous government and the Spanish government
have supported the project economically and politically since its inception.
A virtuous circle of academia–government–industry relations has been
translated into an integrated system which involves universities, research
institutes, governments, private companies, research personnel and infrastructures. The city council of Terresa, home to the School and College of
Industrial Engineering of the CPU and other university institutions through
the Terresa Staryegi c Plan (PECT), has established a collective strategy
for the future of the city. This involves promoting a unified campus, making
it the country's second university city (after Barcelona), and involving the
university as one of the city's defining factors for the future.

Germany

In Germany, complete control over all aspects of education is with the 16
Länder rather than the federal government. In this respect, financial and
administrative responsibilities rest with each individual state. In spite of
this regional aspect of funding, however, OECD (1999, 28) concludes that
there are few requirements from state governments for German HEIs to
engage with the regions. And, although HEIs are funded and administered
at the sub-national level, 'the Humboldtian tradition of German universities affords them a significant amount of autonomy'.

Sternberg's studies of university and industry linkages published in 1998
and 1999 found considerable differences between Länder in the levels of
university–industry linkages, and not ones which would be predicted from
the university–industry-proximity hypothesis. Sternberg (1999, 535)
showed that even in Baden-Württemberg, one of the most economically
successful regions in Europe, the region's very good R&D infrastructure
and rather high technology potential were not reflected in its share of
intra-regional contacts with research institutions of innovative SMEs. In
contrast, the technologically less advanced regional economies of the
Lower Saxony research triangle and of Saxony show higher shares of
intra-regional linkages with research institutions. He concluded that no
statistical evidence can be found for the assumption that prosperous
regions have stronger intra-regional links than peripheral ones. Sternberg
concludes that, in Lower Saxony, one out of two effects which operate

simultaneously in a true innovative milieu are lacking. While proximity effects (reductions in costs) operate, underdeveloped socialization effects (collective learning, co-operation, socialization of risks) are missing.

France

France's national decentralization strategies which began in the 1960s with the formation of DATAR (an autonomous central body in charge of regional development) have since the late 1990s included mechanisms to encourage small companies to increase their links to universities. A clear strategy in France is the establishment of partnerships between universities, industry and political bodies in the French regions. This was articulated in the 1998 report for the Economics Minister (Guillaume 1998). After the decision made by the former EC Director Edith Cresson to favour innovation (Green Book on Innovation, 1995), Jospin's government proposed to develop measures in order to improve start-ups from research institutes and universities. The creation of National Centres for Technology and Innovation was approved in 2000. These are funded at the sub-regional level and are in the national programme of technical resource centres (almost 20 at the moment in France).

Yet France has not adopted such an aggressive national stance on clusters as the UK as each region, in the absence of a defined national policy, adopts its own strategies. For example, the Pôle Universitaire Européen Lille Nord-Pas de Calais brings together seven universities, two research institutes, local governments and chambers of commerce. The main aim of the network, according to OECD (1999, 52), 'is to pursue international relations and communicate the role of the region to the outside world'. (See also Chapter 8 below on Grenoble.) OECD (1999, 136) finds the French system to be interesting in that there are concerns within the university system of the consequences and benefits of decentralization as paradoxically increased decentralization 'requires greater national co-ordination to ensure that different areas stick to the one vision'.

Conclusions

It is at the European Commission level that the ideal of creating a far more integrated system of innovation is enshrined in policy. This is the dominant paradigm. Universities are to be at the heart of the drive towards making Europe able to compete more strongly with the US. To achieve that goal, the emphasis is on greater co-ordination of research and teaching across Europe, networking to overcome barriers to industry working with universities, improving the career opportunities for scientists and student mobility. The territorial role is the second most important paradigm: regions and universities are the major points of delivery of the production and dissemination of new knowledge.

The challenge for European policy makers is illustrated by the differences in the extent to which the integrated model is extant in different countries. At the one extreme the UK and the Netherlands have most fully adopted the new model at national level, and Italy and France least. The picture is complicated by a variety of political systems in which the regional scale provides direction to the university system and by the timing and nature of laws which have enshrined the entrepreneurial university concept which is more established in the US than Europe (Etzkowitz 2003). Germany has the most developed regional tier of government but needs to overcome cultural and organizational rigidities, and the UK in these examples the least. Countries also vary in the quality of science, the dominance of universities and defence and life science research activity in the national system of innovation; each of these has profound implications for points of contact with industry. As Chapter 1 showed, the UK dominates European ranking on university quality, and, in Cambridge and Oxford, has two of the top ten ranked universities in the world.

This chapter has shown that research in both defence and bioscience is concentrated in a few countries and locations. Efforts to create 'mega-centres' which integrate efforts of researchers from different organizations and across geographical boundaries are more pronounced in biotech than in defence.

Evidence on the relationship between proportions of scientists and engineers produced by universities and economic development is confused by the possibilities for mobility and career advancement depending on how the national innovation system is constructed. Europe as a whole compares badly with the US. While the EC (2003b) concludes that Nordic countries including Denmark are investing in higher education and rapidly turning into knowledge-based economies, Belgium and Denmark also have low shares of highly qualified people in their younger populations.

New systems of governance in which universities are being repositioned vis-à-vis both industry and their territories bring with them new sets of accountability, challenging the much-prized autonomy of universities to decide what kinds of organizations they will be. The greater emphasis on evaluation of universities performance both at the European and at the national level is a further indication of the instrumentalist position in society that universities are required to adopt (see Charles 2003). The evidence indicates that autonomy combined with the greater variety and expenditure on university research at Federal and state level is what gives the US the competitive edge over Europe. The implications of this for the longer term are threefold. The first is that the consensus that appears to have been reached between the competing interests of universities and their academics and the other stakeholders in society will not hold and that Europe needs to be aware that the American model also has its internal critics. This is particularly in relation to the increasing ownership and control of business over the university research (see Chapter 5).

Second, unless the emphasis that Europe has placed on upgrading skills is consistent through the careers of scientists and engineers, then Europe will continue to lag behind the US. Third, strategies to involve universities in supporting EU enlargement and convergence processes must be informed by realistic assessments of the capacity of the universities to deliver and the geo-industrial structure of their hinterlands.

5   The United States

Introduction

National policy in the US, as in Europe, emphasizes the role of universities as a driver of economic development. For example, the US Council on Competitiveness (1998, 14) states, 'The nation that fosters an infra-structure of linkages among and between firms, universities and govern-ment gains competitive advantage through quicker information diffusion and product deployment.' This chapter documents how the US system of higher education has evolved to become more integrated especially in science and technology (Noll 1998), and has a clear territorial focus at Federal and state level, while remaining characterized by institutional autonomy.

Distributed innovation systems

The economic and technological leadership enjoyed by the US is accord-ing to Malecki (2005 drawing on Mowery 1983) owed to the three features of its national innovation system. These are its enormous scale; the shifting roles of the three performers of R&D – industry, universities and federal government; and the importance of new firms in the commercialization of new technology. In addition, for far longer in the US than in Europe, uni-versities have had access to measures which have supported the research to innovation process, providing key elements in that infrastructure. Three features which illustrate the history and development of integration between universities and industry within the US national innovation system are legislation and funding, the growing number of joint research centres and public policy towards research collaborations.

Legislation and funding initiatives

National research programmes that have industrial applications date back to the late nineteenth century. The NIH was established in the late 1880s and the Research Corporation in 1912 (Table 5.1). In the mid-1920s,

Table 5.1 Major legislation affecting universities' links with industry in the US

Measure	Date	Effect
Morrill Act	1862	Established Land Grant universities which were dedicated to the support of agriculture and the mechanic arts. Control of universities left to the states. Examples include MIT
National Institutes of Health (NIH)	1887	The Federal focal point for health research
Research Corporation	1912	Set up to help universities patent inventions
National Science Foundation (NSF)	1950	Government responsibility for funding basic research, later specialized research centres were established such as Engineering research centres
NSF	1973	Industry–university cooperative research centres
Patent and Trademark Act (Bayh-Dole Act)	1980	Formalized university ownership of IP and hence capacity to commercialize university research. In universities, innovators were eventually guaranteed 15 per cent of returns on their investment
Economic Recovery Tax	1981	Reduced the cost to industry of funding university research
Small Business Innovation Research Programme (SBIR)	1982	Encouraged small business to explore their technological potential and provided the incentive to profit from its commercialization
National Cooperative Research Act (NCRA)	1984	Eliminated treble damage of anti-trust so that firms, universities and federal laboratories could engage in joint pre-competitive R&D Establishment of Co-operative Research and Development Agreements (CRADA)
Technology Transfer Act	1986	Under CRADAs federal laboratories empowered to co-operate in R&D with private firms and may assign private firms the rights to any intellectual property arising from joint work. Amended in 1989 to allow contractor-operated federal laboratories to participate in CRADAs (Mowery 1998)
Omnibus Trade and Competitiveness Act	1987/8	Advanced Technology Program (ATP). Provided matching funds for industry-led R&D consortia, some of which involve universities or federal labs as participants
Defense Authorization Act:	1993	Renamed DARPA to ARPA; authorizes dual-use technology transfer projects
Technology Transfer Improvements and Advancement Act	1996	Strengthened rights of firms to exclusively license patents resulting from CRADAs
Small Business Technology Transfer Program (STTR)	1997	Expansion of the public/private sector partnership to include the joint venture opportunities for small business and the nation's premier nonprofit research institutions
Budget doubling of NIH	1998–2003	Greater spend on life science research

Sources: Rosenberg and Nelson 1994; Mowery 1998; Bozeman 2000, 634; Shapira 2004a, www.sba.gov/sbir/indexsbir-sttr.html.

policies requiring faculty to disclose their inventions to university administrators were part of a new formalization process (Mowery and Sampat
2001). This pattern began first in the public universities, the University of
California being the first, followed by private universities led by MIT. The
creation of formal technology transfer units began in the 1930s. This new
organization whereby intellectual property was managed to the benefit of
the university meant that technology could be made available to a variety
of firms. Etzkowitz (2003) suggests that this reorganization enabled Stanford University to make available the inventions in physics and electrical
engineering in the period before the Bayh-Dole Act.

While these programmes and legislation laid the foundations for formalized university–industry linkages, the majority of programmes and legislation were initiated either during or after the Second World War, with
the 1960s seeing a massive expansion in government-funded research in
universities. The National Science Foundation (NSF) and other programmes arose during the Second World War as a result of success in harnessing university research to wartime needs (Adams 2002, 275; Shane
2004, 45). As in Europe, radical changes began in 1979 when the government of Ronald Reagan, like that of Margaret Thatcher in the UK,
changed political climate with regard to the function of universities
(Kenney 1986, 28). Between 1980 and 2000, the US Congress passed eight
major policy initiatives dealing with technology transfer and the means of
promoting it (Bozeman 2000, 628). Like legislation in general, legislative
changes were a response to issues arising from well-established trends.

The most famous, the 1980 Bayh-Dole Act, was passed by Congress as
a response to complaints that Federal funding, which led universities in a
more basic direction, also weakened university–firm linkages (Etzkowitz
2003). Thus, Etzkowitz argues, it was the universities that were active in
technology transfer that lobbied for the passage of the law in order to
obtain a stable, regulated environment for the disposition of intellectual
property rights emanating from Federally funded research. The Bayh-
Dole Act permitted government grantees and contractors to retain title to
inventions resulting from Federally supported R&D and encouraged the
licensing of such inventions to industry. Although some Federal agencies
permitted universities to retain title before the Act, this law established a
uniform government-wide policy and process for academic patenting (NSF
2004). The 1981 Economic Recovery Tax, which extended industrial R&D
tax breaks to research supported at universities, also encouraged the take-
up of patents and licences.

The effects of the former were complex and systemic and not confined
to increasing the number or quality of patents and licences. First, there
were reports that the increased rate of university patenting did not seem to
increase the number of important academic patents, but it did greatly
expand the number of marginal patents. Before 1980 academic patents
were on average more important and more general than corporate

patents, judging from citation patterns, but by the end of the 1980s that difference had disappeared. The overall quality of patents from leading universities declined somewhat, but the patents of newcomers were for the most part of less value. Thus, increased patenting did appear to yield decreasing returns. Moreover, only a few of the newcomers were able to replicate the success of the existing patent leaders. Mowery and Ziedonis (2002) argue that any effects of the Bayh-Dole Act on overall academic patent quality reflect the Act's effects on entry, rather than on the incentives of academic researchers and administrators in long-active academic patenters. While there may or may not be a direct relationship with patenting, Florida (1999, 2) argues, that while the Act may have helped universities to commercialize innovations, it may exacerbate the skewing of the university's role towards some notion of driving regional economies.

By 1960, Federal support for basic research amounted to over 60 per cent of the total funding and, by 1965, real resources going into academic research were more than twelve times what they were in the mid-1930s. Rapid growth in the level of funding continued until around 1980, with the real rate of growth about 3 per cent a year. Between 1990 and 2002, inflation-adjusted Federal dollars for academic R&D grew by 66 per cent (Malecki 2005).

Concomitant with this rate of growth was a cultural attitude, and basic research 'not only became respectable, but widely perceived as what universities ought to be doing'. Two indicators of American world leadership in most areas of science were the number of Nobel Prizes and the influx of foreign students – the reverse of the pattern before the Second World War. NSF, however, has accounted for less than one-fifth of Federal support for university research in the post-war period, with NIH accounting for a third and another third accounted for by the Department of Defense, NASA and Department of Energy. In 1989 half of academic research funding went to the life sciences, compared to 16 per cent for engineering – which exceeded physical sciences. By the late 1990s, universities owned 30 per cent of DNA patents (OECD 2001a). The growing involvement of industry in university research is demonstrated by the statistic that, by 1998, corporations sponsored nearly $2 billion in research performed at universities, or nearly 9 per cent of all research performed at US colleges and universities. Noll (1998) prophesied a polarization within the US university system, arguing that declining state appropriations and profits from medical services, a situation made worse by the shrinking of Federal grant support, will work to the detriment of some of the smaller research universities, which may abandon their attempts to maintain this status.

Joint university–industry research centres and research joint ventures

Two particular features of US university–industry linkage infrastructure are legislation which formalizes the intent of collaboration and the large number of joint university–industry research centres.

Joint university research centres date back to the formation of the NSF. A study by Cohen *et al.* for Carnegie Mellon University (CMU) of 1,056 centres with more than $100,000 in funding and at least one active industry partner had total funding in excess of $4.12 billion (see Cohen *et al.* 1994). The centres involved 12,000 staff and 22,300 doctoral level students. Florida (1999) suggests that the popularity of collaboration can be explained either as the corporate 'manipulation view' that corporations seek to control relevant research for their own ends, or that, from the 'academic entrepreneur' view, university faculty and administrators act as entrepreneurs, cultivating opportunities for industry and public funding to advance their own agendas. The Cohen *et al.* study supported the academic entrepreneur thesis. They found that 73 per cent of university–industry research centres indicated that the main impetus for their formation came from university faculty and administrators and only 11 per cent came from industry. These centres, however, existed because of Federal funding. A third policy initiative was the establishment by NSF of several programmes that tied Federal support to industry participation. These include the Engineering Research Centres and the Science and Technology Centers.

Engineering Research Centres receive the most generous public funding – income for the 21 centres was running at about $2 million a year in 1995. As cash contributions from industry averaged only $24,000, the centres were effectively subsidizing R&D in industry (Geiger 2003, 13). Geiger finds that centres are driven by technological opportunities – but that safeguards to the interests of the Centres are built in by vetting by NSF. He finds that in the Industry/University Cooperative Research Centers (IUCRC) programme, the leverage works in the opposite direction. NSF acts almost as a facilitator for far smaller co-operative centres with grassroots support and substantially increased funding for these in the 1980s. Grants from industry are much higher, a minimum of $300,000, while a full NSF grant originally provided $100,000 (later $70,000) of annual support for five years. In 2000 these centres received $5.2 million from NSF compared to $68 million from other, chiefly industry sources. Hence the centres have to meet the real needs of industry. While the state version has been discontinued, those at the Federal level remain. For Geiger, 'the implicit issue seemed to be the problem of targeting investments to stimulate economic development within the state rather than nationally'. To this end the programme explicitly sought to attract smaller firms which fit less well into the centre paradigm. In the 1990s most states moved towards investing in non-university programmes for outright technical assistance. He argues that states and localities face the challenge of capturing returns in the form of economic development from public support for research, which may inhibit a socially optimal investment in discovery.

Like other technology transfer legislation the National Cooperative Research Act (NCRA) was passed in the 1980s. The 1984 Act created a registration process so that research joint ventures (RJVs) can disclose their research intentions to the Department of Justice. By 2002, there were 800 formal RJVs filed under NCRA. On average, 15 per cent of RJVs have at least one university partner and of these over 90 per cent are US universities (Audretsch *et al.* 2002). Like Florida, Audretsch *et al.* conclude that firms with university partnerships are motivated not by desire to control activity but by efficiency objectives. Generally, collaborating firms have greater productivity and greater patenting activity. Hence a key motive of the firm to undertake such collaborations is to have access to university personnel, both graduate students and faculty, and laboratory facilities.

Another collaborative programme is the Advanced Technology Program (ATP), part of the National Institute of Standards and Technology. This is designed to 'bridge the gap between the laboratory and the market place' (www.atp.nist.gov/www/images/icons/misc/bridge.jpg) through research laboratory partnerships with the private sector. It offers early-stage investment to accelerating the development of innovative technologies that promise significant commercial payoffs. The programme assigns rights to the for-profit partner of a university to industry as this can result in universities not being able to apply for patents and removes any motivation for universities to disclose inventions. In 1994 it was reported that this caused universities such as MIT not to accept ATP awards (Stanford University News Service 1994). It has also faced opposition from policy makers. In 2001 the US Congress House of Appropriations Committee questioned its value (Feller 2004, 24).

Diversity versus uniformity and governance

Features of the North American HE system

The US system of higher education is far more heterogeneous than that of any other country. An indication of this is the number of different ways it has been characterized, although a number of features are common to all descriptions. Feller (1999) identifies four features of the American system of higher education: decentralization, competition, regionalism and coupling of research with graduate education. Clark (1992) adds largeness, dual tiers and diversified finance, Davis and Diamond (1997) include institutional pluralism, Shapira (2004a) highlights diverse science and technology policy systems and Malecki (2005) characterizes the system in terms of massive government funding for health and defence-related research, high academic quality and the willingness to invest in long-term development of new and often multi-disciplinary fields.

The US has over 3,600 higher education establishments, 550 of them issuing doctorates, and 125 identified as 'research universities'. The Carnegie Foundation defines these as: 'the presence of doctoral programs, and significant amounts of federal grants' (in Noll 1998). In 2001, the top 200 universities accounted for 96 per cent of all R&D expenditures (NSF 2004). Of these, some 50 accounted for the lion's share of American academic research capacity, public funding in support of university research and the country's Nobel Prizes for science.

Although university-performed R&D accounts for only 12 per cent of the US total, it is also highly correlated with the total R&D performance in a state (Table 5.2). The top ten states in university-performed R&D include the top ten states in total R&D except that North Carolina and Georgia replace New Jersey and Washington. Although R&D expenditures are concentrated in relatively few states, patterns of R&D activities vary considerably among the top R&D-performing locations. Variations in the R&D expenditure levels of states, however, may simply reflect differences in economic size or the nature of their R&D efforts.

NSF (2004) reports that the six states with the highest levels of R&D expenditures – California, Michigan, New York, New Jersey, Massachusetts and Illinois (in decreasing order of magnitude) – accounted for one-half of the entire national effort. Adding (in descending order) Texas, Washington, Pennsylvania and Maryland, the top ten states accounted for two-thirds. As in earlier years, California had the highest level of R&D expenditures in the nation ($55 billion); it alone accounted for over one-fifth of the $247 billion US R&D total. California's R&D effort exceeded by nearly a factor of three that of the next highest state, Michigan, with nearly $19 billion in R&D expenditures. After Michigan, R&D levels for the top ten states declined incrementally to $8.6 billion for Maryland. Although leading states in total R&D tend to be well represented in each of the major R&D-performing sectors, the relative share of each state's R&D performed by these sectors varies. States that are national leaders in total R&D performance are also usually leaders in terms of R&D performance by the industrial sector, which is not surprising because industry-performed R&D accounts for 77 per cent of the distributed US total. Thus, nine of the top ten states for total R&D (all but Maryland) were among the leading industrial R&D-performing states.

Eminence

The US system differs from the traditional European system in that private universities – which comprise the majority – play a far more dominant role in research systems than in other countries. The private Ivy

Table 5.2 Leading US states by R&D performance, R&D by sector and R&D as a percentage of state gross domestic product: 2000

Rank	Top 10 states in total R&D performance[1]		Top 10 states in size of R&D, by type of performer			Top 10 states in R&D intensity (states with the highest R&D/GSP ratio)		
	State	Total R&D (millions of current dollars)	Industry[2]	Universities & colleges[3]	Federal government[4]	State	R&D/GSP (per cent)	GSP (billions of current dollars)
1	California	55,093	California	California	Maryland	Michigan	5.81	325.4
2	Michigan	18,892	Michigan	New York	District of Columbia	New Mexico	5.68	54.4
3	New York	13,556	New Jersey	Texas	California	Washington	4.78	219.9
4	New Jersey	13,133	Illinois	Pennsylvania	Virginia	Maryland	4.64	186.1
5	Massachusetts	13,004	New York	Maryland	Alabama	Massachusetts	4.56	284.9
6	Illinois	12,767	Massachusetts	Massachusetts	Ohio	Delaware	4.22	36.3
7	Texas	11,552	Washington	Illinois	Florida	Rhode Island	4.12	36.5
8	Washington	10,516	Texas	North Carolina	Texas	California	4.10	1,344.6
9	Pennsylvania	9,842	Pennsylvania	Michigan	New Jersey	Idaho	3.87	37.0
10	Maryland	8,634	Ohio	Georgia	New Mexico	District of Columbia	3.97	59.4

Source: NSF 2004, www.nsf.gov/sbe/srs/infbrief/nsf03303/start/htm.

Notes
1 Includes in-state total R&D performance of industry, universities, Federal agencies, FFRDCs, and Federally financed nonprofit R&D.
2 Includes R&D activities of industry-administered FFRDCs located within these states.
3 Excludes R&D activities of university-administered FFRDCs located within these states.
4 Includes costs associated with the administration of intramural and extramural programmes by Federal personnel as well as actual intramural performance.

R&D = research and development; GSP = gross state product; FFRDC = Federally funded research and development center.
Reliability of the estimates of industry R&D varies by state because the sample allocation was not based on geography. Rankings do not take into account the margin of error of estimates from sample surveys.

League universities such as Harvard, Princeton and Yale (Ivy League is the name generally applied to eight privately owned universities (Brown, Columbia, Cornell, Dartmouth, Harvard, Pennsylvania, Princeton and Yale) (etc.princeton.edu/CampusWWW/Companion/ivy_league.html)) have enormous endowed wealth, the result of private philanthropy over two centuries. Although in the early 1990s seven of the top ten universities were private, among the top 104 research universities only 33 were private, the public universities succeeding on the basis of attracting funds from the state, Federal funding and industry (Siegel *et al.* 1999). These authors explain the dominance of private universities in the ranking of the top universities as arising from an important difference between public and private universities – public universities may have less flexibility and may be less focused on university–industry technology transfer than private universities are.

Noll (1998, 16) finds that the US system whereby the close relationship between universities, national laboratories and industry, with universities managing government research facilities, is responsible for the situation whereby 70 per cent of the authors of scientific and technical publications are affiliated to academic institutions – which leads to the situation whereby 'most of the world leaders in the United States are universities'. The pre-eminence of the US research universities (on the criterion of such bibliometric data), compared to Europe, is not just related to funding levels but, according to Herbst (2004), is to do with the structural setting in which the research is undertaken – the 'production–morphology nexus'. Herbst, like Noll (1998), finds a competitive advantage in flexibility: that the rest of the world is bureaucratic and inflexible compared to the US. He concludes that 'European and US higher education cultures can be seen on different shores of development'. US universities have a flat hierarchical set up (of teaching and research), that is, with low student–faculty and low staff–faculty ratios, whereas low performance levels correlate with more pronounced hierarchies below the level of faculty, that is high student–faculty and high staff–faculty ratios ('staff' here referring to administrative and technical support personnel). Thus according to this analysis European universities are much more top-down managed than those in the US and need to become much less hierarchical and more decentralized in order to compete with those in the US.

Defence and biotechnology

The massive government funding for defence and health-related research has involved close integration between universities, industry and the government's own research centres in both cases. Defence spending, according to Malecki (2005), is, in the absence of an explicit industrial or technology policy, the US's implicit technology policy. This has long been the case. The close integration between universities, defence research and industry is illustrated by some statistics from the 1980s in Scherer and Ross (1990). In 1987, 36 per cent of industrial R&D outlays were financed under government contracts, mostly covering military and space development. The manufacturing sector in the late 1980s conducted 97 per cent of all industrial R&D and was then the prime mover in generating technological progress. Since then the share of industrial R&D on both defence and space, although dropping from the peak in the mid-1980s, still contributes millions of dollars to universities and, through both the application of research and the training of scientists, has been associated closely with economic development concentrated in a small number of locations.

For example, defence funding of MIT (which was the largest recipient of research funding in the Second World War) and other universities including Harvard and a growing concentration of industrial laboratories in the Boston area 'offered an intellectual and technological labor pool unsurpassed in the nation, if not the world' (Saxenian 1994, 14). New Mexico's high R&D intensity is largely attributable to Federal (specifically Department of Energy) support of two federally funded research and development centres (FFRDCs), Los Alamos National Laboratory and Sandia National Laboratories (NSF 2004). This spending amounts to being an implicit regional as well as industrial policy (Malecki 2005).

Examples of recent initiatives illustrate how those patterns are being reinforced. In 2004, Congress passed a defence spending bill that included $1.5 million for Purdue University's planned Center for Advanced Manufacturing. Purdue will also benefit from funding in the bill for the Crane Naval Surface Warfare Center, with which it is collaborating on research to reduce the national security threat of shoulder-launched missiles. The money is part of a $418 billion defence package that funds the Pentagon in 2005 and includes emergency war spending (www.boilerstation.com/planet/stories/200407240purdue_planet1090646943.shtml). Other examples include Chevron, which was paid $55.8 million to provide fuel to Utah defence facilities, and the state's universities, particularly Utah State University, which landed $37 million in defence contracts working primarily on missile systems (www.shns.com/shns/g_index2.cfm?action=detail&pk=UTAH-DEFENSE-07-05-04).

Bioscience is the research sector currently most closely associated with national funding of research in universities, which is most influenced by national policies (Cook-Deegan 2000). Funding for research and legislative change which encouraged patenting and entrepreneurship have been the key differences between the US and Europe (Malecki 2005). He argues that it is the funding for the science base rather than the biotechnology industry and the relatively easier environment for academics to start up companies that have laid the foundations for start-up firms to be created out of the science base.

Funding for biomedical research in the US over the three decades has grown rapidly since the late 1970s when 11 per cent of all US Federally funded R&D was directed towards biomedical research (Senker 1996, 221). By the start of the twenty-first century, the National Institutes of Health (NIH) had become 'the world's largest source of support for bio-medical research' (Cook-Deegan 2000, 801). Since then, the NIH have contributed a substantial increase in funding relative to the other main federal funding agencies. Between 1990 and 2003, NIH's funding of acade-mic R&D increased the most rapidly, with an estimated average annual growth rate of 7.2 per cent per year in constant 1996 dollars, increasing its share of Federal funding from just above 50 per cent to an estimated 66 per cent. This compares with the next largest block of academic R&D expenditures, which went to engineering, about 15 per cent in 2001.

The distribution of this funding is uneven. California, Maryland, New York and Massachusetts are the top four states that receive NIH funding for academic science (Cook-Deegan 2000, 805). Unlike other countries, the US has also allocated funds to use the industry as a means of encour-aging economic development. The Experimental Program to Stimulate Competitive Research (EPSCoR) was established to identify, develop and utilize a state's academic science and technology resources in a way that will support the creation of wealth and enhance the life of the state's cit-izens (www.epscorfoundation.org/). It is administered within seven Federal agencies including NIH, NASA and the NSF. Specifically, EPSCoR stimulates sustainable R&D infrastructure improvements at the state and institutional levels to significantly increase the ability of EPSCoR researchers to compete for Federal and private-sector R&D funding, and accelerates the movement of EPSCoR researchers and institutions into the mainstream of Federal and private R&D support. Only those states that historically receive less Federal R&D funding and have a demonstrated commitment to develop their research bases and improve the quality of science and engineering research conducted at their universities and col-leges are eligible to participate in EPSCoR. Bioscience research, in con-junction with the NIH, is a key target. Research activity by itself, however, is not enough to ensure the growth of the biotechnology industry. For example, Atlanta and Houston are major biomedical research centres but with limited commercial activity (Cortright and Mayer 2002).

More than the straight commercial and economic development consid-erations, regulation of particular areas of research, especially stem cell but also agbio, have a direct effect on the US science effort and distinguish the US from other countries. For example, in 2001, the House of Representa-tives voted to ban all human cloning. The House rejected an amendment to the bill that would have carved out human cloning solely for embryonic stem cell research (ESCR) while outlawing its use to produce children. As a consequence, US scientists faced a setback as Federal research grants, whether applied directly or indirectly, were frozen. The freeze was lifted for projects that utilize existing stem cell cultures, but has implications for research. The administration's stance is that embryonic stem cell research is an ethical question. According to the release, taxpayer's dollars should not fund the destruction of human embryos, regardless of the source, including excess embryos slated for disposal at in-vitro fertilization clinics. President Bush has decided to allow Federal funding of embryonic cell stem cell research to go forward, but only on cells already in existence. The Bush decision in respect of Federal funding for ESCR was not a 'freeze' but a limited liberalization of existing policy, under which there had never before been Federal support for destructive embryo research, most recently under the so-called Dickey Amendment, which Congress has passed every year and which makes such funding illegal. Although such policy had major consequences for the university sector as a whole, the decentralized system is illustrated by events in California. In 2004, Governor Schwarzenegger of California put the issue to the vote, following a petition from the people of California. Californians came down on the side of stem cell research by passing a controversial bond measure that devotes $3 billion to human embryonic stem cell experiments and comprises the biggest-ever state-supported scientific research programme in the country.

Accountability

In the US, as in the UK, the reality is that universities are responding to the prevailing political agenda of establishing programmes and offices designed to stimulating economic development through technology transfer (see Bozeman 2000 and Siegel *et al.* 2003). As a result, while university technology transfer offices have gained in political importance, they are also caught up in the tensions between the traditional model of 'open science' and the new 'commercial science model'. In both the US and the UK there is evidence of distress signals from within the system (Bundy 2004). For example Rahm (1993) surveyed 1,134 university technology managers and university researchers in the top 100 research universities. She found that four out of ten technology managers said that firms they had dealt with had placed restrictions on university researchers sharing information with their departments of research centre colleagues. Nearly five in ten of the researchers mentioned this restriction and said that it had 'created a feeling of conflict for them between loyalty to the firm and the university's value of open knowledge'.

Slaughter and Rhoades (1996 in Bozeman 2000) concluded that the external policy environment of co-operative technology and competitiveness is having effects on the structure of academic work, including salary distribution by field and faculty research choices and rewards, and is having a divisive effect between the engineers and scientists on the one hand and arts and letters on the other (see also Florida 1999).

More recently, the US Council on Competitiveness (1998) summarizes concerns as being the low levels of funding for universities in disciplines such as the physical sciences, for laboratory costs and state of the art equipment, and for graduate fellowships in physical sciences and engineering (see Chapter 7 below) as well as tensions in the relationship between business and universities. The latter include the potential dangers in the trend toward exclusive licensing of patented university research, exclusive licensing of genetic information, that patenting practices in advanced materials and other sectors could compromise the open and free exchange of basic research information and the lack of linkages between universities and SMEs. Moreover, there are worries in both the universities and industry about the levels of support for frontier research. Similar concerns are expressed in the Business-Higher Education Forum (2001) and by Bok (2003) (formerly president of Harvard).

Bok (2003) warned that universities are showing signs of excessive commercialization of every aspect of their work. He finds that the need for money is a chronic condition of American universities and that 'the recent surge of commercial activity is best understood as only the latest in a series of steps to acquire more resources', along with financial cutbacks. But, at the same time, there is over-optimism among university officials, and the hoped for profits often fail to materialize while the damage to academic standards and institutional integrity is a reality.

Studies have indeed examined changes in faculty behaviour in the aftermath of their involvement in commercialization activities. In line with Blumenthal *et al.* (1996), Louis *et al.* (2001) find that academic scientists engaged in entrepreneurial activity are more likely to deny requests from fellow academics for research results than other faculty members not engaged in entrepreneurial activities. Similarly, Cohen *et al.* (1994) find evidence both of the publication of research results being delayed and of information being deleted from papers. Delays, often related to patent applications, can be considerable. It can also be related to evidence that a drug is not as efficient as that of a competitor. He recommends that the universities collectively take the lead in establishing shared and enforceable guidelines for limiting disclosure restrictions in research.

A further dimension to the level of increased dependency is when universities lose state aid when benefactors step in and whether this amounts to 'privatisation without any conscious dialog about it means' (see Marklein 2003). The article featured the University of Wisconsin, Madison, which has found that the state has cut back on funding when private sponsorship is used to supplement income. The article reported policies of universities in other states such as South Carolina, Colorado and Wisconsin, which like Texas are looking to free themselves from state controls that place limits on their ability to raise tuition fees or raise private money.

The Madey *v.* Duke University case on academic patent infringement, according to Van Hoorebeek (2004), has focused attention on the society role played by universities. Madey worked at Duke for nearly a decade but resigned in 1998 after being removed as lab director. Madey claims that his removal was predicated on his refusal to use the 'lab's equipment for research areas outside the allocated scope of certain government funding'. Despite Madey's removal from the lab, Duke continued to use some of the lab's equipment, including the equipment embodying Madey's patents. Because of this unauthorized use of Madey's patents, Madey sued Duke for patent infringement (Miller 2003). The denial of the petition for certorari set out in an Amicus brief in June 2003, precluding the experimental use exception for private universities (but not public universities – they are exempt) in the US, 'seals the coffin on the experimental use exception for private universities' (see Miller 2003). This was a mechanism that provided a defence to patent infringement in the US and a mechanism which has parallels around the world. It has a number of potential ramifications for university-level interactions including universities being at the mercy of patent holders, delaying and blocking further research innovation, increasing the cost and duration of research, the demanding of unreasonable returns in exchange for the use of the patents, preclusion of experiments, and stopping on-going research if there is a danger of patent violation and administrative costs.

The complexity of the ethical and political issues surrounding the economic importance of university research is further illustrated by a series of challenges by AUTM to proposals to change existing legislation proposed variously by the NIH (see AUTM 2004b), the American Intellectual Property Law Association and Senate (www.autm.net/about/About AUTM_positions.cfm). Although in the end the NIH decided that it did not have the authority to intervene, the case is still an important indicator of the complexity of the ethical and political issues surrounding the economic importance of university research.

Massification

Three trends are observable in the US. The first is that from within academia critiques are emerging of what Florida (1999) calls the simplistic position that universities contribute to industry through technology transfer. Instead, Florida (1999, 8) argues that regional policy makers should 'reduce the pressure on universities to increase technology transfer efforts' but rather 'ensure that the infrastructure that their region has to offer will be able to attract and retain the top talent and be able to absorb academic research for commercial gain'. This position is supported by Bozeman (2000), who has found that universities' role of human capital and training in technology transfer, including industry's use of students as cheap labour, is becoming more widely recognized.

The second trend is a growing body of evidence to support Florida's argument. For example, NSF (2004) finds a strong association between the geography of the development of high-tech industry in the US and the skills in regional labour markets, with California topping both lists (see Table 5.3 for the distribution of high-tech enterprises by state). The number of high-technology establishments rose from 402,000 in 1998 to 428,000 in 2000 and represented an increasing share of all start-up, growing from 5.8 to 6.1 per cent of total business establishments in the period 1998–2000. The state distribution of this indicator is similar to that of three other indicators: bachelor's degree holders, S&E doctoral degree holders in the workforce, and workforce in S&E occupations.

The third trend is that the US is recognizing that Europe's higher educational system may be more effective in producing graduates in science and engineering, thus putting Europe in a stronger competitive position in establishing, attracting and retaining high-tech companies. Noll (1998, 12) finds that one of the major differences between the US and Europe is that the concentration of higher degrees in the natural sciences and engineering is higher in Europe than in the US, especially since Europeans have begun to place an emphasis on mass higher education to produce a more technically sophisticated workforce. At doctoral level, however, he finds little difference in the distribution of degrees in terms of duration and intensity of study.

Entrepreneurial universities

Commercialization of research began to take off in the period between the First and the Second World War with the increasing amount of involve-

Table 5.3 Quartile groups for high-technology share of all business establishments: 2000

1st quartile (10.53%–6.71%)	2nd quartile (6.54%–5.31%)	3rd quartile (5.21%–4.22%)	4th quartile (4.21%–2.98%)
California	Arizona	Alabama	Arkansas
Colorado	Delaware	Alaska	Hawaii
Connecticut	Florida	Idaho	Iowa
District of Columbia	Georgia	Indiana	Kentucky
Illinois	Michigan	Kansas	Louisiana
Maryland	New York	Maine	Mississippi
Massachusetts	North Carolina	Missouri	Montana
Minnesota	Ohio	New Mexico	Nebraska
Nevada	Oregon	Oklahoma	North Dakota
New Hampshire	Pennsylvania	South Carolina	South Dakota
New Jersey	Rhode Island	Tennessee	West Virginia
Utah	Texas	Vermont	Wyoming
Virginia	Washington	Wisconsin	

Source: NSF 2004, www.nsf.gov/sbe/srs/seind04/c8/c8.cfm?opt=6.

Note
States in alphabetical order, not data order.

ment with industry, although the volume was low and many universities were against faculty benefiting from the exploitation of their research and many academics formed their own companies without involving their universities as a consequence (see Shane 2004). Hence, while entrepreneurial activity has long been embedded in the university system, the 1980s saw a rapid increase across the board in the number of patents, licences, spin-off companies, science parks and university–industry collaborative activity. The institutionalization of the commercialization of the technology transfer process took effect through the widespread establishment of TTOs. Legislative and industrial change, and more recently the political agenda (Florida 1999), are often given as being catalysts for these developments.

Patenting and licensing

Institutions that have been the most successful in commercializing university research – Columbia, University of Washington and Emory – owed their success to biomedical patents. Most important, the distribution of virtually all measures associated with patents remained highly skewed. For example, the top 20 universities in terms of licensing income for 1999 received 74 per cent of all licensing income; the 20 with the most active licences and options had 61 per cent of the total; the top 20 patenters were issued 46 per cent of all academic patents; and the 20 largest TTOs employed 44 per cent of licensing professionals (*AUTM Licensing Survey: FY 1999*). The comparable number of top research performers accounted for 37 per cent of university R&D in 2000). The top universities in each of these categories are not identical, but they substantially overlap. Table 5.4 depicts the leaders of academic patenting and commercial ties generally.

Geiger points to the limitations of the data in indicating economic development. These are that patenting and licensing are exceptional by-products of academic research; and are confined to a very few fields and to a very few institutions – an elite that established patenting offices, developed a campus culture that encourage patenting and built a strong presence in biotechnology. These are the universities of California, MIT, Stanford, Columbia and Wisconsin. Columbia, for example, has earned millions of dollars from its Axel patent for a gene-transfer process used in the commercial production of proteins; Harvard in 1996 received the majority of its royalties from a heart-imaging contrast agent. The University of Washington owed its patenting payoffs to technologies for producing Hepatitis B vaccine and interferon. Such big winners are all the more conspicuous at universities with smaller overall patenting efforts – the anti-cancer drug taxol at Florida State and anti-tumour agents at Michigan State (GAO, *Technology Transfer*).

Powers (2003), using AUTM data, found that private universities and Land Grant universities out-perform other universities on various measures of technology transfer outputs, having undertaken more

Table 5.4 Select data, 16 universities with most licensing revenues: 1999

University – R&D rank		Licensing revenues $ millions	% life science	Patents issued	Total active licences and options	Industry research $ millions	Start-up companies
Columbia	25	95.8	85.7	77	706	3.4	5
Cal System[1]		80.9	66.0	281	1078	177.6	13
Florida State	92	57.3	97.0	5	20	0.7	1
Yale	29	40.8	98.7	37	237	14.4	3
Stanford	8	40.1	81.9	90	872	41.3	19
Washington	5	27.9	80.0	36	207	57.4	na
Michigan State	42	23.7	99.6	63	134	11.2	1
Florida	26	21.6	98.8	58	124	34.9	2
Wisconsin	2	18.0	75.1	79	346	16.1	4
MIT	12	17.1	69.9	154	565	83.1	17
Emory	46	16.2	58.2	44	82	7.5	4
SUNY System[1]		13.6	95.5	53	298	17.5	3
Harvard	23	13.5	94.9	72	388	12.2	2
Baylor Med.	24	12.5	98.4	25	221	17.6	0
New York	55	10.7		30	30	7.7	2
Johns Hopkins	1	10.5	99.7	111	370	46.9	7
Total, all universities		675.5	80.0	3,079	15,203	2,178.2	275
16 univ: % of total		74.0	84.0	39.5	37.3	25.2	30.2

Sources: *AUTM Licensing Survey: FY1999*; Life Sciences % from *AUTM Licensing Survey: FY1996*; R&D$ from NSF 2000 data; Johns Hopkins inc. APL; Geiger 2003, 32.

Note

1. UC campus R&D rank: LA-4; SD-6; B-7; SF-9; D-17; I-67; SB-88; R-108; SC-128. SUNY campuses: B-53; SB-63; A-109. The table also shows only those universities receiving more than $10 million in 1999.

commercially orientated activities. Specifically, private universities were high performers in terms of invention disclosures and running royalities while Land Grants were slightly higher than private ones in terms of licences executed. Consistently with this, in each case relatively few high performers skew the data. Three key factors consistently account for performance differences: research expenditures, the size of technology transfer offices; and their age. He concludes that in fact, after addressing skewness problems and controlling for other resource factors, the evidence seems to suggest no difference in performance for institutional type – but those with larger research expenditures and older TTOs enjoy perform-ance advantages.

Industrial change

During the 1990s, industries that used commercial applications derived from 'use-oriented' basic research in life sciences fields such as molecu-lar biology and genomics emerged and matured. Changes in the US patent regime strengthened overall patent and copyright protection and encouraged the patenting of biomedical and life sciences technology.

The creation of the Court of Appeals of the Federal Circuit to handle patent infringement cases was one factor in the strengthening of overall patent protection. The 1982 court decision (Diamond *v.* Chakrabarty) that upheld the patenting of engineered life forms later extended to genetic material and patenting of more general concepts which 'made active patenting virtually irresistible for universities' (Geiger 2003, 30).

Geiger (2003) reports that drug and medical patents were the chief drivers behind this growth. They accounted for a rise from 18 to 46 per cent of academic patents. But, he argues, these figures understate their importance. Drug and medical patents provide far and away the bulk of licensing revenues for the major participants. For the twenty universities that garnered the highest royalties in 1997, 81 per cent of the income came from life sciences patents. Biotech subsidises patenting in other areas. 'Without these windfalls the current scale of academic patenting could scarcely be supported'. Legal fees for a single patent application averaged nearly $14,000 in the 1990s. Moreover, the potential for royalties was enormous: earnings particularly from biomedical patents meant that licensing revenues in the 1990s increased at roughly twice the rate of university patenting.

Institutionalization

Institutionalization took place with the formation of professional associations of technology transfer officials within university, government and industry sectors. These include the Association of University Technology Managers (AUTM) in 1974, the Federal Technology Transfer Executives and the Licensing Executives Society. Etzkowitz *et al.* (2000) argue that, as a consequence of the formation of these organisations, a 'trilateral network of innovation has been put in place'.

In 1980 only 25 US universities had technology transfer offices. Following the Bayh-Dole Act, many institutions founded a TTO. By 1990 there were more than 200 and more than 2,500 in 2003 (Bozeman 2000; Siegel *et al.* 2003, AUTM 2003). Universities such as MIT and Stanford, which did have offices and had technology transfer activities which had been anomalies within the university system, following the Bayh-Dole Act now became models for other universities to emulate (Etzkowitz *et al.* 2000). These authors state: 'Other schools such as Columbia, which had previously viewed themselves as playing a policy and service role in supplying faculty members going to Washington to serve temporarily in government, now found themselves trying to establish new ties with industry, often in their local region.' While Siegel *et al.* (2002) see the university–industry technology transfer as a mechanism for generating local technological spillovers as well as a source of revenue for the university, the regional role that technology transfer can play in fostering regional economic development is not high on AUTM's list of priorities. Instead, the strategy has been to focus on licensing to established companies, royalty maximization, an increased amount of faculty research support as part of licensing deals and professional service to academic staff (Tornatzky *et al.* 2002, 24). Fogarty and Sinha (1999) found a simple pattern and not one desired by policy makers – that there is a significant flow of intellectual property flowing from universities in older industrial regions such as Detroit and Cleveland to high-tech regions such as Greater Boston, San Francisco and New York metropolitan regions.

Spin-offs

The history of university spin-offs dates back to before the First World War (Rosenberg and Nelson 1994). A small number of high-profile universities such as Stanford and MIT were responsible for large numbers of spin-off firms throughout the twentieth century, while others have had major successes. A growing number of universities are involved in establishing programmes designed to encourage spin-offs but as yet there is no generally accepted model (Sandelin 2002). Of the major success stories, Carnegie Mellon hit the jackpot with its incubation of Lycos, the internet search engine company; it made £25 million in its initial stake in the company when it went public. Yet other universities have not been so successful. For example Boston University lost tens of millions of dollars in its 'ill-fated investment in Seragen' (Florida 1999, 3).

In the first national study of the economic impact of a research university, the BankBoston Economics Department for MIT (1997) reported that by 1997 graduates of the Massachusetts Institute of Technology had founded 4,000 firms which, in 1994 alone, generated $232 billion of world sales. Within the United States, the companies employed a total of 733,000 people in 1994 at more than 8,500 plants and offices in the country – equal to one out of every 170 jobs in America. Eighty per cent of the jobs in the MIT-related firms are in manufacturing (compared to 16 per cent nationally), and a high percentage of products are exported. The five states benefiting most from MIT-related jobs were California (162,000), Massachusetts (125,000), Texas (84,000), New Jersey (34,000) and Pennsylvania (21,000). Figure 5.1 shows where these plants are located. Box 5.1 summarises the impact of MIT on the US economy.

Science parks

The first research parks in the US were founded in the 1950s and were originally set up in order to increase the possibilities and profitability of commercializing university research, and to meet the needs of entrepreneurially-minded academics. The Stanford Industrial Park was

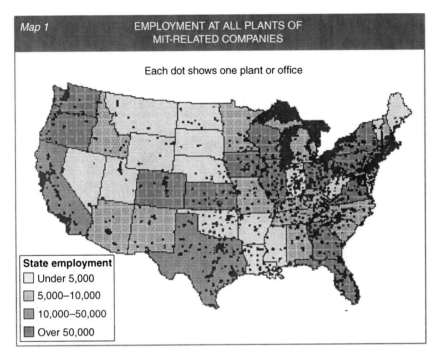

Figure 5.1 The impact of MIT on the economy of the US (source: BankBoston 1997).

established in 1951, 'partly to utilize the university's embarrassingly vast land holdings' (Geiger 2003, 19). The North Carolina Research Triangle Park was created in 1959 as a deliberate attempt to stimulate economic development in North Carolina. These two were the largest and most successful of the 13 that existed in 1969 and 24 in 1979 (Luger and Goldstein 1991). In the following decades, universities in the US became more directly involved in supporting new business development activities, including the establishment of business incubators. By 1992, the US National Business Incubation Association reported that more than 50 universities and colleges had participated in this effort. Using a broad definition of science parks, Kung (1995) found that in 1992 there were as many as 188 centres, 57 Incubators and 103 parks in the US.

Geiger (2003, 20) concludes that in spite of the low-level but important faculty ties with research park tenants, ties do little to enhance faculty entrepreneurship through patenting or forming start-up companies. In areas where research parks are closely associated with research universities, the source of growth is the university. Moreover, the situation for business incubators is little different. At the end of the 1980s Luger and Goldstein found that too many had been created and

---

Box 5.1 The impact of MIT on the US economy

- Eighty per cent of the jobs in the MIT-related firms are in manufacturing (compared to 16 per cent nationally), and a high percentage of products are exported.
- The MIT-related companies, if they formed a nation, would rank as the 24th largest world economy in 1994.
- Massachusetts firms related to MIT had 353,000 worldwide jobs; California firms had 348,000 worldwide jobs.
- Other major world employers included firms in Texas, 70,000; Missouri, 63,000; New Jersey, 48,000; Pennsylvania, 41,000; and New Hampshire, 35,000.
- More than 2,400 companies have headquarters outside the Northeast.
- The MIT-related companies are not typical of the economy as a whole; they tend to be knowledge-based companies in software, manufacturing (electronics, biotech, instruments, machinery) or consulting (architects, business consultants, engineers). These companies have a disproportionate importance to their local economies because they usually sell to out-of-state and world markets, and because they so often represent advanced technologies. Other industries represented include manufacturing firms in chemicals, drugs, materials, aerospace; energy, publishing and finance.
- MIT graduates and faculty have been forming an average of 150 new firms a year since 1990.
- MIT graduates cited several factors at MIT which spurred them to take the risk of starting their own companies – faculty mentors, cutting-edge technologies, entrepreneurial spirit and ideas.
- In Massachusetts, the 1,065 MIT-related companies represent 5 per cent of total state employment and 10 per cent of the state's economic base.
- The companies include 220 companies based outside the United States, employing 28,000 people worldwide.
- Some of the earliest known MIT-related companies still active are Arthur D. Little, Inc. (1886), Stone and Webster (1889), Campbell Soup (1900) and Gillette (1901).

Source: BankBoston 1997.

---

that many should be regarded as failures. By the late 1990s, the trend again was of integrating industry and universities – but using new models (Geiger 2003, 22).

Geiger illustrates this point with reference to the Centennial Campus at North Carolina State University. The plan to create a technopolis is also part of the strategy to advance NC State to be 'one of the country's leading land-grant universities'. The university's integrated strategy is to move academic units to the site, attract major corporations and attract grants for research centers such as textiles and engineering with a further objective of spawning start-up firms. The university is building on its tradition of being more applied than a research university. Tellingly, the university – and Geiger – recognize the potential for conflict of interest, which the university argues that it negotiates from a position of strength (its academic standards) but it is recognized that this model requires a large input of faculty time. The state of Georgia and the Yamacraw at Georgia Tech project is a further novel model of using industry–academic collaboration to further economic growth. In this case the emphasis was on cutting edge research and the training of experts, an investment in human and intellectual capital which survived the depression in the telecoms industry, much as Princeton did (Chapter 8).

The territorial role

In the US, as in the UK, the innovation-led territorial role is front-line policy at Federal as well as state level. Rather earlier than in the UK, the alignment of interests of universities with industry and *regional* economic growth which were described in the 'triple helix model' (Etzkowitz and Leydesdorff 1995) became part of the established rhetoric within universities as well as government (Florida 1999). Etztkowitz (2003) sees a transformation in the broader role of the university as 'regional innovation organizer'.

Bozeman (2000) describes the current phase of policy, which can be dated to the early 1990s, as being similar to that which was influential from 1945 to 1965: that the government role should be closely tied to authorized programmatic missions of agencies. Support for this analysis comes from Shapira (2005a), who finds that US policy has undergone a series of paradigm shifts (Figure 5.2). The latest shift, under the G. W. Bush administration, is one of decentralization, whereby state-based partnerships and the spreading of regional S&T capability are promoted. Now, as in the UK, state policy makers press universities to articulate what they can and do provide to the economic well-being of the state. Powers (2003, 22) finds that the research universities embrace the concept of universities as wealth creators when they believe that it can result in a more favourable financial treatment by the legislators. Overall, the effect of the paradigm shift is that of a technology transfer accretion by all state universities rather than a planned and co-ordinated effort built around the strategic strengths of the various institutions and their specific external environments. This, Powers suggests, results in duplication and inadequate support.

Shapira's (2005a) diagram (Figure 5.2) illustrates a series paradigm shift from the period up to the ending of the Cold War and the beginning of the current entrepreneurial phase to the current climate. In this the focus in the US, as in Europe, is on clusters and on SMEs and technology integration. Unlike in biosciences, spin-offs from defence contracts from the DoD are inhibited by the conditions attached to research funding for example at Johns Hopkins University (Feldman 1994 in Shane 2004).

SCIENCE PUSH >	TECHNOLOGY PULL >	COMPLEX SYSTEMS
Large-firm champions	SMEs > clusters	
Build-up of R&D capabilities • National labs • Universities • Corporate labs • Basic research	Mission-generated R&D • Defense oriented • DoD/NASA/DoE technology drivers • DARPA • Spin-offs • "Technology transfer"	Technology integration • Globalization • International competition • Commercial technology drivers • Post-Cold War environment >? • Innovation systems • Integrated research centers • R&D consortia and public-private partnerships • Incubation • Dual use; supply chain development • Knowledge management • Commercialization and deployment

Figure 5.2 R&D systems in the US: paradigm shifts (source: Shapira 2004a).

Evidence of how states are using their own funds to bolster research in their universities comes from Berglund (1998). By the mid-1990s, states were spending at least $2.7 billion dollars of their own funds on programmes on applied research and technological advance, most of which had regional development aims. In total, by 2001, state and local governments provided 7.1 per cent of academic R&D funding. Since 1980 the state and local share has remained between 7 and 9 per cent. Private academic institutions received a much smaller proportion of their funds from state and local governments (about 2 per cent) and institutional sources (about 10 per cent) and a much larger share from the Federal government (72 per cent). Shares of funding described above, however, only reflect funds directly targeted to academic R&D activities by state and local governments. They do not include general-purpose state or local government appropriations that academic institutions designate to use to fund separately budgeted research or cover unreimbursed indirect costs. Hence the actual level of state funding is higher than these figures suggest, particularly for public institutions (NSF 2004).

The large difference in the role of institutional funds at public and private institutions is most likely because of a substantial amount of general-purpose state and local government funds that public institutions receive and decide to use for R&D. Both public and private institutions received approximately 7 per cent of their respective support from industry in 2001. Since the early 1980s, the Federal share of support has declined.

Yet this latest phase cannot be dissociated with the decreasing level of Federal funding which has been matched by a rise in industry-funded research (NSF 2004), a pattern similar to that in the UK. The effects of this trend have been, according to Florida (1999, 3), that industry has been more involved in sponsored research and universities have been focused more on licensing and patenting their technology and creating spin-offs to raise money. Some of this is ploughed back into the university system in order to strengthen research areas that are of interest to industry (pages 5–6).

The quality of the response to the territorial role varies across institutions. The South Technology Council (STC) (a consortium of Southern states) has been conducting evaluations of science and technology programmes since the mid-1990s. One involved using a reputation approach to determine exemplary institutions (see Tornatzky 2003, 237). The judging panel were asked to identify which institutions they felt were 'actively and successfully participating in, or linked to state and local economic development'. The majority are public, with only Stanford and Carnegie Mellon being private universities. Half are in the top 20 academic institutions in R&D expenditures and all but Carnegie Mellon (85th) are in the top 50. The best practitioners were Carnegie Mellon University, Georgia Institute of Technology (Georgia Tech), North Carolina University, Ohio State University, Pennsylvania State University, Purdue University, Stanford University, Texas A&M University, University of California-San Diego, University of Utah, University of Wisconsin, Virginia Polytechnic Institute and State University. Tornatzky (2003) explains that factors which are associated with this ranking range from mission statements which espouse relationship with industry to programmes which connect undergraduates with local industry. Yet studies of evidence for the enthusiasm of the regional role suggest this has been espoused more by administrators than by faculty, who were much less enthusiastic about business partnerships with industry and a market-driven university (Bozeman 2000, 639).

Examples of universities that have been involved in transforming economies are San Diego, which has gone from a military-dominated to a high-tech economy, Georgia and, more generally, the biotech sector. The University of San Diego's CONNECT programme, established in 1985, is the most successful of a regional strategy (see Walshok 2002). It has been adopted in several other countries such as Scotland where the University of Edinburgh's CONNECT programme is supported by several other Scottish universities, the Scottish Higher Education Funding Council, economic development agencies, business advisers and financial institutions (OECD 1999, 88):

Founded in 1985 at the urging of San Diego's business community, UCSD CONNECT is widely regarded as the nation's most successful regional program linking high-technology and life science entrepreneurs with the resources they need for success: technology, money, markets, management, partners, and support services. Part of the University of California, San Diego (UCSD), CONNECT has a dual role in accelerating growth: it provides added value and delivers targeted, high-level expertise to San Diego's technology business community by teaming up with the region's most prominent industry-specific organizations and individuals, and by partnering with world-class UCSD resources, such as the School of Medicine, Jacobs School of Engineering, San Diego Super Computer Center, and Scripps and Salk Institutes.

CONNECT's services are tailored to meet the varying needs of San Diego entrepreneurs at all stages of their business life cycles and growth. Since its inception, CONNECT has assisted more than 800 technology companies. Its programs serve as a catalyst for the development and exchange of ideas, a forum to explore new business avenues and partnerships, and an opportunity to network with peers.

www.connect.org/about/index.htm

Shapira (2005b) shows how universities are part of the state of Georgia's strategy for regional technology promotion. This includes the development of entrepreneurial research universities such as Georgia Tech and creating knowledge pools for technological innovation. Shapira identifies the following factors: a substantial increase in state technology spending and the evolution into a comprehensive technological development strategy, aimed to make Georgia a premier location for advanced technology development. The vision is that, by 2010, Georgia will be 'Among top five states with a technology-based economy' (sentiments echoed by many of the RDAs in the UK). The Georgia Research Alliance (GRA) is a collaborative state initiative with six research universities in Georgia, established 1991. Its aim is to use research infrastructure to generate business and economic development in targeted technologies, i.e. advanced telecommunications, biotechnology, environmental technologies and existing industries. It includes the encouragement of inter-university collaboration, engagement with industry, the attraction of eminent research scholars and research teams, supplementary endowments (this initiative preceded the 'Bucks for Brains' programme in Kentucky, Chapter 8), the development of research facilities, including new technology centers and a Technology Development Investment programme which funds the university side of collaborative industry research programmes. Investment in the 1990s amounted to more than $200 million by Federal and state government and by industry, including $126 million invested by the state.

Shapira concludes that the GRA has been successful in a number of areas, such as prompting private initiatives – e.g. private incubators, venture capital (VC), and repeat entrepreneurs. These successes have high symbolic value. On the other hand, Shapiro also finds that the effects are geographically concentrated, being mainly focused in Atlanta, and that the Alliance targets advanced research rather than diffusion of knowledge (which also favours Atlanta). He also argues that there are a number of weaknesses in the local system of governance.

Biotechnology is the sector most obviously targeted at the regional level in the US (see for example Malinowski 2000: 17). Some 16 states used a portion of their tobacco settlement to fund bioscience-related research and development (three have also targeted technology transfer and commercialization). Examples are Michigan Life Sciences Strategy, Ohio's bio-medical research and technology transfer trust fund, and the Kentucky 'Bucks for Brains' programme. In Kentucky, $5 million has gone to the Cancer Centre from the state and another $15 million has come from the James Graham Brown Cancer Foundation, a university charity. The effect is that the diversity of funding across the US enables weaker universities to get funding for research and establish centres of excellence in ways that are not possible in the UK.

State-level initiatives are also designed to boost the economy through supporting research and the biotech industry. Nearly every state in the US now has some institutionalized support for the industry. A survey of 77 local and 36 state economic development agencies reported that 83 per cent have listed biotechnology as one of their top two targets for industrial development (Grudkova 2001). Table 5.5 illustrates the complexity of state level initiatives though the examples of California and Massachusetts. The downside of this level of interest is that such an emphasis on biotechnology has resulted in 'bidding wars' between states that attempt to entice firms to relocate by offering financial incentives (Feldman and Ronzio 2001, 11).

Conclusions

This chapter has shown that, since at least the nineteenth century, US universities and industry have shared common interests. The convergence of their separate worlds has increased and, according to many commentators, is a key source of the US's competitive advantage. In addition to the rising costs of research and a more general tendency for industry to externalize its R&D, US-specific factors which have brought about a greater integration of activity within the innovation process are legislative change for example on the ownership and control of intellectual property, the expansion of joint university–industry programmes, massive funding for university research from the Federal government and industry, particularly in defence and more recently life sciences. At the same time, universities' pursuit of an economic agenda has gained legitimacy (Etzkowitz *et al.*

Table 5.5 Selected examples of state-level initiatives in California and Massachusetts: funding, facilities, networking, and taxation

	California	Massachusetts
Types of Funds	*Biotechnology Strategic Targets for Alliances in Research Program* – matches funds for basic proof of concept research *California Technology Investment Partnership* – matches grants up to $250,000 to CA companies that receive federal funding. Healthcare technology companies also eligible	*Bioventure Investors LLC* – a privately managed venture fund. It is the fifth venture fund by Massachusetts Biomedical Initiative (MBI). MBI has received past funding from federal sources
Publicly Supported Venture Capital	*California Public Employees' Retirement System* (largest public pension fund worth $170 billion) created the *California Biotechnology Program* and has invested $285 million in addition to the state's $100 million investment in biotechnology	*Massachusetts Technology Development Corporation* – a state-sponsored venture capital company. It does not usually invest in biotech companies because the size of the fund is not large enough to meet the capital needs of biotech companies but invests in biomedical device and instruments companies
Bioscience Facilities	Three Centers of Excellence in Science and Innovation, including the *Institute for Bioengineering, Biotechnology, and Quantitative Biomedical Research Technology Development Center, Moffit Field* – technology park for biotechnology and high-tech firms	*MBIdeas Innovation Centers* – three locations in Worcester and one in Boston *Mass Biotech Research Park* – one million square feet of building space, over a dozen biotech companies, located adjacent to U of Massachusetts Medical Center *BioSquare* – private research park in Boston; 400,000 square feet of building space *Tufts Science Park* – 106 acres *University Park at MIT* – will contain 1.5 million square feet of office, R&D and hotel space

Biotech Networking and Trade Associations	*California Healthcare Institute* – acts as liaison between government and public for education and policy formulation *Bay Area Bioscience Center* – consortium of university, public officials, educators, and bioscience executives established in 1990 *BIOCOM* – association representing the regional bioscience industry	*Massachusetts Technology Collaborative* – an economic development organization *Massachusetts Biotech Council* – non-profit, works to advance policy and promote education. MBC represents more than 300 companies, institutions, and service organizations in biotech and healthcare *MassMedic* – state's trade association for medical device manufacturers; over 200 members
Tax Policy	*Manufacturers' Investment Credit* – some manufacturers eligible for 6 per cent credit, which can be claimed against tax; unused credit can be carried forward eight years *R&D Tax Credit* – 15 per cent for research done in-house *Net Operating Loss (NOL) Carryover* – biotechnology and biopharma companies given preferential treatment on NOLs. 100 per cent may be carried over for up to eight years	*Credit against excise tax for leased personal property* – R&D companies are eligible *Tax credit for a corporation renting or leasing tangible property* – 3 per cent of the value of qualifying property leased and placed in qualified use during the taxable year *R&D tax credit* – like investment tax credit, R&D tax credit is available to offset excise tax liability

Source: Bagchi-Sen *et al.* (2004).

2000) at the state level. In economically weaker states, such as Georgia, universities are being used to spearhead economic development being closely engaged in evolving state-level governance activities.

At the same time, as in the UK, issues of accountability and concerns about the public good have been documented. Bozeman (2000, 650), for example, has written, 'Public policies of the 1980s and 1990s unleashed the cooperative technology policy genie from the bottle and research shows that some wishes have been granted. But genies, not just wishes, bear watching.' As Powers (2003) points out, some states are so eager to advance an economic agenda that they can turn a blind eye to the conflicts this creates.

6 Labour markets in Europe and the United States

Human Capital is Europe's most important asset
(Spring 2005 European Council)

Introduction

This chapter focuses on perhaps the most important but relatively under emphasized role of universities in economic development – that of the supply, training and mobility of human capital. As this chapter will show, that what industry might need from universities is 'talent not technology' (Florida 2002) is increasingly recognized by the European Commission, at the national level in European countries and in the US, and in both continents in individual regions and localities. Evidence for the importance of access to highly skilled people comes from Simmie *et al.*'s (2002) analysis of innovation in five European cities (Amsterdam, Milan, Paris, Stuttgart and London), which found that, of the 25 reasons why firms would choose to locate the development of a new innovation in their city region, availability of professional experts specializing in technology scored the highest.

The potential for universities to contribute to the supply, training and mobility of highly skilled people is affected by a number of factors relating to the geographical scale at which processes are occurring. The potential supply of graduate labour is mediated by the research and teaching profile of universities and the potential match with the firms within a local or regional economy (see Beeson and Montgomery 1993) which changes over time. The degree of match is influenced by the extent to which labour markets are geographically bounded, to which industries are localized or dispersed, and by inter-disciplinary differences in employee mobility and inter-sectoral variations in firms' propensity to recruit graduates. Employer demand is influenced by many factors, including the national and international economic climate, historic patterns of national development and structural change, and corporate competitiveness, both in the commercial market and in the labour market (Pearson *et al.* 2001). The supply of training is affected by similar sorts of factors, which include the level of demand from local industry or financial incentives by government to meet existing and nascent demands. Mobility has a number of dimensions: universities as 'talent magnets' for both students and highly qualified people, especially in increasingly important international labour markets, through participation in international training and mobility programmes, and allowing facilitation of 'hybrid occupational labour markets' whereby scientists and engineers work in their own firms or in other firms while retaining their academic posts (Lanciano-Morandat and Nohara 2002a). These authors describe the scientific labour market as a 'bridging institution' between academia and industry for the co-production and transfer of knowledge and competences.

The distributed innovation process

The economic argument is that the effectiveness of innovation processes is improved by an increase in the level of skills in the economy through a number of direct and indirect effects (see Chapter 2). The skill composition of the workforce affects the technology used by firms, as skilled and educated workers are better able to absorb knowledge and implement new technologies (see Woznaik 1984; Bartel and Lichtenberg 1987; Dankbaar 2004). Hence, universities may increase local productivity growth, if, as suggested by Lucas (1988), the ability to develop and implement new technologies depends on the average level of human capital in the economy. Therefore, firms in areas with strong universities may have an advantage in implementing new technologies, thereby increasing their growth and potentially further demand for more graduates. This, however, depends on the level of demand in the economy for skills.

A general trend in Europe and the US is the number of jobs requiring S&E skills. In the US, the Bureau of Labour Statistics (BLS) (2001) reported that the S&E labour force was growing by almost 5 per cent per year, while the rest of the labour force was growing at just over 1 per cent. The BLS projected that S&E occupations would increase at three times the rate of all occupations. The projected rise by the BLS was 2.2 million, representing a 47 per cent increase in the number of S&E jobs by 2010. The rates of increase between 1980 and 2000 ranged from 18 per cent for the life sciences to 123 per cent for jobs in mathematics and computer science.

Diversity in innovation systems

Variations by country in the supply of skills, both in absolute numbers and in the relative distribution between academic fields, is a crucial factor in the functioning of innovation processes and national economic performance (Chapter 3). Moreover, industrial training and the ability to attract non-national students and academic staff have also been found to be highly significant in the quality of R&D undertaken by industry in science and engineering.

Supply of graduates

In both Europe and the US, the number of undergraduates, overall and in S&E subjects in particular, is increasing as the link between education and economic development has become a central policy agenda. In 2002, the EU15 produced 2.14 million S&E graduates, compared to 2.07 million in the US. The UK produces the most S&E graduates in Europe (some 504,000), closely followed by France (500,000) with Germany third (300,000). These three countries account for almost two-thirds of the EU total. The UK also has the third highest proportion of tertiary graduates in science and technology per 1,000 of the population aged between 20 and 29 (21.1 per cent), behind Ireland (24.2 per cent) and France (22.2 per cent), compared to 10.9 per cent in the US and 13.2 per cent in Japan. The rate of increase in scientific and technological graduates during the 1990s, however, varied between countries, with virtual stagnation in Germany, moderate growth in the UK and sustained growth in France (Lanciano-Morandat and Nohara 2002a).

Within those broad categories are considerable variations in discipline and recruitment patterns. In the UK for example, HESA data shows that in 2002–3, the UK had a total of 125,860 HE students studying biological sciences. Of these, 5,590 came from other European counties and a similar number from outside the EU. Over a fifth (25,300) were post-graduate students. In spite of the rapid expansion in the area, this is less than the number taking engineering and technology degrees (131,575). Research across the EU for the European Commission shows that there are shortages in particular skills such as IT, and under-utilization of other, expensively developed skills such as life sciences and some areas of engineering (Pearson *et al.* 2001), indicating mismatches in supply and demand for graduates and training. This problem was expected to be exacerbated by the growing demand for bioscience skills. It has been predicted that Europe could have three million biotech jobs by 2005, a huge leap from 400,000 in 1995 (Woods undated).

Moreover, two of the main findings of the Roberts Report (2002, 2) on the supply of people with science, technology, engineering and mathematics skills suggest that the UK system is inefficient in meeting those shortages. These are that there are insufficiently attractive career opportunities in research for highly qualified scientists and engineers, particularly in the context of increasingly strong demand from other sectors for their skills; and science and engineering graduates' and post-graduates' education does not lead them to develop transferable skills and knowledge required by R&D employers.

It was not until April 2004 that the major UK public funding agency for science and engineering in universities, the Engineering and Physical Sciences Research Council (EPSRC), announced that it would be significantly strengthening the links between post-graduates and industry and enabling universities to partner industry more effectively (www.epsrc.ac.uk/ PostgraduateTraining/default.htm). The means chosen to do this is the Collaborative Teaching Accounts. The idea is that, instead of compartmentalizing individual schemes, a university can bid for a single collaborative account and manage the funds awarded across a range of activities and departments. This amalgamates five current schemes – the Engineering Doctorates, CASE, Knowledge Partnerships, Masters Training Packages and research assistant intern secondments. Thus universities which are successful in bidding have greater scope for formulating their own strategies for human capital development, but will require considerable resources to be allocated for this purpose.

In the US, the number of undergraduate engineering degrees has fallen from a peak in 1985 at 77,572 to 59,258 in 2001 (4.7 per cent of bachelor degrees awarded) (NSF 2004). Physical sciences, which at their peak in 1966 accounted for 3 per cent of bachelor degrees awarded, have declined steadily to 1.1 per cent. Graduate enrolment in S&E programmes, however, has increased. Levels reached a new peak of nearly 455,400 students in 2002, having recovered from the downward trend of 1994 to 1998 (NSF 2004). This represents a 6 per cent gain over enrolment in 2001 and a 5 per cent gain over the previous peak, in 1993, of about 435,700 students. The number of post-doctoral appointees in S&E fields in US institutions reached a total of 32,100 in 2002, also an all-time high. Table 6.1 shows the breakdown of graduate student enrolment in the US.

Graduate enrolment in the US in 2002 grew in all major S&E fields and in nearly all subfields. Engineering and mathematical sciences led in percentage gains, both rising more than 9 per cent over the previous year. Other fast-growing fields were computer sciences and biological sciences, which each increased by 6 per cent. At master's level, engineering accounted for 13.5 per cent, physical sciences 8.3 per cent and biological sciences 16.0 per cent. The number of doctoral degrees in engineering peaked in 1996 with 6,309 before declining to 5,501 in 2001 (13.5 per cent compared to 10.6 per cent). The number of doctoral degrees in physical sciences declined slightly too, thus representing a declining share of doctoral programmes (8 per cent in 2001 compared to nearly 10 per cent in 1986), when biological sciences accounted for 16 per cent of doctoral degrees awarded. Overall, the number of S&E doctoral degrees awarded by US academic institutions in 2001 was essentially the same as in 1993. Moreover, only about a quarter are employed in firms, while nearly two-thirds were employed in academic positions following graduation but were increasingly faced with having to accept temporary academic posts. This is a similar situation to that in the UK but in the UK the rate of post-doctoral graduates leaving the university is much higher owing to the

Table 6.1 US graduate student enrolment in science and engineering, by enrolment status and sex, and post-doctoral students in science and engineering: 1992–2002

Characteristic	1992	1993	1994	1995	1996	1997	1998	1999	2000	2001	2002	Per cent change 2001–2
All graduate students	430,517	435,723	431,142	422,466	415,181	407,630	404,856	411,182	413,536	429,242	455,355	6.1
Full time	290,408	293,905	292,979	287,171	284,039	280,669	278,943	283,893	291,355	304,021	325,669	7.1
First time	83,102	79,280	78,038	74,364	73,448	73,600	74,373	75,447	78,332	82,411	86,921	5.5
Other	207,306	214,625	214,941	212,807	210,591	207,069	204,570	208,446	213,023	221,610	238,778	7.7
Part time	140,109	141,818	138,163	135,295	131,142	126,961	125,913	127,289	122,181	125,221	129,656	3.5
Men	280,305	279,185	272,031	262,256	253,510	245,619	241,429	242,786	243,057	251,812	266,521	5.8
Women	150,212	156,538	159,111	160,210	161,671	162,011	163,427	168,396	170,479	177,430	188,834	6.4
Post-doctoral	23,883	24,665	25,787	26,160	26,569	27,264	27,876	28,980	30,224	30,194	32,075	6.2

Source: www.nsf.gov/sbe/srs/infbrief/nsf04326/start.htm.

shortage of longer-term posts (Lanciano-Morandat and Nohara 2002a). These authors reporting on NSF data for 2000 find that overall in the US the recruitment of PhDs by industry is increasing, but varies by subject. For example, the share of PhDs in engineering entering industry is greater than that of PhDs in science: 57 per cent of those with doctorates in engineering were working in the private sector in 1997 compared with 40 per cent for computer science and 20 per cent for the life sciences. In Germany far fewer doctorates in engineering stay in academia. Enders (2001) in Lanciano-Morandat and Nohara (2002a), shows that one year after obtaining their doctorates, some 60 per cent of engineering graduates are employed in the private sector, while 60 per cent of biology and mathematics PhDs stay in the public sector, mainly in universities.

For the European Union to compete with the US, the targets are to increase the number of students, eliminate the unnecessary fragmentation and compartmentalization in research and teaching policies, raise the quality of education and encourage mobility between students and industry and between member states through the establishment of European Higher Education Area (EHEA). This policy links the goal of improving economic performance to human capital formation from undergraduate to professional development. Its objectives were set out in November 2001 when the Directorate General of Education and Culture of the European Commission released a working document, 'From Prague to Berlin, the EU Contribution', which outlined ten concrete measures the Commission would take in order to bring the Bologna process forward (www.bologna-berlin2003.de/pdf/Zgaga.pdf). The most radical of these is the adoption of a system of easily readable and comparable degrees with first degrees no shorter than three years and a system of credits; a European Credit Transfer System (ECTS), and the elimination of remaining obstacles to the mobility of students and teachers.

Within Europe member states are at different stages in being able to comply with these measures. The UK, for example, is in some ways ahead of the Bologna process, particularly in the structure of new degrees, in the standard three-year undergraduate degree and in accreditation of qualifications. The UK has introduced two-year foundation degrees, making them the main work-focused higher education qualification. These are not bachelor's degrees but could be upgraded to bachelor's degrees with four more terms of study. The UK with its standard three-year degree programme, which is what the Bologna process requires, will not have to make fundamental changes like other countries such as Germany, France, Italy and Eastern European countries, where the norm is degrees taking five, six or seven years. On the other hand, a concern for the UK is whether one-year master's degrees will be seen as being of less value. Some problems in harmonization of procedures for validating degrees are likely as the UK's system is generally not one which measures length of time in study as opposed to the outcomes of that study (SBS 2004b).

The adoption of the Bologna process is likely to be more difficult in Germany than in the UK because of the split in German higher education between universities and Fachhochschulen which have degree courses of different lengths and different balances between theoretical and practical education. Typically initial university degrees take five or six years to complete. Germany does, however, have a more established tradition of participation in student programmes such as Erasmus which may be important in the propensity of German students to capitalize on employment opportunities in the EHEA.

France's reform of its higher education system will make it more like the proposed European higher education system. This is being implemented on the basis of a new legal framework informed by a set of decrees in 2002 (www.esib.org/BPC/Countries/france/France2.pdf). The major features of reform include a new degree (the master's degree which can be professionally or research orientated); the organization of all the higher education studies into semesters and course units; the general implementation of ECTS in the design and meaning of new degrees; the delivery of the Diploma Supplement if international mobility is at stake; the general principal of regular national assessment of HE institutions; and the broader principle of validation of previous studies and personal experiences of students.

Graduate education and training

Different models of university systems produce different kinds of connections via the scientific labour market between universities and industry. Some are more hierarchical than others. Lanciano-Morandat and Nohara's (2002a) study illustrates a number of distinctive features of the organization of career paths in different countries.

In German extra-industry research institutions the academic labour market is organized by the supervisory authorities, which operate on two different levels: 'the federal government lays down a general framework of rules and procedures governing the university system, a framework within which the individual Länder or states are able to develop a certain number of options. The Länder are also very active in negotiating professors' salaries, since they are requested by the universities to find the necessary funds' (Musselin 1990 in Lanciano-Morandat and Nohara 2002a). The relationship with industry is determined by the university career path leading to the status of professor that is the obligatory route for all academics and which allows individuals subsequently to be considered for positions of responsibility in extra-university research institutions funded by the state or by industry, such as the Max Planck Institute, the Helmholtz Centres and the Fraunhofer Gesellschaft and so on. It is through these public or semi-public research organizations that German industry receives a steady flow of professors, doctoral students and post-docs as part of a process of cross-fertilization that reflects the close co-operation between science and industry.

Lanciano-Morandat and Nohara (2002a) find that in the US, the academic labour market is characterized both by different missions of teaching and research institutions and by the tenure system, which offers young academics in research institutions an incentive to produce knowledge. Unlike in France or Germany, 'where the discourse is egalitarian and where the universities are all supposed to be of comparable quality and to award degrees of the same value' (Brisset-Sillon 1997), universities in the US are systematically ranked, which has the effect of hierarchizing and segmenting the academic labour market (page 14).

Yet, at the same time, an increasing share of undergraduate, doctoral and post-doctoral students in European and American universities are being supported by joint industry/university programmes. Dedicated national programmes designed to increase the degree by which such skill acquisition is subsidized by the state include those in which university personnel supervise graduate or undergraduate students who are located in the collaborating firm's premises. Some of the best-known examples include, at the undergraduate level, the Co-op scheme which began at Waterloo University in Canada. This has now spread worldwide and aims to achieve closer relations between business and universities by requiring undergraduates to spend one or more terms in monitored employment. At the doctoral level examples include France's CIFRE scheme and the UK's CASE (Co-operative Awards in Science and Engineering). (Les conventions industrielles de formation par la recherche (CIFRE) partnerships are managed by ANRT (National Association of Technical Research) on behalf of the Ministry in charge of Research. The programme allows a doctoral student to carry out his or her thesis in a company by carrying out a research and development programme in connection with a team of researchers within the company.) An example of post-doctoral programmes is the UK's TCS (now the Knowledge Transfer Partnership (KTP) programme) (see Chapter 3). (This is dedicated to helping SMEs and industry in general innovate through collaboration with the universities, colleges and research organizations that could be of value in developing new products, services and processes. See www.ktponline.org.uk.) Mason (2000) found that British doctoral students are more likely than their French counterparts to be involved in industrial projects, particularly with SMEs in electronics and biotechnology industries, which has a knock-on effect of increasing the likelihood of students looking to industry for employment on the completion of their studies.

An increasing number of international student programmes are designed to increase interaction and integration of cultures between universities or public research centres and industry (see below). Profit-orientated programmes provided by universities for in-service training for employees in industry or business include extension programmes and continuing professional development (CPD).

In the US, a study by the Battelle Memorial Institute and the State Science and Technology Institute (2001, 18) reports that bioscience work-force initiatives have been introduced addressing the skills supply issue. These include the establishment of two-year associate's degree pro-grammes, for example, in Massachusetts and 13 other states, and changes in curricula at colleges and universities to reflect better the workforce needs of bioscience firms. Examples of changes in higher education include a PhD programme in biotechnology offered by two universities in Maine and a new master's programme focused on biotechnology in New York, and outreach programmes for bioscience companies to determine skill training and education needs (Florida and New York).

Mobility

Improving mobility is a central plank in the EU's and many countries' labour market and educational policies. Numerous OECD countries have designed policies for attracting various types of talent (students, researchers, IT specialists, research scientists etc.), such as tax incentives, repatriation schemes and improving the attractiveness of academic careers (OECD 2004). Bachtler (2004) finds that talent attraction of star acade-mics, researchers and highly skilled workers is increasingly replacing inward investment attraction as a key role for regional development agen-cies (Young and Brown 2002).

The objective of improving mobility in Europe has been addressed by a number of vocational training programmes. In recent years there has been a growing emphasis on adult education and training (Table 6.2).

Take-up of these programmes is uneven, as participation in the Erasmus programme illustrates (Table 6.3). France, Spain, Germany and Italy have the largest numbers of students going to study elsewhere, the UK has less than half the number of those countries, while Sweden with a population of nearly nine million has proportionally far fewer than Belgium with just over ten million. Mason (2000, 26) argues that student mobility between EU countries increases the chances of host country employers recruiting foreign national engineers and scientists after they have graduated from universities with which they (the employers) are familiar. He does, however, find that student mobility is still marginal and that mobility per se does not necessarily have beneficial effects. In 2000, only 2.3 per cent of European students were pursuing their studies in another European country and, while the mobility of researchers is higher than that of the average of the population concerned, it is still lower than it is in the US. Mason also reports that many European countries are char-acterized by a high degree of labour immobility even within national borders. Such difficulties are conceivably more likely to be overcome in

Table 6.2 European Union industry–university training and mobility programmes

Programme	Objectives
The Community programme for Education Teaching and Training (COMETT) (1989–95)	Co-operation between universities and industry in the development and provision of training in fields involving advanced technology. Many of the COMETT projects deal with manufacturing, research and medical technology. Transnational exchanges of expertise and training resources are a fundamental element of COMETT projects. In addition to organizations in the twelve member countries of the EC, organizations in the seven members of the European Free Trade Association (EFTA) are also invited to participate in the programme.
Leonardo Da Vinci (Leonardo). Initially 1995–99, extended to 2000–6	To raise the quality of vocational education and training in Europe. The Programme comprises three vocational sectors: • initial vocational training • continuing adult education for working life • co-operation between university level education and enterprises.
Socrates	European Union education programme that supports European co-operation on a range of educational projects. The higher education section of SOCRATES II ('ERASMUS') continues and extends the European Community Action Scheme for the Mobility of University Students (the 'ERASMUS programme'), established in 1987. More emphasis is consequently placed on teaching staff exchanges, transnational curriculum development and pan-European thematic networks. Wider dissemination of and participation in the results of this work are sought through specific support. ERASMUS also encourages universities to associate other public and private bodies from their surrounding regions with their transnational co-operation activities, thereby enhancing opportunities for inter-regional co-operation between the participating countries. From 1987/8 to 1999/2000, about 750,000 university students have spent an Erasmus period abroad and more than 1,800 universities (or other higher education institutions) are presently participating in the programme. The EU budget of SOCRATES/Erasmus for 2000–6 amounts to around €950 million (of which approximately €750 million is for students grants). Additional funds are provided in each country by public authorities, by the universities themselves and by other organisations.
The European Universities Continuing Education Network	'to contribute to the economic and cultural life of Europe through the promotion and advancement of lifelong learning within higher education institutions in Europe and elsewhere; and to foster universities' influence in the development of lifelong learning knowledge and policies throughout Europe'.

Source: Europa.

Table 6.3 Erasmus student mobility numbers: 2000/1–2002/3

Home country	2000/1	2001/2	2002/3
Austria	3,026	3,026	3,312
Belgium	4,417	4,551	4,653
Bulgaria	398	622	612
Cyprus	0	72	91
Czech Republic	2,001	2,533	3,002
Denmark	1,750	1,752	1,847
Estonia	255	274	302
Finland	3,286	3,291	3,402
France	17,179	18,220	19,396
Germany	15,890	16,641	18,494
Greece	1,922	1,974	2,115
Hungary	1,996	1,736	1,830
Iceland	134	147	163
Ireland	1,648	1,708	1,627
Italy	13,237	13,951	15,217
Latvia	182	209	232
Liechtenstein	12	17	7
Lithuania	624	823	1,001
Luxembourg	28	30	33
Malta	92	129	72
Netherlands	4,162	4,244	4,241
Norway	1,007	970	1,010
Poland	3,691	4,323	5,419
Portugal	2,569	2,825	3,171
Romania	1,899	1,965	2,701
Slovakia	505	578	654
Slovenia	227	364	422
Spain	16,383	17,405	18,258
Sweden	2,726	2,633	2,656
United Kingdom	9,028	8,479	7,957
Total	110,274	115,492	123,897

the case of highly qualified occupations than in any other type of occupation, particularly if the cross-border movement takes the form of job changes within particular multi-national enterprises. Therefore mobility in the EU is so far not a major influence in developing a 'hybrid labour market'.

Compared to the US, the potential for integration of the interests of universities and industries in Europe is limited by the quality of the research or study environment and by terms of employment. European universities offer researchers and students a less attractive environment than in the US. The EC (2003a, 77) states that 'In several countries, such as Finland, Italy, Germany and Austria (and until recently France), mobility between universities and industry is frequently hampered, especially for the academic partner. Most university professors and other employees have the status of civil servants, and are neither encouraged nor allowed to work temporarily within industry'. Moreover, Mason finds that the labour markets for qualified scientists and engineers in various EU countries are linked in important ways to non-EU countries, casting doubt on the existence of a specifically 'European' labour market. He reports that evidence shows that many Europeans migrate to the US.

For example, the UK has a low level of international mobility within the EU. Consistently with the pattern of relatively low participation in Erasmus programmes, Mason (2000) reports that the UK has been found to be rather less committed to the process of 'Europeanizing' science and engineering activities than many other EU countries. In particular, the logic of the UK's university finance regime tends to promote the recruitment of non-EU foreign students (who pay full tuition fees) against recruitment of EU students who are eligible for public subsidies. Furthermore, one of the many consequences of the greater pressure on British national laboratories to generate short-term commercial income – at the expense of involvement in basic and strategic research – has been a reduction in interactions with non-national qualified scientists and engineers. On the other hand, Mason concludes that, in terms of British performance in high-tech industries such as electronics, the results of cross-country comparisons show that the UK's relative lack of involvement in cross-border student mobility and knowledge flows within Europe is more than offset by the impact of non-EU foreign investment in the UK together with the advantages to internal knowledge transfer which arise from high levels of mobility between enterprises.

Moreover, in their study of electronics firms in France and the UK, Mason *et al.* (2004) found that the greater proactivity of UK academics in seeking out industrial funding was in part responsible for faster and broader external network building with firms diversifying their knowledge-sourcing activities. Mason *et al.* suggest that this may account for the improved position of the UK's electronics industry over France. They also conclude (page 70):

> in the British case some of the mechanisms contributing strongly to high levels of labour mobility and university-enterprises research interactions – such as the prevalence of temporary contracts for young researchers in higher education and the financial pressures on universities in general – are associated with a relatively weak level of investment in basic and strategic research in the UK. In the long-term, this could prove to be an Achilles heel contributing to deficiencies in knowledge generation and the ability of UK-based establishments to absorb relevant knowledge produced elsewhere.

The US in proportion attracts many more students from other countries at advanced levels in engineering, mathematics and informatics, and is successful in retraining more persons with doctorate qualifications: some 50 per cent of Europeans who obtained their qualifications in the US stay there for several years, and many of them remain permanently. Yet, in spite of the fact that many European academics have studied in the US, this has not in any major way brought the European system in line with that of the US. Herbst (2004, 17) argues that European universities 'cannot easily replicate the learning path that propelled the US research university to prominence'.

The growth in the S&E labour force has been maintained at a rate well above the rate of producing S&E degrees because a large number of foreign-born S&E graduates have migrated to the US. Between 1990 and 2000 the proportion of foreign-born people with bachelor's degrees in S&E occupations rose from 11 to 17 per cent; the proportion of foreign-born people with master's degrees rose from 19 to 29 per cent; and the proportion of foreign-born people with PhDs rose from 24 to 38 per cent. This is one area where the US is performing less well than competitor countries. Since the 1980s other countries have increased investment in S&E education and the S&E workforce at higher rates than the US. Between 1993 and 1997 the OECD countries increased their number of S&E research jobs 23 per cent, more than twice the 11 per cent increase in S&E research jobs in the US (www.nsf.gov/sbe/srs/nsb0407/start.htm).

The US tops five countries which are host to more than 70 per cent of all foreign students in OECD countries. The country attracts 29 per cent of foreign students, followed by the UK (14 per cent) and Germany (12 per cent). English-speaking countries account for over 50 per cent of the OECD total (OECD 2001a). In 2004, a survey by the US Council of Graduate Schools found that graduate schools saw a 28 per cent decline in applications from international students and an 18 per cent drop in admissions, damaging many universities' graduate programmes. The number of admitted students from China dropped 34 per cent; from India, 19 per cent; and from Korea, 12 per cent from 2003 to 2004. In engineering, which was particularly badly hit, the number of admitted students dropped 24 per cent. Programmes in the sciences reported application decreases averaging 20 per cent. Explanations include changes to the visa application process after '9/11', a perception that the US has grown less welcoming of foreigners and increased competition from universities abroad (www.usatoday.com/news/education/2004-09-07-grad-schools-foreigners_x.htm).

Accountability

Co-existing with the increasing emphasis of the universities as suppliers of skills to the economy is a changing construction of accountability, with a growing emphasis on the territorial role, albeit with geographically uneven impacts. The example of policy debates conducted in the UK and the US illustrates how responsiveness and accountability to industry has become a central theme in policy making.

The UK

Whereas university departments and individual academics have the responsibility for course and lecture content, the advent of new-style of degree courses, such as foundation degrees, brings with it a clear intent that design must reflect the needs of employers and that this strategy should be developed at the regional level. The 2003 White Paper on *The future of higher education* proposed that employers should have input to the design of two-year foundation degree courses. The LDA response to the White Paper identifies a clear role for RDAs to help co-ordinate a private sector response, particularly where competing interests might inhibit such involvement, or to support HEIs themselves more directly. Moreover, the intention is that there should be greater co-operation between regions, with the suggestion that cross-regional co-operation in the design of foundation degree courses would be particularly beneficial.

The political realization of the importance of training is illustrated by the Framework for Regional Employment and Skills Action (FRESA) (now replaced by Regional Skills Alliances) which the regional developments have been obliged to formulate with their partner organizations. For example, the 2002 FRESA plan for the South East identifies a number of objectives or priorities linked to improving the coherence of the relationship between HE or FE institutions and the business community. This quotation from the FRESA document is typical of the kinds of responsiveness envisaged:

> Colleges and universities should be granted more flexible funding to respond efficiently and effectively to employer requirements and raise the attainment of vocational and intermediate skills at level 3, key to raising productivity. Funding formulae also needs to reflect the increased demand for short 'bite sized' courses.
>
> (www.seeonline.net/learning/ActionSouthEast/Publications)

While the RDAs have been given an important role in skills development, the RDAs' Skills Development Funds amounted only to £26 million between the eight RDAs and remains small. Moreover, the potential co-ordination of activity between universities and industry is limited because Learning and Skills Councils are not responsible for training in the HE sector or for addressing graduate-level training needs. Organization at the regional scale, moreover, is not without problems. Within the UK, because of the complexity of regions as defined by RDA boundaries, demand for HE skills might be at the local rather than the regional level (Potts 2002, 997).

A swingeing criticism of the UK system of education and confusion of objectives, the simplication of role of education and the direct relationship between the amount of education in a society and economic growth comes from Wolf (2002, 249). Such criticisms can be levelled also at the Bologna process. Her argument is that expansion in higher education is ineffective in economic terms compared to investment in core skills at primary and secondary levels, and has little to do with social justice and quality of life. She argues that 'low level, uniform funding of a vast sector precludes first-rate facilities in which to train first-rate students and deters such students from entering university research and teaching'. Similar problems exist throughout the system: it has been argued that the UK 'government's skills strategy is qualification-led rather than skills-led' (Willis quoted in Tysome 2003a). Moreover, the downside of massification of HE in the UK is that, although it is designed to feed professional, managerial, associate professional, technical and some craft occupation labour markets, it has the negative effect that the rest are seen as low-status and low-paid work (Keep and Mayhew 2004).

The US

Recent debates have been around the extent to which the US government should subsidize training to overcome the shortage of qualified scientific and engineering workers, an issue relevant to all countries because of its implications for how universities should be required to tailor their teaching to meet the needs of industry – and hence be accountable if those needs are not met. The issue has been the subject of the 2003 National Science Board (NSB) report, *The Science and Enginering Workforce: Realising America's Potential*, and a paper by Romer (1999) as well as by economic strategy reviews by individual states such as Connecticut.

Romer's argument is that the supply response of American HE has not only been inadequate, it has also been perverse, in the sense of withholding supply when demand is rising, as was demonstrated above (see Stodder undated). It has erred by subsidizing the private-sector demand for scientists and engineers without asking whether the educational system provides the supply response necessary for these subsidies to work. Romer puts forward the view that university politics have constrained science and engineering departments from adequately expanding their student enrolments, pushing them instead to over-invest in 'quality' and scholarly research – although he points out that, as in the UK, undergraduates in natural sciences and engineering must be convinced that this kind of degree can lead to better career outcomes than the 'dead-end postdoctoral positions that have become increasingly common in some fields' (page 32). He finds that the challenge for the universities is not to increase the total number of PhDs but to increase the proportion of them that can put their skills to work in private-sector R&D. Likewise Stephan (2001, 203) argues that 'science has a long tradition of producing graduates who have a contempt for jobs in industry. This widespread attitude has contributed to poorly-functioning labour markets for newly educated scientists – especially in the life sciences, where post-docs are bountiful.'

Stodder (undated) looks at the evidence in relation to two of Romer's points. He finds that, in contrast to Romer's assertions of universality, there are sector and regional (state) differences in supply conditions. His study related educational supply to educational demand through associated job clusters within 47 states and Washington DC. He found that post-graduate degrees in sciences are highly responsive to research spending – the supply rises when research funding increases. On the other hand, associate degrees in engineering are highly responsive to salary – much more responsive than demand. It follows that the demand target to the appropriate incentive and degree level will be met with an elastic (responsive) supply. His conclusion is that for some scientific and engineering labour markets, educational supply may be more salary-elastic than industry demand. In such cases subsidizing demand at the state level rather than supply will provide more employees at a reasonable cost in the shortest possible time. Directly subsidizing supply, however, yields a longer-term increase in the stock of human capital and reduction in wage differentials, with lags of up to a decade.

Stodder argues for directing demand towards the basic end of professional qualifications, to associate degrees and short-terms certificates, and concurs with the Batelle Report (2001) that there is a need to expand business input into the education process. He finds that this is the practice in leading states such as California, Maryland, Illinois and Virginia, whereas some richer states lag behind in the provision of associate degrees. Connecticut for example, with the highest income per capita in the US, provided no associate degrees in the sciences in 1996–7. Thus Stodder's study is a partial qualification of Romer's study in that it shows that the market insensitivity of US HE does not hold everywhere for the supply of S&E workers. But it does confirm Romer's thesis in that, for post-graduate degrees in the basic sciences, supply is sensitive to research expenditures rather than to salary increases and for bachelor's degrees in engineering; the educational supply does appear 'perverse', reacting to salary increases with *fewer* not more degrees produced; the supply of engineers is most sensitive to salary pressure in the associate degree programmes; and there is likely to be a regional demand effect as programmes at associate and certificate levels have already the shortest time-to-market.

If the trends identified in *Indicators* 2004 continue undettered, Stodder argues that three things will happen. The number of jobs in the US economy that require science and engineering training will grow; the number of US citizens prepared for those jobs will, at best, be level; and the availability of people from other countries who have science and engineering training will decline, either because of limits to entry imposed by US national security restrictions or because of intense global competition for people with these skills. The US has always depended on the inventiveness of its people in order to compete in the world marketplace.

Now, preparation of the S&E workforce, for example by universities, is a vital arena for national competitiveness (see also NSB 2003).

Stephan (2001) finds that that a barrier to this objective is a lack of information. She suggests that US universities should collect data on job placements in industry and make it available to students. The US has no nationwide database of occupations sorted by comparable level of skill – the US sorting of Occupational Employment Statistics (OES) is merely by industrial area, which hinders policy formation (Stodder undated). This problem is being addressed state by state. For example, the state of Connecticut has established its own grouping of occupational clusters relating to education supplies and occupational demands through the Southern Technology Council (STC). The STC was faced with problems of collecting data from institutions in its attempts to understand why so many young talented people were leaving the Southern states and not being replaced by migrants from elsewhere, and had to rely on sample data from the National Science Foundation (see Tornatzky 2003 on this point).

Moreover, as in the UK, in the US the issue of the number of university places is politically sensitive. Bundy (2004) reports that, in his Higher Education Policy Institute lecture, Robert Reich described how state governments have cut higher education spending, while the Federal government has slashed Pell grants to poor students, and how there is extensive social stratification within the university system. While the US has engaged in massification of the university system, students from the richest 25 per cent of families are more than ten times more likely to attend college or university than those from the poorest quartile.

Defence and biotechnology

The expansion in the number of research units in the life and agricultural sciences has been matched by a growth in the number of students taking courses in these subjects and a decline in subjects with defence applications such as physical sciences and engineering. The populations of students in particular locations are therefore also changing depending on the degree of specialization of institutions.

In the UK, the number of students in biological science has risen sharply from 81,750 in 1996–7 – the earliest date for which data are available – to 149,520 in 2004–5 (a 54 per cent increase). Engineering, in contrast, rose by only 3,000 students and physical sciences rose by only 4,000 to 78,685 in 2004–5, up from 74,496 in 1996–7 (5.4 per cent) (www.hesa.ac.uk). In the US, the number of biological science undergraduate degrees nearly doubled between 1985 and 1998, before dropping back to 62,089 in 2001 when they, with agricultural sciences, accounted for 6.3 per cent of bachelor degrees awarded (www.nsf.gov).

In the US, the geographical distribution of both life science students and defence is highly uneven. Of the three states which feature in Chapter 8,

California is ranked top in the number of doctorates in S&T, including those in life sciences as well as in academic R&D. Kentucky is 33rd in both undergraduate and doctoral degrees, 30th in academic research but well above the national average in spending on life science research. New Jersey ranks 14th, 12th and 17th respectively and has a lower than the national percentage of academic R&D devoted to life sciences. With regard to state rankings in research and development funded by the DoD, and by extension the number of staff and students working on defence related research, California is ranked first, Kentucky 40th and New Jersey 11th (www.nsf.gov).

Territorial role

The potential for policy intervention to develop a territorial role for universities based on graduate recruitment and retention, training and CPD is that regions will gain if university graduates stay locally and lose if they leave and are not replaced by sufficient numbers of incoming graduates. Patterns of each vary considerably by country, by region and by institution, depending on which areas offer the best jobs and career prospects. To illustrate how they vary, examples are given from the UK, France, Denmark, Germany, Sweden and the US.

The UK

Belt *et al.* (2000) found wide variations in the proportion of students who stayed in the region to go to university and of graduates who stayed in the region following graduation. This is illustrated in Table 6.4.

Table 6.4 Proportion of graduates remaining in region of study after completing degree and proportion of these who originate from the region

Region	Proportion of graduates remaining in the region after study (%)	Proportion of those remaining who originate from the region (%)
Scotland	42.7	89.5
Greater London	41.2	62.9
Northern Ireland	37.3	99.5
Wales	35.7	68.3
Rest of South East	33.7	65.1
North East	33.2	68.8
North West	33.1	68.2
Yorkshire and Humberside	30.4	50.4
South West	29.7	60.4
East Midlands	29.2	52.2
West Midlands	28.5	62.6
East Anglia	22.2	47.7

Source: Belt *et al.* (2000).

Of the English regions, graduate retention of migrating students tends to be highest in Greater London and the rest of the South East, reflecting the superior job and career prospects in these regions. On the other hand, East Anglia, which includes Cambridge, has the lowest proportion of students staying in their home region to study, the lowest proportion staying in the region after study and the lowest proportion of those remaining who originate from the region. This situation is more extreme than in any other English region, with 42.8 per cent more students going out of the region to study than coming into it, and with only 17.8 per cent of students living in the region also studying in the East of England (East of England Development Agency (EEDA) 2002). EEDA's response to Lambert argues that the net loss needs to be reversed given the very high graduate skills shortages. In contrast, the North East has a low popularity as a destination for graduates of other regions but a relatively high retention of graduates from local institutions. The South East and East of England contribute to the success of London by flows of graduates into employment (see McCann and Shepherd 2001).

A weakness in the UK generally is insufficient training and graduate recruitment by SMEs. Nationally, between 30 per cent and 40 per cent of firms employ no graduates but this varies between areas (CURDS 2000). Thus intervention is appropriate for better training of undergraduates, of graduates and of employees in industry, enabling SMEs to retain graduates and make the best use of them, facilitating technology transfer through mobility within the labour market and linking into the further education sector to ensure a strong value chain of skills. Central to these activities are (1) the identification of where HEIs jointly can offer training and (2) an intelligence-gathering role about vacancies and availability of personnel. At the same time, other problems in the UK are inter-agency competition, an overemphasis on delivery at the regional rather than the local scale, plus fragmentation of effort and vested interests not wanting to lose their patch (Potts 2003).

Some examples of where universities have identified industrial demand for vocational courses are given in Box 6.1 (Lawton Smith 2003c):

- In the South East, the Oxford Brookes Motorsport degree is supported by the major motorsport companies in the region.
- The University of Westminster has developed a number of degrees that address the particular needs of industry, for example BA (Hons) in fashion merchandising and management, and City University offers an MSc in mathematical trading and finance.
- Collaboration between the five university careers services in the North East have sought to raise awareness of graduate employment opportunities to regional employers and of regional SME employment opportunities to students.
- The Graduates North East (GRANE) website started in 2002 has been

the chief output of the RDA-funded Graduate Retention in the North East programme. It provides links to the university careers services websites and other websites but does not offer a single website for employers and students through which to pass on information about job and placement opportunities.

- Since 1995 Newcastle and Northumbria University careers services have collaborated on graduate recruitment and have been fully sharing vacancy information. Around 1,000 graduates per year have received advice.
- Yorkshire Universities have established a forum of ten universities and three HE colleges to work together to extend their contribution to the region. One project is HLS for Success ESF Objective 3 Project. The purpose of this project is to build capacity within HE institutions to deliver a Virtual Business School (VBS) for the region.
- In the East of England, a number of HEIs have links with FE colleges to encourage continuing education. Anglia Polytechnic University is the leader in the field with 20 FE partner colleges.
- Oxford University's Department for Continuing Professional Development draws on Oxford University academics to deliver master's level courses and part-time PhDs aimed at the high-tech sector. The strategy is to offer part-time modular courses in new technologies or areas where R&D is in development, for example bioinformatics, where it is not known what the skill set is.
- The University of Greenwich Biopharmskills project was established in June 1999 with £474,900 funding for the development phase from SEEDA and £225,000 matched funding from the university. It forms part of SEEDA's skills development programme to plug critical skills shortages within specific sectors of the economy.
- In London, the Southern Key Skills Group comprises 11 universities and 'brings together regional higher education institutions' key skills coordinators to share experiences in policy development and implementation of key skills work and to provide support and disseminate findings regarding key skills provision'. This is in line with government policy (the UK's 2003 White Paper *The future of higher education*) that employers should have input to the design of two-year foundation degree courses.

France

Compared to countries such as the UK, the French system of higher education is distinctive in that it is much more local and regional (OECD 1999, 134). High levels of students attend home universities and up to two-thirds of graduates are retained in the region in which they studied. There are, however, inter-regional variations reflecting the size and structure of the university sector and the economic-industrial environment. For example, the Ile-de-France (Paris region) attracts many students from other regions and retains 80 per cent of its graduates, whilst regions such as Languedoc-Rousillon generally lack the ability to both attract students and to retain graduates.

In 1990 the 'University 2000' project was launched, a long-term plan for the development of training nationwide. Grenoble has strong local patterns of recruitment and so does Sophia Antipolis where the contribution of universities to the scientific labour market has been of increasing importance since the relocation of research institutes and doctoral programmes of the University of Nice. This increased training capability and reduced reliance on an inflow of highly qualified workers facilitated the development of local-university research linkages in which students play a significant role (Lawton Smith and De Bernardy 2000, 104).

Denmark

In Denmark, Maskell and Tornqvist (2003, 136) report that both the Copenhagen region and the Scania region have been able to attract more graduates than they export, thus maintaining a balance of academic trade. This is especially so for the Copenhagen region, which has benefited from a net immigration of graduates educated outside the region. This has benefited industry as well as public administration and the legal profession. A major outflow has taken place within natural science (school teachers and veterinarians). The authors find, however, that, in the Oresund region, in general firms do without university graduates: more than three-quarters of firms employ no graduates, while the R&D-intensive industries employ proportionally more than other types of firms. Moreover, they found a distinct sub-regional difference: in all sub-sectors of manufacturing studied, industry in Scania had a higher proportion of graduates than the same sub-sectors in the Copenhagen region. This result was ascribed to a different division of labour between the manufacturing and the knowledge-services providers and the size of the local market. They conclude that it is not the abundance of university graduates employed in industry that can explain the relative success of the dominant R&D extensive, low-tech parts of the manufacturing industry in the high-cost environment in the Oresund region. They point out that knowledge intensity is a much broader concept and firms might employ huge stocks of accumulated knowledge without employing a single graduate. They conclude that the economic role played by universities in one of the most prosperous and advanced regions in the world is mainly indirect. It is achieved through influence exercised on public governance, on civic culture and on informal institutions rather than on private sector firms directly.

Germany

Leifner *et al.* (2004) identified two changes to the German pattern of student recruitment which are influencing where students chose to study.

First, the vast majority of students (82 per cent) go to within their home region. The absence of income from student fees mean that there are fewer opportunities for universities to raise money to cover costs and to offer more expensive – but different – courses. Second, German universities are not selective; they have no influence on the motivation and knowledge-level of first-year students, although that is changing under modifications to the Higher Education Acts in several states. Thus, as in the UK, growing transparency about differences in quality and reputation following the growth of university rankings may affect where students choose to study.

Sweden

Following a different line of the relationship between universities and their supply of graduates, that of institutional factors which influence the levels of graduates in the local labour market, Lindholm Dahlstrand and Jacobsson (2003, 80) examine the changes in the supply of capabilities approximated by changes in the volumes and orientation of graduates and MSc and PhD levels in Gothenburg. They found an indirect process whereby local firms, in relying on the local labour market for engineers and scientists, generate spin-offs. This market in turn is greatly influenced by the responsiveness of Chalmers University. They argue that the extent of the local availability of specialized labour has a direct bearing on the size of industrial activities in fields demanding such specialized labour – in this case electronic engineers in microwave technology. The knock-on effect of this is that the responsiveness of Chalmers is therefore expected to influence, via its influence on the labour markets, the 'size' of the training ground, and therefore the potential number of technology-based engineers. They found, however, that, during the period when demand was high, the responsiveness to growing electronics opportunities in electronics and computer engineering was weak. As a consequence the volume of technology-based engineering was limited and skewed towards the region's traditional strength in mechanical engineering. They explain the poor responsiveness by reference to the centralized nature of Swedish education, by which the Department of Education controlled the volume and specialization of undergraduate education in great detail, and the absorption by Ericsson Microwave of many of the available engineers, which also had a negative effect on technology-based entrepreneurship.

The US

The case of San Diego illustrates further Stodder's assertion about state differences in supply conditions. San Diego has a very large population of graduate student enrolments, particularly in scientific subjects, and of post-doctoral doing research. This is an important resource for the region's growing population of high-tech firms, which in 1999 employed 11,000 people. Here it is continuing education rather than graduate education that provides one of the main inputs into innovation (Walshok *et al.* 2002, 40). These authors cite an earlier study which shows that continuing education enrolments are significant and can dwarf regular full-time undergraduate and enrolments combined. Furthermore, on a per capita basis, regions with thriving high-tech clusters have higher extension (CPD) enrolments in science and technology programmes than regions without them.

CPD/Extension programmes are becoming more part of individual states' economic development strategies. While much of the academic and policy focus is on the university sector's role in educating and training its own cohorts of students, it is slowly becoming recognized that universities have an increasingly important role in updating skills more generally. In the modern world, skill requirements are changing so rapidly that traditional skills and traditional ways of training and re-training are becoming outdated. Workers at all levels need to adjust to changes in technology methods of production and to expand their range of skills, thus providing continuous skills improvement. This is true in skills ranging from technicians through to R&D managers to CEOs. And workforce training should be so directed that 'all workers progress steadily up the ladder to fill jobs requiring higher skill sets than they currently possess' (Lee and Walshok 2002, 1).

Lee and Walshok argue that in the case of San Diego in California, the University of California at San Diego (UCSD) and Riverside have well-developed self-supporting Extension and Continuing Education Programmes which represent a significant contribution to human resource development in the state. In 2001 enrolments were running at 163,303 in UCSD and 64,670 at Riverside. While the nature of the programmes offered in each region reflected the industry mix, most of the students were working adults in the prime working decades of their lives. The authors conclude that the role of the University of California in workforce education and training, especially in science and technology-related skills and competencies, has been understated.

In a study which does not appear to have been replicated in Europe, research by Quigley and Rubinfeld (1993 in McCann and Shepherd 2001, 136) found considerable variations in spend on universities depending on whether graduates were more or less mobile. They found that there was less spending when graduates were more likely than not to leave the state following graduation. In such locations, the reduced ability to retain students after graduation reduces the returns to public investment in higher education, and state government have responded accordingly.

Conclusions

This chapter has focused on the supply, training and mobility of human capital as the three components of what is probably the most important contribution of universities to innovation and economic development. It has shown that the supply of S&E graduates is increasing, particularly in biological sciences, engineering and computer sciences, notwithstanding decline in some subjects such as physics and chemistry in the UK (Chapter 4). This is one area where Europe leads the US (Malecki 2005). Beyond that, a number of substantial differences are apparent between Europe as a whole and the US, and within Europe between different countries, just as there are between the different states in the US. For the EU, the establishment of the EHEA, as well as the ERA, is intended to improve cohesion and overcome fragmentation.

In addition to reform in the structure of undergraduate and graduate education, training and programmes designed to improve the flow of people, skills and knowledge to industry, with a growing but still underdeveloped focus on vocation and life long learning compared to the US, are central to EU and member state policy agendas. Examples from particular countries illustrate national weaknesses and the challenge for European policy. The US training model is becoming pervasive, but there are problems with demand and leakage at post-doc as well as PhD stage. The share of PhDs that industry absorbs varies from country to country (Lanciano-Morandat and Nohara 2002a). The chapter has presented arguments that in both the US and the UK there are significant cultural and other barriers which limit the propensity of students to be recruited by industry.

International student mobility has the benefit of increasing the likelihood of industry recruiting foreign engineers. Mason (2000) is sceptical about how far Europe has advanced in encouraging mobility between member states, with the US a more attractive destination. Indeed the attraction of foreign talent is crucial to the US university system and the economy (Malecki 2005).

It is also shown that engagement of universities with the economy at territorial level varies enormously. Stodder demonstrates vast differences within the US in patterns of retention, patterns replicated in Europe, reflecting both the impact of different structures of university systems (e.g. Germany compared to the UK) and the location of demand from industry.

Finally the chapter has also shown that the normative agenda implicit in most of the discussion is not without its downsides. Wolf (2002) and Keep and Mayhew (2004) in the UK and Bundy (2004) in the US all point to the confusion of objectives arising from placing so much emphasis on universities and training. The results are an increasing social stratification within university systems and knock-on effects on segmentation within labour markets, both of which lead to social polarization.

7 Grenoble and Oxfordshire

Introduction

The purpose of this and the following chapter is to explore in some detail what can be learned about the differences in relationships between universities and their territories by using case studies as examples. In this chapter Oxfordshire (the UK) and Grenoble (France) are discussed, and Stanford, Louisville and Princeton in the US in the next.

Oxford and Grenoble are twinned towns. Their twinning reflects their similar rank in their respective national innovation systems, that of second ranking after their capital cities as research poles of public sector research. Grenoble specializes in physics, electronics, engineering, biotechnology and medical sciences (Druilhe and Garnsey 2000) and Oxfordshire in physics, chemistry, materials, biochemistry and medical research.

In comparing the potential for the territorial role, however, the units of analyses are the Grenoble city region and the county of Oxfordshire. This reflects pattern of population and of the research base in each. Grenoble's population is some 626,000 compared to 607,500 in Oxfordshire. Whereas in Grenoble the majority of research facilities are located in and around the city because it is surrounded by mountains, in Oxfordshire the research base is more dispersed. In Oxfordshire, two of the universities (Oxford and Oxford Brookes) are in the much smaller city which has a population of some 134,600 people, while the major research laboratories are to the south of the city and a third university (DCMT at Shrivenham, part of Cranfield University) is to the south-west.

While the research bases and populations are similar, their locations are very different, a factor which is significant in the overall pattern of economic development. While Oxford is within easy reach of London, Grenoble is in France's South East and its scientific fortunes are in part linked to France's decentralization strategies in the 1950s. Another difference is that although both have strong manufacturing bases: in Oxfordshire until the mid-1990s this has been low-tech – cars, blankets and food – while in Grenoble manufacturing has long been high-tech (energy, electrical engineering), dating back to the early twentieth century (see Dunford

1989). Neither is strongly oriented towards defence research, but in Oxfordshire there is perhaps more than is generally recognized.

The chapter will show how, although the research bases of Oxfordshire and Grenoble have some similarities, they are very different in the ways in which they function in teaching and research and in their territorial roles. The evidence to support this comes from a number of sources. These include a CNRS-funded study (1999–2001) undertaken by the late Michel de Bernardy and the current author. Interviews were conducted in six research laboratories and universities in Grenoble and four in Oxfordshire. For this book, the information has been updated with interviews with senior academics and administrators in Oxfordshire's universities and laboratories and further desk research. For Oxfordshire, much of the discussion is focused on Oxford University, which has had the greatest, and an increasing, impact on the local economy in recent years.

Grenoble

Grenoble is a major international centre of public and private sector research. It has five major international laboratories and eight national facilities employing some 18,200 people. The majority (about 13,700) work on fundamental research, operating in a wide range of fields ranging from atomic energy to telecoms and computing. It has four universities with a combined student population of 59,200. Two of Grenoble's universities, UJF and INPG, have developed strong specializations in teaching and research in science-based subjects including maths, computer science, electronics, physics and process engineering. INPG has nine engineering schools. These strengths are reflected in the series of collaborative arrangements with other local institutions, which are both locally established and are part of national programmes. The institutions and their specializations are shown in Table 7.1.

Grenoble also has one of France's largest concentrations of research in the private sector. Firms include Xerox, Open System Foundation, Sun Microsystems, ST Microelectronic, Hewlett-Packard and Schneider-Electric. The number of inward investors is increasing dramatically. In 2000, some 212 companies were partly or wholly foreign-owned, compared to 180 in 1999 and 145 in 1996. Of these some 68 are US companies, accounting for 15,600 jobs, many of them in large research laboratories. The active population of Grenoble-Isère is younger and better trained than the national average. The relatively high level of qualification is due to the large number of leading international firms operating here, the presence of one of France's top universities and the overall attractiveness of the location (www.grenoble-isere.com).

Although both Grenoble's and Oxfordshire's national laboratories were established after the Second World War, those in Grenoble were located in a city that already had a highly skilled workforce and an

Table 7.1 University and Scientific Pole of Grenoble – 'Pole Scientifique'

Laboratory	Specialization
International laboratories	
European Synchrotron Radiation Facility	Materials research, ranging from biomolecules to nanomagnets, and ancient Egyptian cosmetics to metallic foams
IRAM (Institut de Radio-Astronomie Millimétrique)	Astronomy
GHMFL (Grenoble High Magnetic Field Laboratory)	Physics
EMBL, European Molecular Biology Laboratory	Molecular biology
ILL Institut Laüe Langevin	Neutron science and technology
National laboratories	
CEA-Grenoble	Atomic energy
LETI (Laboratoire d'Electronique de Technologie de l'Information) CEREM	Microelectronics
CNRS (Centre National de la Recherche Scientifique)	National scientific research funding body
CRSSA (Centre de Recherches du Service de Santé des Armées)	Medicine
INRIA l'Institut National de Recherche en Informatique et en Automatique	IT and automatics industry
CNET (National d'Etudes des Télécommunications)	Telecoms
INSERM	National Institute of health and medical research: a publicly-owned establishment of research in scientific and technological matters, 4 federative units of research in Grenoble, including CEA and UJF
IMAG Institut d'Informatique et Mathématiques Appliquées	A federation of research institute for applications of mathematics, including INPG and UJF
TIMA (Techniques of Informatics and Microelectronics)	Computer architecture, largest French independent research laboratory in the field of design and testing of circuits and systems
Universities	
INPG (Institut National Polytechnique Grenoble)	
UJF (Université Joseph Fourier)	
Stendhal	
UPMF	

Source: www.grenoble-isere.com.

orientation to R&D. De Bernardy (1999) explains the development of Grenoble as a scientific city as resulting from the actions of a local scientific elite which was instrumental in attracting big scientific complexes throughout the second half of the twentieth century. A major role was played by Professor Louis Néel, director of the Centre d'Etudes Nucléaires de Grenoble (CEA-G) from 1956 to 1970. In 1956 he created and subsequently developed CEA-G, as part of the French Atomic Energy Commission, and subsequently was responsible for decisions which integrated networks between different elements within the public/private research base. He and other leading scientists were able to defeat other competitors by winning the location of large devices, allowed under territorial planning rules. Arrivals included CEA-G (1965) and CNET (1974), both of which relocated activities from Paris under decentralization programmes under DATAR (Délégation à l'Aménagement du Territoire et à l'Action Ré), established in 1963 to co-ordinate regional policy. A more recent arrival is the European Synchrotron Research Facility (ESRF) (1989). Commercialization of the nuclear research programme began with the establishment of LETI in 1967. This was to be achieved primarily by developing new technological processes in microelectronics that would be licensed by industry. The period 1970–6 saw the privatization of all CEA activities through the formation of CEA Industrie (Lawton Smith 2000). De Bernardy's conclusion is that this series of activities and achievements, even when helped by local politicians, never reached the point where it amounted to a deliberate local policy.

Grenoble's specialization in advanced semiconductor manufacturing processes has resulted from the collaboration between LETI, other government laboratories and major French firms. LETI is partnered with CNET and SGS-Thomson in a regional consortium, the Grenoble Submicron Silicon Initiative (GRESSI). The group was created in 1991 and boasts an annual budget of $60 million and a staff of 200 researchers (www.cordis.lu/paxis/src/lyon_grenoble.htm). GRESSI's main programmes are work on CMOS and nonvolatile memories, silicon-on-insulator (SOI) technologies, and sub-0.1-µm research, including Coulomb blockade devices.

Early in the new century, LETI and INPG established Minatec, a €400-million innovation and education centre in micro and nanotechnology. A total of €150 million was scheduled for investment in Minatec between 2002 and 2005 to fund the new infrastructure, in addition to the €250 million invested by CEA-Léti and INP Grenoble. Moreover, during the last ten years the microelectronics industry has invested €4 billion in the Grenoble-Isère area. Minatec will be giving new impetus to courses in micro- and nanotechnology at INP Grenoble, which launched its first microelectronics courses at the end of the 1970s.

In all, almost €35 million will be invested in training at Minatec, which will be taking more than 1,000 student engineers, masters, PhDs and interns. New courses, focusing specifically on emerging technologies, are already on offer, as part of initial and continuous training schemes. Several projects are under study to focus more attention on nanophysics and nanoscience, and respond to rapidly evolving demand in research and industry. The initiative has had the decisive support of local authorities – Isère Departmental Council, Rhône-Alpes Region and Grenoble Urban Area Council and City Council (www.minatec.com/minatec_uk/).

Autonomy and accountability

While units have been set up to facilitate the patterns of technology transfer both in the universities and in the national laboratories, there are considerable tensions concerning the university–industry interface. Support provided by the liaison unit at UJF (UJF-Industrie) ranges from providing simple advice to the whole transfer process. A specific 'assessment committee' chooses projects that will be supported for six to 12 months with technical and economical expertise, protection of results, constitution of the means for developing prototypes, search for industrial partners and marketing training etc. As at Oxford University, a policy has been established on how to share the financial rewards from the commercialization of IP, and how to allocate and guide funds through rules in order to avoid waste or illegal practices. But, unlike in the UK, universities in France are generally not prepared to extend the introduction of profit to individuals. Instead external incomes are oriented to the laboratory. Hence the incentive for academics to establish new firms is not as strong as in the UK. Moreover, the study found that the downside is that there is a growing trend for firms to demand to be exclusive partners for the outcome of research results when a contract is agreed, thus threatening academic freedom.

In the 1999–2001 study, the Head of UJF-Industrie reflected on the growth of university–industry interaction: 'In Grenoble, after an important period of growth of relationships between firms and university, a certain stability is observed and that in itself raises some questions on what we are about to do'. Depending on the interpretation, it can direct different policies but there are concerns about aspects of informal or non-professional management of the relationship around the three issues:

- interface between the university as an entity and industry for the purpose of technology and knowledge transfers (more institutional aspects)
- interface between research academics and various facilitating services (incubators, technical structure, start-up funds)
- interface between laboratories and their actors and the supervision at the level of the university: the internal relationships and the ethical or 'disciplinary' aspects.

Like the universities, the national laboratories in Grenoble have extended the technology transfer function and developed a professional service in order to manage those relationships that need a wide range of competencies: IP, laws, management, ethics, adaptation or translation of researcher language to SME and vice versa. This problem must be mutually addressed and, even though each institute keeps its own facilities (ASTEC, CEA Valorisation and various testing technical platforms at CEA-G for example), a regional policy is being gradually developed to foster technological development through inter-institutional collaboration. The comment was made by the Head of UJF-Industrie that while these arrangements make spin-out easier, this does not disguise the fact that there is a vicious circle between sponsor's funds and official public help which often impose conditions that make projects impossible.

Defence and biotech

Grenoble does not have defence research establishments per se but some of the research in the national laboratories, for example in microphontics, micro- and nanotechnology, has defence applications. Life science research in Grenoble, as in Oxfordshire, is expanding rapidly and with it a number of strategies to facilitate the commercialization process. For example, the Grenopole Rhone-Alpes, a functional genomics network launched in the year 2000, links nearly 60 laboratories. Two further networks are being built up: Cancerpole is a network of cancer R&D expertise and will receive €60 million from regional and national funding, and Nanbio is a programme that will bring nanoscience into biology. All three poles will use public/private partnerships to provide funding for priority research projects. Grenopole also supports an exploratory genomics centre split between Lyon and Grenoble to develop research and application in bioinformatics (Goodman 2003).

Massification and training role

One of the key differences between the locations is the relative roles played by universities and research laboratories in training graduate students. Grenoble has 55,000 students, compared to Oxfordshire's 35,000, a main difference being that Oxfordshire's nuclear laboratories have far smaller student populations than their equivalents in Grenoble. In 2003 Grenoble's universities had only 14 per cent of students on post-graduate courses in the 14 doctorate schools in the city. The research laboratories such as CEN-G and TIMA supervise the majority of students, and provide close links between the laboratories and industry. For example, TIMA's post-graduates take a large part of the responsibility for contracts with firms while they work on their thesis, a guarantee that specific research will be developed with benefits to the firm via a patent, the employment of the post-graduate and other forms of transfer. Between 1984 and 1998, 100 theses were completed in TIMA. Of the students graduating, 37 found their first job in Grenoble. Of these 23 were integrated into a research team in Grenoble (12 within TIMA) and ten were recruited by SGS-Thomson (Lawton Smith 2003a).

In comparison to Oxford, the universities, national laboratories, industry and the communities of the city region in Grenoble are far more integrated into a regional technological strategy. In particular, all of the universities and schools in Grenoble have pooled their energies with the objective of making Grenoble France's leading centre for training in micro- and nanotechnology. The two main players are INPG and the Université Joseph Fourier (UJF). Some five-year courses are organized in partnership. Their objective is to offer students courses ranging from two to eight years after matriculation in micro- and nanotechnology (materials, components, systems-on-chip (SoC), biotechnologies, etc.) as well as their applications (telecommunications, multimedia, etc.), information technology and software. Table 7.2 shows courses in micro- and nanotechnology on offer in Grenoble.

Entrepreneurial activities

That formal research co-operation with industry is well established is demonstrated by the levels and variety of income from industry through various means including licensing, secrecy agreements and contracts for both UJF and INPG. Income more than doubled in the period 1992–9. INPG alone had managed 556 contracts with firms since 1995 for Fr226 million, ranked fifth in a league table of the best engineering schools for links and contracts with firms in 1998 (*Review Industrie et Techniques* 797). The largest increase is in income from licensing. This grew from Fr1 million in 1995 to Fr13 million in 1999 in total before the shares between universities (15 per cent), laboratories and individuals are broken down. Grenoble-Isère is the top French department for patent registration in electronics, electricity and instrumentation and for engineering science publications rated by the Science Citation Index. In 1998 235 patent requests were filed in Isère (i.e. a quarter of the total for the Rhône-Alpes region) (www.grenoble-isere.com/index2_uk.html).

The two locations differ markedly in the entrepreneurial activities of the national laboratories. Whereas Oxfordshire's laboratories have produced only around ten firms (Lawton Smith and Ho 2005), many more firms have emerged from their equivalents in Grenoble and where entrepreneurial activities of the science base are underpinned by the local state. By the late 1990s, this strategy had had some success: 29 new firms had been recently created in the numeric imaging activities of which ten were from universities, five from INRIA, six from CEA, one from ILL, one from France Telecom and six from other firms within the region.

Table 7.2 Undergraduate, graduate and professional courses in micro- and nanotechnology in Grenoble

Initial training: engineering degrees, and post-graduate: and PhD courses	Grenoble's Graduate School of Electronics and Radioelectricity (ENSERG), specializing in microelectronics and data processing Grenoble's Graduate School of Physics (ENSPG), specializing in physics and biotechnology The Telecommunications Department of INPG, specializing in telecommunications The Doctoral School of Electronics, Electrical engineering, Automation, Telecommunications and Signals (EEATS)
Continuous training	Centre for Continuous Training in Microelectronics and Microsystems
Initial training: engineering courses for micro and nanotechnology and the associated applications in other schools belonging to the INP Grenoble group	Grenoble's Graduate School of Computer Science and Applied Mathematics (ENSIMAG): software engineering, computer systems, communications and calculation systems Grenoble's Graduate School of Electrochemistry and Electrometallurgy (ENSEEG): science of materials and surfaces, microsystems Grenoble's Graduate School of Electrical Engineering (ENSIEG): signals and systems Graduate School of Advanced Industrial Systems (ESISAR) in Valence (Drôme): computing and networks, embedded computing INPG Doctoral College post-graduate and PhD courses
Courses at UJF	Institute of Technology (IUT1) courses starting two years after matriculation Institute of Science and Technology (ISTG), courses starting three and five years after matriculation; industrial computing and instrumentation (i), and materials science and engineering (SciGMa) with a joint micro- and nanotechnology option in the third year (starting in 2003) Training & Research Units (UFR) ranging from four to eight years after matriculation Doctoral College with post-graduate and PhD courses
Continuous Training Department at INP Grenoble	• access to engineering degrees (ELAN programme) • access to executive positions (Formatech and MIDEP programmes) • Technological Research Diploma (DRT), Multimedia Project Leader Diploma (DHET), etc. University Centre for Adult Education and Training (CUEFA), Continuous Training and Apprenticeship Department (SFCAA) at Université Joseph Fourier.

Source: www.cordis.lu/paxis/src/lyon_grenoble.htm.

Reflecting the research base specialisms, the fields of production are mainly oriented to microelectronics, computers and the internet. Since the turn of the new century, the rate of spin-off has been sustained by a change in national seed funds and venture capital.

LETI is the only French research centre with a spin-off policy. The laboratory has been the origin of about 30 new companies since the early 1980s, with around ten between 2000 and 2004. In those 30 years more than 1,500 jobs have been created. The most famous is the international firm STMicroelectronics, world number four in semi-conductors (Cheney 1997). Other companies spun off from LETI include field emission display (FED) pioneer Pixtech, integrated read-write head manufacturer Silmag, and Soitec, a leader in the burgeoning silicon on insulator (SOI) market. Protein'eXpert is a spin-off from Grenoble's institute of Structural Biology; it was founded in 2000 and by 2004 had 25 employees.

TIMA records five spin-off companies (http://time.imag.fr/valorization/Spinoffs.asp). The earliest was established in 1997. The five companies are:

- MEMSCAP, 1997. The company started with seven engineers, mainly composed from researchers from the Microsystems Group of TIMA Laboratory (CAD of micro electro mechanical systems)
- AREXSYS, 1997. Merged with TNI-Valyosis in July 2001 (innovative hardware/software co-design solution for embedded system and system-on-chip (SOC) designs)
- iRoC, 2000 (technologies unique and global design solutions for integrating Robustness on Chip)
- MND, 2003 (semiconductors)
- NanoSPRINT s.a.r.l., 2005 (innovative provider of virtual representation solutions for science and technology).

In the Rhône-Alpes region linkages between universities and national laboratories and industry are being built by support provided for seed funding, business advice and incubators, and for developing structured poles such as the biotechnologies pole around Lyon as well as the micro- and nanotechnologies. National schemes are the main source of funds for early stage capital. For example, national seed funds are delivered through local organizations including the national seed fund for electronics and materials, EMERTEC; the national seed fund for informatics and I-Source in Grenoble is hosted by INRIA.

With the exception of the biomedical sciences, Grenoble has had business incubators for science-based industries associated with national laboratories and universities for far longer than Oxfordshire. Since 1986 the ASTEC incubator has generated some 80 firms located near CEN-G in order to benefit from various facilities like heavy apparatus, measures and prototyping capacities, expertise by direct relations. ASTEC is now linked to GRAIN (Grenoble Alpes Incubation), the regional incubator located in

Grenoble. GRAIN works with EMERTEC. As a common initiative at the local level, GRAIN brings together the two previous incubators and has greater resources. This increases the number of projects introduced in the incubator. It supplies advice and aid to companies, providing market research assistance and development of business plans and, through investment opportunities, assisting their financial start. Nearly one-third of all the projects selected by GRAIN concern bio-industry. More recently a biotech incubator, Biopolis is being established and is due for completion in 2006. It will provide specialist premises and business support (Goodman 2003).

The territorial role

The role played by the regional authorities in supporting research in the attempt to bring coherence to the region's infrastructure is far more advanced than in Oxfordshire. Since 1999, the regional council has doubled its financial support for research, contributing €43 million in 2003. The territorial role is enshrined in the activities of the Groupement d'intérêt public (GIP). This grouping was created in 1992 by the universities, the communities, the research laboratories and major companies to support scientific developments within the scientific community and the sharing of resources and projects. Grenoble Universités was set up to encourage dialogue between the universities as a means of supporting the emergence of innovative solutions and to set up actions that would be in the public interest (see www.grenoble-univ-rech.org/pole/).

As everywhere else, there are barriers to the successful realization of strategies, for example, local SMEs do not necessarily have the absorptive capacity (Cohen and Levinthal 1990) to collaborate with the institutions, scientific research does not necessarily translate into economic development. Other factors relate to the geographical location of Grenoble. Saperstein and Rouach (2002) conclude that Grenoble faces a number of challenges and problems in staying competitive and attracting multinationals. Regional factors include infrastructure – there is no TGV from Lyon and being surrounded by mountains isolates Grenoble. It faces competition from Lyon and Sophia Antipolis. Nationally, Brittany, Lorraine, Paris and Sophia Antipolis are competitors for high-tech activity. Internationally, Grenoble is not a major European city and is in competition with Munich, Dublin, Barcelona and Stockholm.

Oxfordshire

Three features mark Oxfordshire's scientific innovation system: a high concentration of research, especially in biomedical sciences; success in the application of research; and until recently a specialized largely non-university- and non-local-authority-based innovation support system. The research base encompasses three universities (Oxford University, Oxford Brookes and Cranfield DCMT at Shrivenham) and seven laboratories to the south-west of the city in the Didcot area (United Kingdom Atomic Energy Authority (UKAEA) Harwell and Culham, Joint European Taurus, Central Council for Research Laboratories (CCLR), Rutherford Appleton Laboratory (RAL), Medical Research Council (MRC), National Radiological Protection Board (NRPB) and the Institute of Hydrology). Collectively these institutions employ around 13,200 people (Table 7.3).

Oxfordshire's first laboratory, Harwell (nuclear energy, fission), was established in 1946 on an old airbase, located within reach of Oxford University. Other laboratories funded under a range of government departments were established in the next three decades. These include the atomic energy fusion laboratory Culham in 1961, RAL in 1957 (education and science) and the National Radiological Protection Board in 1970 (health and social security) (see Lawton Smith 1990). The latest big science project is the Synchrotron X-ray laboratory which is being developed at RAL.

Oxford University

Oxford is the one of the UK's premier universities and was established in 1214. Oxford consists of a central university (including the central and departmental libraries, and science laboratories) and 39 colleges and seven permanent private halls (PPHs). All teaching staff and degree students must belong to one of the colleges (or PPHs). These colleges are not only

Table 7.3 Research laboratories and universities in Oxfordshire (2002)

Name of research centre/university	Location	Number of employees	Sector
Research laboratories			
UKAEA	Culham and Harwell	920 combined	R&D
RAL	Chilton	1,700	R&D
Environment Agency	Wallingford and Oxon	324 combined	Government/ regulatory
NRPB	Chilton	260	R&D
Universities			
Oxford University	Oxford	7,773	Academic
Oxford Brookes University	Oxford	2,278	Academic
DCMT – Cranfield University	Shrivenham	191	Academic/ military
	Total	13,186	

Source: Author's survey.

houses of residence but have substantial responsibility for the teaching of undergraduates and post-graduates. Some colleges accept only post-graduate students and one college, All Souls, does not accept students at all. Oxford's collegiate system came into existence through the gradual agglomeration of independent institutions in the city of Oxford (www.fact-index.com/u/un/university_of_oxford.html).

By research income and human capital it is one of the UK's top four universities (the other three are Cambridge and two London colleges, UCL and Imperial). It has more academic staff working in world-class research departments (rated 5* or 5 in the RAE 2001) than any other UK university. It had the highest research income of any UK university in 2002–3 (www.ox.ac.uk/research). External income has risen sharply in recent years, rising by 28 per cent between 1998–9 and 2002–3 (Table 7.4). Major funding came from the Wellcome Trust and cancer charities. The university specializes in genomics – 50 per cent of university research groups work on genomics. The university is increasingly part of internationally distributed innovation systems as overseas industry income is increasing while UK industry income is declining. On the other hand, commercialization activities, with the exception of spin-offs, are not advanced. While the university's licensing income has reached £10.2 million, on a global scale, however, compared for example to Stanford University (Chapter 8), Oxford still has a long way to go to catch up.

In 2000–1 Oxford University's externally funded research amounted to £142 million. Of this almost £100 million was directed towards research in the life and medical sciences.

Like other UK universities, public funding for research has been declining as a proportion of university research income, particularly under the successive Conservative governments (1979–97) to reach a low point in 1997. While research income from external sources pays for salaries and travel and so on, it does not replace worn-out equipment. (In 2005, the UK research councils have moved to provide full economic costing for research.) Oxford has, however, benefited from programmes which have been jointly funded by government and the private sector, including

Table 7.4 Oxford University income from industrial sources FY 1998–9 to FY 2002–3 (£ million)

	1998–9	1999–2000	2000–1	2001–2	2002–3
UK	11.8	12.5	13.6	11.7	11.4
Overseas	5.8	7.8	8.9	8.2	9.0
Total Industry	17.6	20.3	22.5	19.9	20.4
Total University Research Income	117.5	129.6	142.4	149.7	162.9

Source: Oxford University Research Services Office.

charities such as the Wellcome Trust to address these problems: JIF (Joint Infrastructure Funds) (1998–2001) and the on-going SRIF (Science Research Investment Funds). (The Science Research Investment Fund (SRIF) is a joint initiative by the Office of Science and Technology (OST) and the Department for Education and Skills (DfES).) For example, the Chemistry Department's new building is funded through a £60 million JIF bid, the biggest JIF grant. The drawback of these awards is that they are not recurrent and provide only 75 per cent of total funding for each project. These and short-term research grants of three years' duration also do not solve the general problem of maintenance.

One of Oxford University's major strengths is its interdisciplinary and interorganizational research across a wide range of technologies in physics, chemistry, engineering, materials, IT and life sciences. In 2001, Oxford's Department of Engineering Science was awarded a Faraday Partnership in Automotive and Aerospace Materials. Partners are Oxford Brookes and Cranfield Universities, the Motor Industries Research Association, the Oxford Trust (a local charitable trust), and the Heart of England Business Link. Box 7.1 shows Oxford University's interdisciplinary research centres.

Box 7.1 Interdisciplinary research at Oxford University.

- Faraday Partnership in Automotive and Aerospace Materials, a collaboration between universities and industry to develop new materials required for future low-energy consumption, pollution-free transport systems supported by the DTI and the Engineering and Physical Sciences Council (EPSRC), aims to build effective networks between academia and industry to provide a continuous exchange between skilled scientists, engineers and technologists of research results and advanced technologies.
- Oxford Internet Institute, set up in 2001 as the first truly multidisciplinary internet institute based in a major university, aims to carry out research and make policy recommendations about the effects of the internet on society.
- MRC IRC for Cognitive Neuroscience promotes interaction between research groups in aspects of basic and clinical neuroscience. Its main interests concern the mechanisms by which the brain forms representations of the outside world, stores information as memories and programmes movements. The Centre encourages work in all areas of cognitive neuroscience, across all relevant disciplines.
- Oxford Centre for Environmental Biotechnology (OCEB) was inaugurated in 1997 as a collaboration between research workers in the Department of Engineering Science, the Department of Plant Sciences, and the NERC Institute for Virology and Environmental Microbiology (IVEM). The objectives of OCEB are broadly to develop biological

science and technology and the associated process engineering to reme-
diate environmental problems in soil, water and air.

- Quantum Information Processing Interdisciplinary Research Collaboration (QIPIRC) received EPSRC funding of £9 million over the next five
  years to further the understanding of the fundamental laws of quantum
  physics.
- Oxford Centre for Gene Function (OCGF) will be a multidisciplinary
  international centre of excellence for postgenomic science. Funded by a
  £10 million JIF award and a subsequent grant of £1.7 million from the
  Wolfson Foundation, it will involve substantive collaboration between
  research teams from the departments of Physiology, Human Anatomy
  and Genetics and Statistics. It will provide an integrated approach to
  the study of gene function, which will facilitate the discovery and development of novel targets for therapy. The state-of-the-art building of
  about 3,000 sq m, will combine leading experimental research groups
  totalling around 70 scientists.
- IRC 'From Medical Images and Signals to Clinical Information' focuses
  on the development of clinically efficient IT systems for clinicians and
  researchers who, increasingly, have vast amounts of images and measurements at their disposal which they need to analyse effectively in
  order to diagnose and treat their patients in the best possible way.
- The IRC Bionanotechnology is a collaboration between six departments within the University of Oxford (Departments of Physics, Chemistry, Biochemistry, Engineering Science, Physiology and Materials),
  together with the Universities of Glasgow and York, Cambridge, Not-
  tingham and Southampton, and the National Institute for Medical
  Research. The Centre aims to investigate naturally occurring biomolecular nanosystems, from the level of single molecules up to molecular
  machines, and to apply this knowledge to produce artificial electronic
  and optical devices.
- Institute of Nanotechnology will offer state-of-the-art facilities,
  opportunities for collaboration, cross-disciplinary transfer of ideas and
  support for those involved in nanotechnology research and applications.
- Princeton/Oxford Partnership in Materials Science. Formal programme
  of undergraduate student exchange, academic collaboration and sharing
  of research facilities.

Source: Oxford University.

One of the key differences between Oxfordshire and Grenoble and one
which limits the county's territorial role is the potential for collaboration
with local MNCs. Oxfordshire has a small number of research laboratories
of foreign-owned companies. These include the European research laboratory of Sharp and Dow Elanco's research laboratory. Genzyme, the US
biotech company set up its UK headquarters in Oxfordshire in 2000, but
has a service rather than research function. Yamanouchi, the Japanese
pharmaceutical company, relocated its R&D activities back to Japan in

2002. Overall, in 2003 some 93 of Oxfordshire's 1,400 high-tech firms employing 36,700 people were foreign-owned, over half of them US-owned. Employment in these firms represented almost one-fifth of all high-tech jobs in the county (Chadwick *et al.* 2003). The majority of these firms have been acquired by foreign companies rather than established in the county. One explanation for the low level of influx of foreign companies to the county is Oxfordshire's strict planning rules (Lawton Smith *et al.* 2003).

Accountability

The UK allows each university to set their own terms of trade by which the commercialization of research is undertaken. From 1 October 2002, Oxford University formally changed its statute to a position where the university claims ownership of all intellectual property of staff, students and visitors to the university. This new statute, in asserting the right to determine the distribution of income derived from any profits made from patents, licences, other intellectual property and of course spin-off companies, changed the basis of accountability of its staff and students to the university, from one of relative freedom to determine the ways in which research should be commercialized to one which is regulated by the university. The rules are now that:

(1) The University claims ownership of all intellectual property specified in section 6 of this statute which is devised, made, or created:
(a) by persons employed by the University in the course of their employment;
(b) by student members in the course of or incidentally to their studies;
(c) by other persons engaged in study or research in the University who, as a condition of their being granted access to the University's premises or facilities, have agreed in writing that this Part shall apply to them; and
(d) by persons engaged by the University under contracts for services during the course of or incidentally to that engagement.
(2) The University's rights under sub-section (1) above in relation to any particular piece of intellectual property may be waived or modified by agreement in writing with the person concerned.
6. The intellectual property of which ownership is claimed under section 5 (1) of this statute comprises:
(1) works generated by computer hardware or software owned or operated by the University;
(2) films, videos, multimedia works, typographical arrangements, field and laboratory notebooks, and other works created with the aid of university facilities;
(3) patentable and non-patentable inventions;

(4) registered and unregistered designs, plant varieties, and topographies;

(5) university-commissioned works not within (1), (2), (3), or (4);

(6) databases, computer software, firmware, courseware, and related material not within (1), (2), (3), (4), or (5), but only if they may reasonably be considered to possess commercial potential; and

(7) know-how and information associated with the above.

7. Notwithstanding section 6 of this statute, the University will not assert any claim to the ownership of copyright in:

(1) artistic works, books, articles, plays, lyrics, scores, or lectures, apart from those specifically commissioned by the University;

(2) audio or visual aids to the giving of lectures; or

(3) computer-related works other than those specified in section 6 of this statute.

8. For the purpose of sections 6 and 7 of this statute, 'commissioned works' are works which the University has specifically employed or requested the person concerned to produce, whether in return for special payment or not, but, save as may be separately agreed between the University Press and the person concerned, works commissioned by the University Press in the course of its publishing business shall not be regarded as 'works commissioned by the University'.

9. Council may make regulations:

(1) defining the classes of persons or naming individuals to whom section 5 (1) (c) of this statute shall apply;

(2) requiring student members and such other persons as may be specified in regulations to sign any documents necessary in order to give effect to the claim made by the University in this Part and to waive any rights in respect of the subject-matter of the claim which may be conferred on them by Chapter IV of Part 1 of the Copyright, Designs and Patents Act 1988; and

(3) generally for the purposes of this Part.

10. This Part shall apply to all intellectual property devised, made, or created on or after 1 October 2000 and is subject to the provisions of the Patents Act 1977.

(www.admin.ox.ac.uk/statutes/790-121.shtml#_Toc28143157)

Alongside these rules, the university has established a highly professional technology transfer system, in the form of Isis Innovation, Oxford University's wholly owned technology transfer company. In 2001 Oxford won an award for being the UK's most entrepreneurial university (see below).

Defence versus biotech paradigm

Oxford University like many other universities has defence-funded research but the level of funding is dwarfed by that of income for bioscience research. In 2002–3 the university gained £117,553 from the Defence Research Agency, Defence, Science Technology Ltd and the MoD combined. It also had an award of £46,000 from the US Office of Naval Research. In contrast, it received £7,281,705 in grants from the Biotechnology and Biological Sciences Research Council (BBRC). Harwell undertook defence research in its early years but its remit changed entirely to energy research.

Defence research is concentrated in Cranfield DCMT, which undertakes specialized and generic research to be carried out on defence technology and equipment.

The Centre for Photo-Analysis and Photo Manipulation of Materials has been formed by Cranfield University in an initiative funded under the remit of the Science Research Investment Fund (SRIF) from the Higher Education Funding Council of England (HEFCE). The Centre is an inter-disciplinary venture involving four departments: Engineering Systems Department (ESD), Department of Materials and Medical Science (DMMS), Department of Environmental and Ordnance Systems (DEOS) and Department of Aerospace, Power and Sensors (DAPS). Its primary objective is to consolidate and strengthen the research facilities at Shrivenham and to establish an international lead in the area of novel photo-materials chemistry, photo-fabrication and analysis and modelling.

The aims of the Centre are:

- to offer a service to local industries in the areas of process and structural health monitoring using low-cost and non-contact fibre optic sensor systems
- to custom-design, synthesize and characterize organic, inorganic and composite materials
- to enable technology transfer and exploitation of technologies developed in the Centre
- to design and offer specialist career development and progression courses in partnership with local industries
- to offer a consultancy service to local industries.

The Centre has a staff of 22 and a research portfolio totalling £1.5 million, and collaborates with a number of industrial sectors including aerospace, civil engineering, manufacturing, chemical and defence. Funding has also been secured to make possible the purchase of state-of-the-art equipment such as excimer lasers for micro-machining materials, a suite of thermal and spectral characterization facilities, environmental scanning electron microscope, dynamic contact angle, nano-indenter and quasi-static and fatigue test machines. In addition to servicing the research needs of the Centre, the facility will also be made available to local industries and schools for training and consultancy.

Oxford University is one of the major UK centres for life sciences research, and one which is characterized by interdisciplinary research and by initiatives to commercialize that research. Biomedical research (from research councils, charities and industry) accounts for the largest share of external income. In 2002–3, major grants came from the charities such as the Wellcome Trust (£37 million) (over a fifth of all external research funding) and the British Heart Foundation (£4.1 million) and the drugs companies such as Merck (£4 million) and Bayer (£1.68 million). The university has at least 14 interdisciplinary centres in the biomedical field and runs programmes in genetics, immunology and epidemiology with 700 graduate students. Specialization is increasing in genetics and genomics. In June 2004, the university was awarded £500,000 for research into stem cells (Blueprint 2004).

Moreover, strong links between the research base and hospitals, such as the John Radcliffe, ensure easy access for the clinical studies that are necessary for putting research into action. Oxford's hospitals have a long record of providing excellent 'testing grounds' by hosting commercial trials as well as NHS trials. Building on this relationship, in 2002 Oxford was awarded £750,000 over five years to establish a Genetics Knowledge Park (GKP) funded by the Departments of Health and of Trade and Industry, one of the initial six Genetics Knowledge Parks. It is a partnership between Oxford University and the Oxford Radcliffe Hospitals NHS Trust. The aim of the GKPs is to translate advances in genetics research into clinical practice. As well as the research and application remits, the parks are intended 'to cause the transfer of technology and skills between research groups, the NHS and private sector' (www.dh.gov.uk/Publications AndStatistics/PressReleases/PressReleasesNotices/fs/en?CONTENT_ID= 4013031&chk=7neKRv). Isis Innovation has staff dedicated to supporting the biomedical sector and manages a bio innovation fund (Oxford University BioForm).

Massification

Oxford's universities and government laboratories in the county are part of the explanation why Oxfordshire has proportionately the second most highly qualified labour market in England and Wales: over a quarter (27 per cent) of Oxfordshire's residents are qualified to degree level (NVQ level 4). Its student S&E labour market has a different orientation to that of Grenoble. It is more focused on the universities than on Oxfordshire's research laboratories, which have far smaller student populations than their equivalents in Grenoble. Table 7.5 shows the student populations in the major institutions.

The student body at Oxford University is increasingly international, particularly at post-graduate level. The University recruits over 1,000 foreign undergraduate students per year (1,029 in 2002–3). The largest

Table 7.5 Student populations in Oxfordshire: 2002–3

	Undergraduates	*Post-graduates*	*Student totals*
Oxford University	11,069	5,626	17,097[1]
Oxford Brookes	12,510	5,702	18,212
DCMT – Cranfield University	300	700	1,000
Rutherford Appleton laboratory		20 CASE awards	20
UKAEA Culham	–	16	16
Totals		17,690	36,345

Sources: Oxford University Annual Report 2002/3 and author's survey of institutions. NB: only those with graduate students are included. For example, the NRPB does not have a formal graduate programme.

Note
1 includes 375 additional students.

cohorts come from Germany (141), North America (151), Asia (168) and Far East Asia (200). The overseas post-graduate body is three times as large (3,085 in 2002–3). Some 771 students come from Europe and 2,314 from outside the EU. North America dominates, accounting for over one-third of non-EU students with 901 in residence plus a further 239 additional students. The emphasis on graduate studies at Oxford has been increasing, with the university setting up seven new colleges dedicated to post-graduate studies in the last 30 years. Post-graduates currently account for more than one-quarter of the student body.

The move towards an increasingly graduate focus has been accelerated because the university finds that it is no longer cost-effective to teach undergraduates. Schooling costs Oxford more per student than the current fees and government subsidies cover, and even with the government's proposed additional top-up fee of £3,000 from 2006 (from the 2004 figure of current flat-rate tuition fee of £1,125), there would still be a deficit per student. In 2004, it was estimated that Oxford's undergraduate teaching is in the red by £24 million (Nülle 2004). Davis (2004) cites David Palfreyman, bursar of New College and Director of the Oxford Centre for Higher Education Policy Studies (Oxcheps), who argues that Oxford will need to charge undergraduate fees of up to £10,500 a year from families of the higher income brackets to maintain its international status; the true cost of teaching an Oxford undergraduate for a year was £18,600, which the University currently subsidizes by 47 per cent. The effect is that there is a freeze on undergraduate numbers but an increase in the number of post-graduates, particularly from overseas. The university's major target market for recruitment for post-graduates is the US and it is therefore in competition for the best students with Harvard, Stanford, Yale and Princeton (personal communication Dr Jeremy Whiteley, March 2004). It has been suggested in the education press that if Oxford wants to rival the major US universities, its 36 independent colleges should follow the example of Yale and Harvard and establish a single in-house 'investment club' – which would make it better placed to go private or offset the impact of top-up fees with more scholarships for poor students (see Tysome 2004, 8).

A high proportion of Oxford University's students stay locally on graduation, whereas those from Oxford Brookes University are more likely to leave. HESA data shows that one-third of both Oxford University (32.62 per cent) and Oxford Brookes University (34.6 per cent) students stay in the county after their first degree. These figures reflect the much greater propensity for Oxford University graduates to stay on for further degrees as they include those students who stay on to post-graduate studies: one-quarter of all Oxford undergraduates go on to further study. The availability of jobs in London exerts a strong pull on Oxford University's graduates: over a quarter (26.3 per cent) are recruited to London. One-fifth go overseas. Fewer Brookes students moved to London (16.2 per cent) and only a very small proportion (less than 4 per cent) go abroad.

The university is also in a global market for best academics. For example, it competes to attract the top bioscience people, of whom there are estimated to be only 250–300 in the world. A barrier to recruitment is that academics (dons) at Oxford are paid about one-third as much per teaching hour as in the US, are bereft of teaching assistants and have only two support staff at their disposal, compared to five per professor in the US. Moreover, the beginning salary for Oxford's dons is typically £14,100 (Nülle 2004). Oxford, however, has begun to respond. In order to compete, the university is much more flexible in rewarding staff than ten years ago, being able to pay higher salaries. Until the beginning of the 1990s there was a single professorial salary. The university is now able to offer distinction awards to keep people and recruit the best people. Moreover, the university is constantly aware of the need to fulfil infrastructural requirements underpinning recognition to keep staff happy (personal communication, Dr Jeremy Whiteley 2004).

The training role of the university has gradually expanded but is nowhere near as extensive as in US universities for example. Initiatives are small-scale. For example, in 1995, the Physics Department introduced OUTINGS (Oxford University Training in Industry Graduate Scheme), initially funded by the department and now receiving DTI funding. This scheme organizes placements for science post-graduates with local high-tech companies, ensuring that they gain business experience and networking opportunities with potential employers. The university so far has not done what Oxford Brookes University has done and created undergraduate degrees that have the support of industry. Oxford Brookes offers a Motorsport degree supported by the motorsport industry, reflecting Oxfordshire's 'pole position' in Motorsport Valley (Henry and Pinch

2000). Recently, however, the two universities have begun a collaboration that seeks to address the county's technician shortage through a programme based at Oxford University's Begbroke Science Park.

Industrial in-service training is available in the dedicated programmes run by Oxford University's Department of Continuing Professional Development, a component of the Department of Continuing Education. Courses are held in engineering, computation, biomedical sciences, information technology, mathematics, law and the applied social sciences. Specially tailored courses are available for companies and professional groups. Oxford Brookes offers a 'Business for bioscience' web-based course – hence not a locally based programme. CPD is not yet, however, mainstream to either Oxford's universities or to the regional development agencies. The former head of Oxford University's Department of Continuing Professional Development, Dr Mark Gray, said this of policy shortcomings:

On the policy side, I should note that our representations to DfES, to SEEDA and others in the last few years have all tended in one direction, namely noting that the lack of direct support (other than under special initiatives such as HEIF and HEROBAC, and from the research councils in target sectors) for skills development in high skill and high technology areas is seriously affecting the ability of the region to develop, retain, retrain and motivate key science and engineering professional staff. My own view is that the region's professional scientific and technology staff are well served in a few areas, but not served with enough volume or variety across the whole GOSE region. Our concern here is that as science-based businesses play an increasingly important role in the region, and as science moves faster and toward greater integration of life, physical and computational and mathematical sciences, the region could be left with excellent basic skills provision for the unemployed and the low skill occupations but less than adequate provision for the underemployed and, more seriously yet, the employed experts the region needs to retain a science lead. The argument against funding the work (a Treasury one) is that such provision ought to be near market and that there would be a welfare loss from public provision. That would be true if universities were tasked – and were expecting themselves – to compete with private training providers. Instead our role is to anticipate the development of new science based businesses and the evolution of existing sectors and to develop innovative new course structures for them – that in my view necessitates public goods provision and public, pump priming, funding. While the CPD Centre is an excellent example of how a university can do this without ongoing funding – and do so largely without loss – that is not proof that this provision should be regarded as near market enough to end public funding. *If I could*

*change one thing it would be to have the region take the development of
high level skills provision as seriously as it takes (through SEEDA and
the LSCs) the development of basic skills and level 1 and 2 attainment
levels.*

(Miles and Lawton Smith 2004)

Perhaps the most marked difference between Oxfordshire and Grenoble is
in the number of graduate students supervised by the national laboratories, reflecting the very different position occupied by these organizations
in France in the national innovation system. While UKAEA Culham
supervises a small number of graduate students, the number of graduates
supervised at Harwell fell sharply in the 1990s when the laboratory was
split and the largest component was privatized and moved into the commercial sector. A more important link to the economy was the training
provided under the apprenticeship programmes run by the UKAEA at
Harwell. These ended in 1993 with the closure of the nuclear reactors.
Until then, Harwell was a source of skilled people for other local organizations such as RAL, Esso Research, National Power etc. and for Oxfordshire companies such as Oxford Instruments (Lawton Smith 2003a).
Culham and RAL still train apprentices, who are often recruited by, for
example, the motorsport companies. A recent development is RAL's plan
to establish a technician training academy in collaboration with other
major employers in the county. For that to happen it will require funding
from the local Learning and Skills Council.

The entrepreneurial role

Oxford University is the UK's 'most entrepreneurial university' as judged
in a competition by Brainspark 2001 (see www.xacp.com/news_detail.
asp?news_id=82). Indications of Oxford University's increasingly entrepreneurial role are the growing numbers of patents, licences (though these
are small compared to some of the top US universities) and spin-off companies. Data from Oxford University Research Services Office reveals that
over the period 2000–3 the grand total of income from 34 licences
amounted to £10,230,059. Examples of licences include a licence to BTG
FactorIX protein and a licensing agreement with research sponsor Searle
Phamaceuticals in the year 2002–3 for £500,000, which took the total
income from licences to £1,399,384 in that year.

Since the 1980s, the university and its colleges have launched a series of
initiatives to increase entrepreneurial activity. They include Isis Innovation, the university's wholly owned technology transfer company established in 1988, the Oxford Science Park (1990), Entrepreneurship
Programmes at The Saïd Business School, Venturefest and Oxford
Consulting.

In March 2001, Oxford launched Oxford University Consulting, a wholly owned subsidiary that markets academic expertise. Contracts are already under negotiation with companies ranging from global enterprises to locally based start-ups. Academics are allowed to consult for 30 days per year.

Venturefest was created to bring together new innovators, entrepreneurs, managers and their potential sponsors. It gives scientists the opportunity to find out how to promote their ideas commercially. It has helped promote Oxford as a global centre for business innovation and development, which is underpinned by Oxford University's reputation as a world-class seat of learning. The event was developed in association with Oxford University's Saïd Business School and the Departments of Engineering, Chemistry, and Medicine. Dr Peter Johnson, University Lecturer in Business Development (then Visiting Fellow of Balliol College), originated Venturefest in 1999, and the event was first held in St Catherine's College in 1999. The intention to broaden the engagement with the local business community and research communities is reflected in the fact that the venues for 2001 and 2002 were Culham and RAL, and in 2004 and 2005 were on land owned by Unipart.

The Saïd Business School was established in 1996 and has since developed a number of initiatives to foster entrepreneurship. These include its teaching programmes and Oxford Science Enterprise Centre (OxSec). OxSec was established in 2001, part funded by the Office of Science and Technology and the University of Oxford, to encourage entrepreneurship amongst the science and technology communities in Oxford. It aims to encourage entrepreneurship by giving university members the vision and skills to deal with the reality of business. The most recent is Entrepreneurship Saïd established in 2005 to integrate the teaching, research and practice of entrepreneurship in Oxford University (www.science-enterprise.ox.ac.uk/html/Default.asp).

Isis Innovation

Isis Innovation did not become the driving force for commercialization of the university's research activities until 1997 with the appointment of Dr Tim Cook, a successful entrepreneur and business angel in his own right. Under his leadership, Isis Innovation has expanded and now has the largest number of commercialization staff of UK universities (Minshall and Wicksteed 2005) and has been very successful in attracting government as well as private funding for spin-off activities, being awarded funds from all of the major government programmes designed to increase the rate of university spin-offs. The success of Isis Innovation in managing the spin-offs process and patenting and licensing activities is indicated by Table 7.6. Box 7.2 gives the names of companies formed through Isis Innovation and some of the major firms which originated from Oxford University before Dr Cook's arrival and the refocusing of Isis Innovation.

The data shows that Oxford University generates three times as many as the UK average of two university spin-offs a year. Between 1998 and 2003, 33 firms formed through Isis Innovation had a combined market capitalization of over £308 million. In 2002, Isis estimated that the total market capitalization of spin-offs formed since 1988, including such firms as PowderJect and Oxford Asymmetry/Evotec OAI, had a combined value of £2 billion. By 2004, 37 spin-offs had been established through Isis Innovation, with a total job creation of some 5,000. Moreover, the survival rate is very high; very few of the spin-offs supported by Isis Innovation have failed. The table also shows the investment in spin-off companies and licensing activities.

Isis Innovation has been highly successful in attracting outside funding to support its enterpreneurship activities. Since 1997 Isis Innovation has raised £4 million from Universities Challenge Fund. Under this scheme, the University's £1 million was matched by £3 million from the Treasury, the Wellcome Trust and the Gatsby Foundation. In 1999 Oxford University established the Isis College Fund, making £10.7 million available to Oxford spin-offs in their second round of financing. In 2000 Isis Innovation set up the Isis Innovation Angels Network. By October 2000, 18 angels had signed up with £19 million in funds and 36 new applications. Isis has also won £300,000 from DTI Biotechnology Challenge Fund to establish BioForm, a dedicated unit for creation and growth of biotech firms.

Since 1997, the majority of companies formed through Isis Innovation

Table 7.6 Oxford University spin-offs

Year ended March	1999	2000	2001	2002	2003	5 years
University investment	£500,000	£1 million	£1 million	£1 million	£1 million	
Staff	9	17	21	23	34	
Projects	243	319	415	476	627	
Patents filed	51	55	63	82	65	316
Licences/options	18	21	36	42	71	188
New companies	3	6	8	8	7	33

Investment in spin-out companies	
Business Angel Start Up Investment	£25 million
Venture Capital Follow on Investment	£153 million
Total Capitalisation of Spin-outs	£308 million
Current University Equity in Spin-outs	£10.8 million

Oxford University Challenge Seed Fund	
Investment (Proof of Concept/Seed capital)	£4 million
Business Angels Co-investment	£21.4 million
Number of Projects	68
Licences	4
UCSF Equity holding in	21 companies

Source: www.isi-innovation.com/spinout/index.html

Box 7.2 Companies formed through Isis Innovation.

2003
Oxford Consultants for Social
    Inclusion Ltd
Riotech Ltd
ReOx Ltd
VASTox Ltd

2002
Oxford Risk Research and
    Analysis Ltd (ORRA)
BioAnalab Ltd
Oxford Immunotec Ltd
Oxitec Ltd
Glycoform Ltd
Zyentia Ltd
Spinox Ltd
Minervation Ltd
Pharminox Ltd

2001
Inhibox Ltd
NaturalMotion Ltd
Novarc Ltd
Oxford Ancestors Ltd
Oxford ArchDigital Ltd
OxLoc Ltd
The Oxford Bee Company

2000
MindWeavers Ltd
Mirada Solutions Ltd (now part
    of CTI Molecular Imaging Inc)
Oxford BioSensors Ltd
Oxford BioSignals Ltd
PharmaDM
ThirdPhase Ltd (now Cmed
    Technology Ltd)

1999
AuC Sensing Ltd
Avidex Ltd
Dash Technologies Ltd
Oxonica Ltd
Oxxon Pharmaccines Ltd

1998
Celoxica Ltd
Prolysis Ltd
Sense Proteomic Ltd (now Procognia
    Ltd)
Synaptica Ltd

Pre-1998
Opsys Ltd (now Cambridge Display
    Technology) (1997)
Oxagen Ltd (1997)
Oxford Biomedica Ltd (1996)
Oxford Gene Technology Ltd (1995)
PowderJect Pharmaceuticals Plc (now
    Chiron Corporation) (1993)
Oxford Asymmetry Int Plc (now Evotec
    OAI) (1992)
Oxford Molecular (now Accelrys Ltd)
    (1989)
Oxford Glycosciences Plc (1988)
Oxford Lasers Ltd (1977)
Oxford Instruments Plc (1959)

www.isis-innovation.com/spinout/index.html

have three characteristics in common: they are companies, they have Oxford University IP and are backed with non-public sector cash. However, using other definitions, including counting those formed by graduates of the university, many more companies have their origins in Oxford University. Examples include Littlemore Scientific Engineering founded in 1954 by Professor Edward Hall, Research Machines (computers) formed by Oxford graduate Mike Fischer and Cambridge graduate Mike O'Regan, in 1973, Sophos (anti-virus software) in 1985 and Powder-Ject in 1993 (vaccines, needless injection system) (acquired by Chiron in 2003). The most famous – and most successful in terms of employment – is Oxford Instruments, formed by Dr Martin Wood in 1959, then a Senior Research Officer in the Clarendon Laboratory. The company now employs around 2,000 people worldwide (Lawton Smith *et al.* 2003).

Some departments are more entrepreneurial than others. The Department of Chemistry, for example, has contributed over £40 million in cash to the University as a result of its spin-out activities. In addition it holds substantial equity in eight recent spin-outs. This return comes from the successes of Oxford Molecular and Oxford Asymmetry International, both of which had successful initial public offerings, floating on the London Stock Exchange, and later sold. In addition a novel partnership with IP2IPO Ltd (formerly Beeson Gregory) produced £20 million towards financing a new £60 million Chemistry Research Laboratory.

The IP2IPO partnership was described by the *Financial Times* as 'the way universities should be financed in the future'. Under this arrangement, in return for an upfront sum IP2IPO receives half of the university equity in Chemistry spin-outs and technology licences until 2015. The typical equity split in spin-outs is: founders 30 per cent; management 20 per cent; the university 25 per cent; and the academics 25 per cent. Since 2000, six new companies have been created: Inhibox; Pharminox; Zyentia; Glycoform; REOX; and Vastox. Close ties between the department, Isis and IP2IPO are maintained through the chairman of the department, Professor Graham Richards, who is a director of Isis Innovation and of IP2IPO Ltd (www.chem.ox.ac.uk/commercialisation.html).

A study by the current author (Lawton Smith and Glasson 2005) has identified 114 science and engineering based spin-offs from Oxfordshire's universities and public laboratories. Of these 12 are PLCs, the rest are limited companies. They collectively employ at a conservative estimate 9,000 people, about 3.5 per cent of the county's workforce, with a turnover of over £1 billion. Non-Oxford University spin-offs include Psion (UKAEA Culham) and Exitech (RAL).

Science parks

Oxford's first science park, the Oxford Science Park, opened in 1991 and is a joint venture between Magdalen College and the Prudential Assurance Company. It is home to over 50 companies, operating in computer hardware and software, bioscience and electronics, and Phase II of the Park's development is under way. The Oxford University Begbroke Science Park was opened in July 2000. The Park houses the industrial arm of the Department of Materials, and a number of companies have already established Technology Centres on site, funded by (amongst others) the Toppan Printing Company of Japan, Luxfer and Infineum. This science park hosts the University's Faraday Centre. The Begbroke Directorate, Oxford University Begbroke Science Park is sponsored by the Higher Education Innovative Fund (HEIF) set up by the Higher Education Funding Council for England (HEFCE). Its objective is to try to improve the interface between academic research and academic activities and business and commerce. It is the prototype of what the government would like to see in the way of third-leg funding. Initial funding has been extended under HEIF2 and HEIF3 programmes.

The Directorate specializes in high-tech engineering. It has established four institutes in high-tech aerospace automotive, environmental technologies and ICT. It currently comprises some 12 people. Of these, the Directorate employs three types of Enterprise Fellows whose task it is to engage in the process of improving the interface between the university and business and commerce. Industrial Research Fellows have a remit to spin out companies; Business Development Enterprise Fellows work with ISIS Innovation and help with the Industrial Research Fellows. The Directorate has a strong commitment to training and works closely with the CPD department. One of the two Knowledge Transfer Enterprise Fellows works directly for the Department of Continuing Education.

The territorial role

The institutional innovation support system in Oxfordshire until recently was primarily non-university-based and led by The Oxford Trust, a local charitable trust. The non-university activities form part of an interconnected set of initiatives to support high-tech industry in Oxfordshire, of which academic enterprise forms a part. They include the Oxfordshire Investment Opportunity Network (OION) and a number of incubators and science parks (see Waters and Lawton Smith 2002). Although locally led, most of the dedicated biotech initiatives are at least in part funded by central government. These include the Oxfordshire BiotechNet (established under the DTI's Biotechnology Mentoring and Incubation Challenge). Initially a network, it has established the Oxford BioBusiness Centre, Littlemore Park (on land owned by Yamanouchi Pharmaceuticals). Later the Oxford Bioscience Network (now based in Oxford Brookes University) was formed. The most recent, and the only one without central government funds, is The Oxford Trust's Biosciences Network, an initiative led by The Oxford Trust. Its steering group and specialist sub-groups are designed to bring local interests (academia, the government labs, industry and local government) together with a view to identifying the needs of the sector and identifying how they can be met. Even with the last, the local-research-to-innovation system is fragmented. While entrepreneurs, including academic entrepreneurs, might meet other local actors, there is no formal setting by which representatives from the universities, government laboratories and local authorities can meet with entrepreneurs to discuss local strategies. There is still no coherent overview of how the sector should be supported and by which organizations. This is clearly not the case in other locations, for example Boston (Cooke 2002).

Oxford University's territorial role became explicit in 1999 when Oxford University was awarded more than £1 million over four years from its bid to the Higher Education Funding Council for England's HEROBAC initiative. This funding enabled the university to set up a new post, the Regional Liaison Officer, to act as a 'one-stop service', forging stronger links with regional agencies and promoting the services which it can offer to meet business needs. The appointment underlines the university's commitment to play a more prominent part in local economic development (Oxford University Gazette 1999). An indication of how this works is that, in addition to being heavily involved in the management of Venturefest, the Head of the Regional Liaison Unit and Dr Tim Cook are both members of the Oxfordshire Economic Partnership's management board and are extensively involved in local networks (see Lawton Smith *et al.* 2005).

At the regional level, the RDA, SEEDA, is a partner in the Faraday Centre and, like others, its Economic Strategy articulates that it will encourage universities and industry to work together (seeda.org.uk). At this stage, it is difficult to see where in fact the RDA is making a difference. Moreover, in 2005, it made a decision to cease supporting the BioBusiness Incubator.

Conclusions

These two case studies illustrate how profound differences in national innovation systems and local/regional patterns of engagement lead to distinctive roles and functions of the universities and research laboratories within distributed innovation systems. Oxfordshire's and Grenoble's research bases have a similar number of scientists and engineers. Both have diverse specializations and comprise engagement at the highest levels within distributed innovation processes with an emphasis in both at the blue-sky end of the spectrum in the universities and government laboratories, but in Grenoble a greater emphasis on applied research. Biomedical research is of growing importance in both locations but defence activity is also a contributor to the profile of the research base. An increasing trend in both is the establishment of interdisciplinary research centres, particularly in biotechnology, but also in engineering sciences. In both places then, there is evidence of a plurality of engagement within an increasing range of actors in innovation processes.

The economic link, however, is much more direct in Grenoble – its research laboratories, and much more recently its universities, have been linked to firms in its hinterland through collaboration, courses and students. The city region has a long history of integrated innovation processes though regional consortia involving research and training. The territorial role is grounded in the nucleus of activity built by Professor Neel. The commercialization of research in Grenoble's research laboratories has been achieved through four main factors: (1) central government strategies with regard to the technology transfer function of laboratories such as LETI and INRIA; (2) a history of incubation activities dating back to the 1980s which include the involvement of SMEs; (3) the presence of national and international MNCs which have located in Grenoble to collaborate with the laboratories; and (4) since the early 1990s, a close relationship between the science base and the regional and local authorities. For the universities, the legal framework and incentives for entrepreneurial activity were not in place until the late 1990s. They, like the laboratories, particularly UJF and INPG, are actively involved in developing the networks of training which are the bedrock of technology-based economic development activity.

The Oxfordshire case illustrates how the degree of autonomy allowed to individual universities affects their overall strategy towards positioning within international research and research commercialization systems. For Oxford, the ability to respond to global challenges depends on prestige and ability to attract resources as well as internal cultures. Oxford's response to new agendas is to reposition itself towards competing in the global elite, moving towards research and away from its traditional undergraduate focus.

The case also illustrates how the national system, as in France, is crucial in the decisions made by individual organizations to adopt a territorially active role. Oxford University's territorial role would not have developed without national funding incentive structures. But also important was the person whom the university appointed to head Isis Innovation. In Dr Cook they appointed a man who has driven the commercialization strategy forward and who has been a prime mover in local networks that combine both the university and the business and government communities (see Lawton Smith 2003b). At the same time Oxford University's income from commercialization activities, other than spin-offs, is very small-scale compared to the major US research universities. Unlike in Grenoble, in Oxfordshire the research laboratories until recently have not been involved in stimulating local economic development and now only in a limited range of activities including science and technology parks, hosting Venturefest and training technicians. Far less attention is paid in Oxfordshire to how the universities' central function of teaching might be harnessed to further human capital development at the local level.

The greater autonomy of UK universities compared with those in France is reflected in Oxford University's rate of spin-off formation. In Grenoble institutional entrepreneurship is the dominant form of spin-off, largely from the research laboratories. University academics have only recently been 'encouraged' to be entrepreneurial. Moreover, the greater restrictions on researchers have led to a brain drain rather than to scientists staying local and enjoying dual incomes (university salaries and entrepreneur income). On the other hand, in both, state investment in the biosciences is having a notable impact on the growth in the number of firms in that sector.

National policies on the function of national laboratories have a major and differing impact on patterns of engagement with the local economy, for example in the case of the atomic energy laboratories. In France, the policy has been one of renewal of research in national and international scientific activities, keeping core strengths together, while at the same time there has been a strategy of spinning out new firms. As a consequence, many more firms have originated in the research laboratories in Grenoble than in Oxfordshire. The sudden change in UK government policy in the early 1990s, which brought about the removal of the research function of the Harwell laboratory, considerably reduced the size of the science base and that of the training element – the supervision of doctoral students. Moreover, Oxfordshire's laboratories, unlike those in Grenoble, have had no remit to work with local SMEs and therefore have not in this way increased local innovation capacity. Nor, in the absence of a concentration of large foreign high-tech firms, is there the likelihood of linkage arising from geographical coincidence through either collaboration or recruitment of the post-graduate cohort as in Grenoble. On the other hand, there is an increasing availability of property on business and sciences parks on the sites of the Harwell and Culham laboratories. While this may act as a means of encouraging firms to stay in the county, it does not in itself add to the skill base – a crucially important component of any innovation system. Finally, and most important, the major difference between Grenoble and Oxfordshire is the scale of operations in the former that involve collaboration between the universities, research laboratories and industry – and the regional and city authorities. Hence the territorial role is part of the system of governance.

8 Stanford, Louisville and Princeton

Introduction

The three case study universities in this chapter – Stanford on the west coast, Louisville in one of the Southern states (Kentucky) and Princeton on the east coast – occupy very different positions within the US national and state/regional systems of innovation. Stanford and Princeton are both private universities but come from very different traditions. Stanford is often described as the driving force for Silicon Valley's evolution, while Princeton, an 'Ivy League university', although famous for its undergraduate teaching and research, has come very late to its territorial role. Louisville is a relatively unknown university in a state that is famous for the Kentucky Derby and the 'Louisville Lip' (Mohammed Ali) but which is interesting in this context because of the 'Bucks for Brains' programme designed to stimulate economic growth through its universities. Each of the three illustrates responses to changing political agendas in which the territorial role is increasingly prioritized at state, but not necessarily at the national, level. The chapter proceeds by identifying student and research profiles of the three universities and then takes each case study in turn beginning with the west coast and moving east.

The universities, student populations and sources of income

The student bodies differ considerably by size, ratio of undergraduates to graduates and in recruitment patterns. These three combined represent considerable differences in the way each university functions within distributed innovation systems and with their territories. Louisville has the largest student population and Princeton much the smallest, with around a third of Louisville's students. Reflecting its research orientation, Stanford has more graduate students than undergraduates, the reverse of the ratio at the two other universities. Princeton has a higher ratio of graduate students to undergraduates than Louisville (Table 8.1). Princeton and Stanford have a far stronger orientation to research than Louisville, hence the potential for research engagement with industry.

Table 8.1 Student numbers, Stanford, Louisville and Princeton Universities: 2002–3

	Undergraduates	*Post-graduates*	*Total*
Stanford	6,654	7,800	14,454
Princeton	4,635	1,997	6,632
Louisville	14,475	4,764	21,089
		Professional degrees	
		1,850	

Sources: University websites.

This orientation is further demonstrated by the pattern of income. Stanford and Louisville represent the extremes of research income, research standing, endowment income and degrees of accountability to their respective states. Stanford is one of the top ten research universities in the US, ranked eighth in the list of the top 100 academic institutions in R&D expenditures in 2001. Princeton was 80th, reflecting its small size, and Louisville was not in the list at all (NSF 2002). Stanford is ranked second (behind Harvard) in a recent world ranking of the top 500 universities (see Chapter 1). While Stanford and Princeton are major players in international and national innovation systems, Louisville is much more embedded in a regional innovation system, receiving a higher percentage of state funding for research than either of the other two (7.2 per cent). Stanford receives 1 per cent and Princeton 2 per cent. Overall, the University of Louisville receives 38 per cent state appropriation, 18 per cent tuition fees, 9 per cent money from endowments. The rest is related to grants, contracts, medical school, and clinical dollars. Sources of income are shown in Table 8.2.

One of the major differences between European universities and those in the US is in the endowments that are used for research. Stanford has endowment of $8.6 billion, which yielded $28,275,787 of non-athletic endowment income in 2003–4. Louisville's total endowment rose from $183 million in 1995 to $492 million in 2002–3. In comparison, Oxford University's 36 colleges have combined assets of £1.6 billion ($2.2 billion) St John's College, the richest, has assets of £202 million ($282.8 million) and The university has endowments of £424 million ($593.6 million).

Table 8.2 Stanford, Louisville and Princeton Universities' income sources: 2002–3 ($ million)

	All sources	*Federal*	*State/local*	*Industry*	*Academic institutions*	*Other*
Stanford	483	384.00	5.0	35.0	31	27
Princeton	149	79.00	3.0	8.0	42	17
Louisville	115	53.67	8.3	5.7	14	–

Source: NSF and University of Louisville website.

Stanford University

Silicon Valley is located on California's San Francisco peninsula and radi-
ates outward from Stanford University. It is bounded by San Francisco
Bay on the east, the Santa Cruz mountains on the west and the Coast
Range to the south east (Tajnai 1996). At the start of the twentieth
century, California's Santa Clara County was an agricultural economy.
Stanford University was founded on 8,800 acres of land donated in the
early 1890s by Leland and Jane Stanford, who specified that it could not be
sold. The standard story of Stanford is that it played a major territorial
role in developing Silicon Valley, and that Frederick Terman, who was the
first chair of electrical engineering, then Dean of engineering and who
started a series of initiatives at Stanford University which Etzkowitz
(2003) sees as exemplifying the stage-wise institutional evolution of academic enterprise, was a major driving force. Recent re-evaluations have suggested a complex picture that dates back to the early part of the twentieth
century (see Lenoir *et al.* 2002) and suggested that Terman's role was
replicated across the US (Moore and Davis 2001). (Gordon E. Moore is
one of Silicon Valley's founding fathers. He was one of the 'Traitorous
Eight' who left Shockley Semiconductor to start Fairchild Semiconductor
in 1958. He was also co-founder of Intel.)

Distributed innovation systems

To begin this case study, two quotes from Lenoir *et al.* (2002) summarize
their view of the interdependent relationship between Stanford University, the Federal government and industry, showing not only how different
actors interact within distributed innovation systems but also how their
roles change over time.

> We view Stanford as perhaps the paradigm case of a university deeply
> integrated into networks of mutually beneficial, symbiotic exchange
> with industry, forming what might be characterized as a university-
> regional innovation complex. The flows of influence and dependence
> have been both ways: Stanford has contributed to the emergence of
> Silicon Valley through the flow of people, ideas, and technology. On
> the other hand Stanford has also been profoundly shaped by Silicon
> Valley. Through connections with industry Stanford research pro-
> grams have been pushed toward new frontiers. Silicon Valley has con-
> tributed to Stanford by providing funds for research, by posing
> research questions that push the boundaries of fields such as materials
> science, microprocessor architectures, and database design, and by the
> movement of technology, technical know-how, and people from
> industry to the University.
> Even preliminary discussions made it clear that Stanford has played

different roles at different times in the rise of Silicon Valley and that Stanford has developed different types of relations with the Valley's high-tech sectors. In some industries, such as microwave component and system manufacturing or biotechnology, the University played a major role in educating key scientists, engineers and entrepreneurs who made major innovations such as the klystron and nuclear magnetic resonance instrumentation. In other industries, such as semiconductors, Stanford initially played a more modest role, acting more as the recipient than as the initiator of incentives for new lines of research.

The origins of Silicon Valley go back to the early part of the twentieth century. Sturgeon (2000) argues that a Stanford graduate, Cyril Ellwell, who founded the Poulsen Wireless Telephone and Telegraph Company in 1909, had more influence on the origins of Silicon Valley than Frederick Terman. In his account, Silicon Valley grew out of the area's amateur radio community in the first three decades of the twentieth century. Partly because of its strong maritime orientation, starting in the 1900s and 1910s, the Bay Area was one of the largest centres for amateur radio in the US. The local hobbyist community produced technologists and entrepreneurs who set up vacuum tube and radio system corporations – such as Heintz and Kaufman, Eitel-McCullough (Eimac) and Litton Engineering. In the postwar period, the electronics manufacturing complex on the Peninsula was shaped by subsequent groups of entrepreneurs and technologists in semiconductors and computing. These groups, who predated Terman, came from the east and had, at first, little to do with the University. In time, this industry recruited Stanford graduates who 'installed and maintained technology imported from the eastern United States and supplemented it with their own inventions and products' (Etzkowitz 2003).

Moore and Davis (2001, 2) are equally less certain of the key role of the University in innovation and economic development, attributing the central element in the Valley's trajectory to 'the founding of a previously unknown type of regional, dynamic, high technology economy'. They argue that its success lies in a progression of effort, discovery and learning. In particular they argue that the university's scientists learning to be managers and the evolution of the technologist manager have been critical in this process.

Sandelin (2002), on the other hand, finds institutional factors to be important. He argues that the relationships such as those developed by the Office of Technology Licensing and other proactive efforts are linked to the success of technology transfer and formation of university-linked start-up companies. He supports this claim by providing evidence of considerable and diverse funding for corporate Stanford, for activities relating to income for training, industry-funded research and, above all, from gifts to the university. In the fiscal year 1999–2000, revenue to Stanford totalled

$172 million. The breakdown shows that Stanford does not receive huge amounts of industry income directly for sponsored research – only $42.1 million came in industry-sponsored research – but industry does pay for training on a large scale. Some $11.3 million came from company subscriptions to the Stanford Center for Professional Development and $17.7 million from Industry Affiliate Programs. The largest amounts come from gifts. While $64 million came in donations and gifts through Stanford's Office of Development, total donations in that year exceeded $300 milllion, with a higher proportion from wealthy individuals.

Quality versus quantity

U.S. News and World Report (2004) ranked Stanford second to MIT only in overall quality in US universities. The Report's college rankings place four Stanford engineering departments/programmes in the top two: aeronautics & astronautics (ranked top), computer science and mechanical engineering (both ranked second), and the environmental engineering programme within the civil and environmental engineering department (ranked top) (see soe.stanford.edu/about/facts.html). This quality is arguably a legacy of Terman's philosophy, that quality of research is based on extremely talented people, and the institutionalization of that philosophy under the leadership of the university's president J. E. Wallace Sterling from 1955 to 1965 'led to Stanford experiencing unprecedented growth in national academic prominence and prestige' (Lenoir *et al.* 2002).

Lenoir *et al.* (2002) describe in detail the 'Terman model' of 'steeple building' – that is building academic 'steeples of excellence' by bringing on and utilizing the talent of others while retaining a high degree of independence from industry sponsors. Although government grants and contracts were used to finance the growth of faculty research, Terman pursued what he termed 'salary splitting'. The strategy was to pay for half of the salary of a new faculty member from grants and contracts. Research associates and other personnel working on sponsored projects would be entirely covered from contract funds. In addition, building expansions and equipment would be funded on contract. His primary goal was to build the premier research programme in electronics (or other potential 'steeples of excellence'). This was to be accomplished by getting the very best talent in the field and building a graduate programme around them – which was as important as any other component of the programme. Terman's approach was that, instead of receiving research funds to pursue specific problems defined by a sponsor, he wanted both government and industry to invest funds in the research directions defined by the core faculty of the lab. Even with industry funding, Terman rejected funds for specific applied industry problems in favour of funds to pursue a general research direction of interest to a company. A company funding the research would have privileged access but not exclusive rights to the research results.

Defence and biotechnology

Defence research was crucial in Stanford's expansion in the Terman era. Terman used defence money to leverage the growth, first of electrical engineering, then at the School of Engineering when he became dean, and then used broader Federal funds in very similar ways to leverage the growth of other parts of the University after he became provost (see Rosenweig 1998 in Lowen 1998). In the 1950s and 1960s the Engineering School accounted for the largest sector of government grants and contracts. Within the Engineering School, electrical engineering was the major recipient of government funding, around 90 per cent in the mid-1960s, falling gradually to around 70 per cent in the 1980s in the post-Vietnam period, when roughly 80 per cent of the operating budget for electrical engineering was covered from grants and contracts. The percentage of the operating budget covered from grants and contracts to the Hansen Labs and the Electronics Lab was between 90 and 98 per cent in this period. After the Cold War, funding for the research programme was replaced by industry, including local industry (Lécuyer 2002). Moore and Davis (2001), however, do not find the Stanford story exceptional. They argue that while it is true that some electronics firms did grow out of this defence-related university research and the San Francisco Bay Area did find itself home to a growing electronics industry, the clustering of science-based firms around universities was common throughout the country. Likewise other universities set up industrial parks and Terman's own efforts were replicated in other places around the country.

From the 1980s, the Engineering School experienced an intensification of its relations with industry and more specifically with Silicon Valley – in a variety of ways. The main impetus for this reorientation was industrial grants and contracts, which represented a few percents of the school's research budget in the late 1970s and grew roughly to 10 per cent of its total research funding at the end of the 1990s. Much of this funding was funnelled through new organizational mechanisms such as consortia. These consortia, which pooled funding from a number of industrial firms, supported several research groups. Examples of these consortia include the Center for Integrated Systems, the Stanford Institute for Manufacturing Automation, the Center for Telecommunications and the Center for Photonics. Later medical sciences and biotechemistry research became the fastest-growing areas and appeared to have followed the Terman model (Lenoir and Ueyama 2002). They find that whereas faculty research might have pursued any number of new areas, rather than pursuing, for example, work on drosophila or other organisms, Stanford biochemists and molecular biologists focused on problems related to human genetics and molecular medicine. Their preliminary interviews have pointed to discussions in numerous faculty meetings at the end of the 1970s where programmatic decisions of this sort were discussed – and not without dissent.

Moreover, concerns about orienting the work of the department toward technology transfer are also reported to have been hotly debated in these meetings.

Lenoir and Ueyama (2002) argue that a crucial element in transforming the medical school was the founding of the biochemistry and genetics departments. The departments of radiology, biochemistry, and genetics all fit the Terman model in the style of their growth. As prime recipients of government funding, particularly from the NIH and NSF, these departments were the first medical school departments to finance their growth and operating budgets almost entirely from government grants. They also evolved important relations with industry and made extensive use of the Honors Cooperative Program in building teaching components of their programmes directly linked to the emerging biotech industry.

The shift from defence to life science research as a source of research funding and commericalization activities has been dramatic. Rosenberg and Colyvas (2002) find that the Academic Medical Center (AMC) is now the dominant contributor, within the Stanford University research community, to technological innovation. The reason for this focus is straightforward. They point out that whereas in 1970 one-eighth of the patents issued to universities were for biomedical inventions, by 1990 the percentage had doubled. Currently, over 60 per cent of all university licences are based upon biomedical invention and the dominant source of patent royalties.

Accountability

Even within Stanford, misgivings exist about the economic and territorial role that universities are expected to assume. For example, Donald Kennedy, President Emeritus of Stanford and a professor of biological sciences, was quoted in 1994 at a conference at Stanford University: 'The universities have been cast in a very utilitarian role in recent years ... It's widely believed by universities and their regents that if only they did the right thing, they could be the next Silicon Valley, I think that's heavily overstated and there's going to be deep disappointment in universities when it doesn't happen'.

Moreover, Tornatzky *et al.* (2002, 160) find that Stanford's relationships with industry in the past were not well managed and that problems over accountability and responsibility were rife. They cite a 1995 faculty study of industry relationships in medical sciences. This reported 'a growing mistrust ... [based on] perceived differences in motives and mission that are not based on fact'. It said that Stanford was perceived as one of the worst American universities to deal with, especially on the topic of ownership/patent status of intellectual property. Subsequently, the Office of Technology Licenses (OTL) was given responsibility for managing industry-sponsored research, which improved organizational efficiency. He does, however, find that the position on intellectual property rights at Stanford increases flexibility missing in other universities.

The policy on IP at Stanford – as generally in the US – is for the university to claim ownership:

> As a general proposition, the University's patent policy requires that all potentially patentable inventions conceived or reduced to practice in whole or in part by members of the faculty or staff (including student employees) of the University in the course of their University responsibilities or with more than incidental use of University resources be disclosed on a timely basis to the University. Title to such inventions is assigned to the University, regardless of the source of funding, if any. Inventors may place their inventions in the public domain if they believe that would be in the best interest of technology transfer and if doing so is not in violation of the terms of any agreements that supported or related to the work (http://www.stanford.edu/dept/DoR/rph/5-1.html).

Massification of education and the teaching role

As already indicated, an important feature of Stanford's link to its expansion through its engagement with Silicon Valley is the postwar expansion of lucrative graduate education programmes both in technical education and more recently in business and management. Lécuyer (2002) argues that professional education is arguably Stanford's most significant contribution to Silicon Valley from the mid-1950s to the late 1970s. More recently the Stanford Graduate School of Business has played a significant role in the evolution of Silicon Valley (Rowen and Sheehan 2002).

Lécuyer (2002) argues that Stanford's professional education programmes found their origin in the educational demands of the local tube, instrumentation and communication industries during the Korean War. In the early 1950s, Hewlett-Packard, Sylvania and other electronics corporations on the Peninsula put considerable pressure on the university to set up evening programmes in electronics for their rapidly growing workforce. At first, Terman resisted these demands on the ground that evening courses would provide an education of dubious quality and be detrimental to the school's prestige. But, as the pressure grew intense, he allowed engineers working at local firms to take regular classes at the university on a part-time basis. This proved to be a mistake. The University experienced a large influx of industrial students. These students far outnumbered regular students in most electronics courses. They proved also to be costly, as tuition did not cover the cost of their education.

To solve these problems and at the same time serve the needs of local firms, in 1954 Terman set up the Honors Cooperative Program, a graduate course of study intended to train the most talented research and development engineers in industry. Under this programme, co-operating firms nominated employees for admission to the university. While Stanford theoretically had the final say on their selection, in practice the university seems to have followed the firms' recommendations. Students obtained a master's degree in two years (they could also work for a PhD degree). The programme was particularly remunerative for the university. Industrial students paid double the normal tuition. In addition to the regular tuition, firms paid a matching fee of a similar amount to the university. In order to ensure a steady income stream, Stanford instituted a quota system whereby each firm had to commit itself for a specific number of units over a period of five years. These steady revenues helped the School of Engineering create twenty faculty positions between 1954 and 1974. Hewlett-Packard, the Stanford Research Institute and the local branches of Sylvania and the General Electric Corporation (GE) were the first firms to participate in the programme. Within a few years, the programme attracted a substantial number of electronics and aerospace firms in Silicon Valley. By the early 1970s, more than 30 firms sponsored honours co-operative students, in order to provide training and to address recruitment problems by attracting top students with the offer of free places. Lécuyer (2002) finds that by 1974 the programme had enrolled approximately 2,000 students a year from local industrial firms and had granted graduate degrees to some 1,500 engineers in local industry.

Yet Moore and Davis (2001, 11) find that the Honors Cooperative Program was secondary in importance to the opportunities that semiconductors represented and that 'the size of the opportunity and the learning about firm-building and market building that took place in the semiconductor industry would have overcome a less welcoming environment'. Although they find that Stanford's main role in the industry was to produce students of outstanding quality, they argue that, 'In a country with such mobile labour markets as the US, the local presence of a university seems hardly to have been a necessity'. In sum their conclusion is that the best way to think of the primary role of the university in this and other regional high-technology economies is 'as an economic institution responsive to the manpower and intellectual needs of the marketplace' (page 12). They argue that Stanford has been exemplary in responding to the needs of the industrial community, and that the synergistic relationship increased in the 1990s so that large numbers of advanced degree scientists and engineers work directly in the Valley.

The Stanford Graduate School of Business was established in 1925 at the instigation of Herbert Hoover, later President of the US. Hoover had decried the lack of management education on the west coast and, in an entrepreneurial act for the times, proposed starting a business school at Stanford. He enlisted the aid of his business friends to raise the money and open the School (www.gsb.stanford.edu/news/about_us.html). In the postwar period it developed a reputation as an analytical powerhouse but posed an obstacle for its ability to address the highly entrepreneurial types of Silicon Valley firms (Rowen and Sheehan 2002). They report that this changed after the mid-1980s. In 1985 there were two or three such courses while in 2000–1 there were 17, comprising around one-third of second-year course-hours. The GSB has not been alone in the university in offering courses on entrepreneurship; other schools such as Engineering, Medical and Law offer courses. The Center for Entrepreneurial Studies was established in 1996 with the mission of supporting research, curriculum development and student programmes on entrepreneurship and venture capital and the entrepreneurial activities of alumni and students.

The entrepreneurial role

Rather than the entrepreneurial role at Stanford being recent, in the 1930s the university took steps to formalize a system by which the intellectual property generated in the university and in firms related to the university was held by the university as a common commercial resource. A number of significant electronic devices, with theoretical as well as practical implications for the study of electrons and radar systems, were invented in the physics and electrical engineering departments just before the Second World War. Etzkowitz (2003) points out that, 'rather than the patent positions being split among competing firms and used to exclude access, the university served as a repository of economically commercially useful knowledge that was made available to all firms in the region'.

Defence research played a major role in the expansion of entrepreneurial activity in the postwar period. In 1945 the microwave lab began as a division of the Physics Department. The new centre built upon Stanford's prewar work in electronics and much funding came from Federal research funds. At this time Terman initiated a three-pronged financial strategy that included accessing federal funds for defence-related research, making contracts with industry in exchange for access to research results, and the development of university land. Federally funded research centres were also expanded with industrial support. Stanford entered into an agreement with the GE to build an extension of the microwave lab. In return, GE received first rights to the Stanford patents from the linear accelerator, the right to call upon Stanford researchers for assistance in accelerator design, and office space at the university so that its representatives could closely monitor developments.

Sharpe (1991) identified that it took the Korean War in the early 1950s to transform this academic empire into big business. In light of the national emergency, the military services reviewed their university contracts and decided to complement selected programmes with applied (and classified) contracts. Stanford, already high on the list for its contributions to travelling wave tubes (TWT) and high-power klystron studies, received $300,000 (subsequently increased to $450,000) a year for translating its basic research into practical devices and systems (Etzkowitz 2003). In seeking to further capitalize on Stanford expertise, GE and Sylvania, as well as other companies, set up microwave tube divisions near campus and often hired Stanford faculty and graduates to staff them. Former students became heads of these divisions, while others went into business for themselves. By 1960 one-third of the nation's $40 million annual TWT business (virtually all of it for defence) was located near to the university.

It was not until 1955 that semiconductors became a major sector in what was to become the Silicon Valley area, and it was in this field that entrepreneneurship grew rapidly. The start of the solid state era is attributed to Terman, who wrote a letter to transistor inventor William Shockley at Bell Laboratories to invite him to participate in 'independent research and development activity in transistors' near Stanford. In this letter, Terman told Shockley about the university's objectives and of all the benefits of being located nearby. William Shockley, who would share the Nobel Prize in 1956 for the invention of the transistor, recruited Robert Noyce, Gordon Moore, Jean Hoerni and others to set up Shockley Semiconductor in Palo Alto. In 1957 eight of Shockley's recruits left to form Fairchild Semiconductor (www.stanford.edu/dept/OOD/CORPREL/maximize.html).

The Stanford Industrial Park, the US's and the world's first university-owned science park, founded in 1951, is an indicator of the entrepreneurial activity connected to Stanford University. It was made possible by the original bequest of land. The idea of the park developed when Varian Associates, which had its origins in the university, made a proposal to the university to build its facility on university land in order to be close to faculty and facilities in the university. Terman enthusiastically supported this development. Subsequently the university developed an 800-acre park later entitled the Stanford Research Park (Tornatzky *et al.* 2002). By 1962, the park had 25 companies on site (Saxenian 1994), and there were 140 companies employing 23,000 staff in electronics, software, biotechnology and other research fields in 2003 (www.stanford.edu/home/stanford/facts/lands.html).

The existence of the park, which illustrates a demand for sites for entrepreneurs, and the evidence on the number of university spin-offs, suggests that a culture of enterprise had been established in the university by the 1970s. From 1971 to 1993 over 300 full-time surviving companies had been founded by members of the university community (Leone *et al.* 1993 in Tajnai 1996). In the last several decades, over 1,200 full-time companies have been founded by members of the Stanford University community including Hewlett-Packard, Cisco Systems and Yahoo! – three top Silicon Valley companies founded or co-founded by those with a current or former affiliation with Stanford University, as an alumnus or alumna or faculty or staff. In FY 2001, the largest companies on the list were responsible for generating 42 per cent ($106.3 billion) of the total revenue of the Silicon Valley 150 – an annual list of the largest Silicon Valley firms. And as a group, the Stanford-affiliated companies experienced a loss ($9 billion) that represented 10 per cent of the aggregate loss of the Silicon Valley 150 companies (www.stanford.edu/group/wellspring/). It is important to note that, on an individual basis, there were many firms on the list that reported income rather than loss for 2001. The Stanford-founded companies on the list had a total market capitalization of $332.5 billion, or 36 per cent of the total market capitalization of the Silicon Valley 150 firms. Table 8.3 contains a ranking of the top companies founded or co-founded by Stanford affiliates, in descending order of revenue.

Rowen and Sheehan (2002), however, are cautious about this data and have a number of reservations. They find that the number of start-ups from Stanford is impossible to calculate accurately. Three main problems exist. The first is the definition of Silicon Valley – given that the university's research and teaching activities are not geographically bounded. Second, defining a 'Stanford' start-up or product is problematic given that most companies and ideas for products have multiple sources. The third is causation. For example, does the high level of entrepreneurship exhibited by GSB graduates during the 1990s reflect changes in the School, changes in the character of the students or increased opportunities in the Valley? The authors conclude that some combination of these has been involved. They found that, of the founders listed as graduates of Stanford on the Wellspring of Innovation website, 379 hold an MBA from Stanford; many of these also hold bachelor's degrees and/or JDs or MDs from Stanford. Nevertheless, they noted that GSB graduates who started a company within four years after graduating comprise the majority of the site's listing for alumni from that School.

Territorial role

In the Stanford model the university does not give preference or actively seek local licences (Tornatzky *et al.* 2002, 162). He argues that in practice, however, strong ties between Stanford faculty and students and local businesses meant that 'a strong regional market exists for new inventions'. Moreover, the pattern is for start-ups to remain in the state, reinforcing those strong ties. He also reported that Stanford was found to be an exemplar of a university which actively participated in local economic development (see Chapter 5).

The Stanford University Office of Technology Licensing (OTL), however, has a societal role as well as just that of commercialization. Sandelin (2002, 39–53) reviews its history. He finds that its mission from the beginning has been to promote the transfer of Stanford technology for society's use and benefit while generating unrestricted income to support research and education. Thus, the primary focus of OTL has not been to maximize income generation but to facilitate putting into use for society's

Table 8.3 Ranking of the top companies founded or co-founded by Stanford affiliates

Company	Revenues 2001 ($ million)	Net income 2001 ($ million)	Market cap on 28 March 2002 ($ million)
Hewlett-Packard	44,211.0	751.0	34,855.0
Cisco Systems	18,290.0	−2,294.0	123,953.1
Sun Microsystems	14,059.0	−563.0	28,651.1
Agilent	7,257.0	−241.0	16,216.5
SGI	1,684.5	−405.0	836.4
Electronic Arts	1,562.2	36.3	8,765.7
Atmel	1,472.3	−418.3	4,735.2
Cadence Design	1,430.4	141.3	5,664.5
Intuit	1,372.4	−48.1	8,158.8
Nvidia	1,371.4	177.1	6,413.3
Adobe Systems	1,168.6	185.7	9,531.8
Maxim Integrated	1,111.4	211.6	18,152.6
Symantec	1,011.3	−60.4	5,861.8
BEA Systems	975.9	−35.7	5,503.3
Network Appliance	819.3	−4.3	6,804.0
Cypress Semiconductor	819.2	−407.4	2,809.2
Varian Medical Systems	787.3	71.7	2,755.8
Rational Software	751.4	−57.7	3,077.2
Varian	751.2	46.1	1,268.6
eBay	748.8	90.4	15,829.0
Yahoo	717.4	−92.8	10,989.2
Read-Rite	659.8	18.9	369.7
Aspect Communications	449.4	−151.8	205.1
Extreme Networks	444.5	−128.1	1,191.8
Silicon Storage	294.0	−29.0	964.0
Ariba	293.9	−2,494.3	1,194.6
Mattson Technology	230.1	−336.7	264.5
Affymetrix	224.9	−33.1	1,679.0
Incyte Genomics	219.3	−183.2	790.2
ONI Systems	195.7	−188.3	873.4
Dionex	184.3	29.4	521.2
Actel	145.6	−4.7	496.6
E.piphany	125.7	−2,609.4	538.2
SonicWall	112.0	−20.9	861.9
Zoran	107.7	−36.1	778.5
Rambus	107.3	24.4	781.3
Net.com	101.9	−48.6	113.9
Totals	106,272.1	−9,104.0	332,456.1

Source: www.stanford.edu/group/wellspring/economic.html.

benefit the innovations developed at Stanford. Thus, the OTL accepts and invests in inventions that may have small income potential but nevertheless will bring incremental value to the public. For example, while the OTL accepts and pursues over one-third of the invention disclosures it receives, the for-profit Research Corporation Technologies (a licensing agent for a large number of universities) accepts less than 5 per cent.

The OTL also engages in a number of activities that are not income-generating, such as serving on committees, assisting in policy formulation and reviews and providing advice and consultation on intellectual property questions from members of the Stanford community. When the OTL was established in FY 1969–70, it was agreed that 15 per cent of gross revenue would be allocated to offset costs of operation. Using this measure of financial breakeven, the cumulative 15 per cent amounts did not exceed total costs until FY 1988–9, or 19 years from the formation of the OTL. By FY 2000–1, the cumulative total had reached over $45 million. This surplus has been used to cover patent cost write-offs to fund the OTL Research Incentive Fund, to fund invention enhancement via the Birdseed and Gap Funds and for other uses as determined by the Dean of Research. In FY 1981–2, the software distribution centre (SDC) was formed. It served as a place where faculty could arrange for the distribution of software they had created and which others were requesting. This software was offered 'at cost' to non-profit organizations, and for a modest fully paid royalty to for-profit organizations. It also encouraged the submission of invention disclosures for software programs that had potential for licensing to third parties, such third parties then to develop commercial versions (with useful documentation) for sale to end customers and with royalty payments to the OTL based on product sales. It should be noted that this effort resulted in a number of software licences (with copyright and sometimes affiliated trademark protection, but no patents) which have total royalties in excess of $1 million.

The benefits to Stanford resulting from the formation and operation of the OTL have been many. By the end of FY 2000–1, the OTL had received total revenues of $496 million and had total expenses of $29 million. Revenue from the DNA invention accounted for $255 million, and this was shared equally with the University of California as their faculty member, Herbert Boyer, was a co-inventor with Stanford's Stanley Cohen. Genetech, the world's first biotech company, was founded in 1976 to exploit this technology. Since its establishment, OTL has distributed over $300 million to inventors and to support research and education at the university. Royalty growth in the early years was, compared to later years, relatively modest – from $55,000 in the first year to $655,000 in FY 1980. During this period, there were no significant earned royalties from product sales. Typical was the FM sound synthesis invention licensed to Yamaha in 1974, where product introduction, and thus earned royalties, did not start until 1984. Eventually this invention produced over $22 million in royalties, but most of this amount came in the late 1980s and early 1990s.

A very few inventions produced most of the royalties, and, with the exception of the Yamaha licence, the vast majority of royalty income came from medical-related inventions. Medical industries tend to have products with relatively large gross margins that can afford an earned royalty and still produce acceptable profits. These industries also do not have the patent proliferation that exists in some other industries (e.g. consumer electronics or computer products) where many patents may have to be licensed to market a product. While income from the RDNA licences comprised the largest share of royalties, non-RDNA royalties also grew during the decade FY 1991–2001 (from $8.4 million to $38.6 million).

An incident at Harvard University in the early 1980s resulted in a policy that Stanford would not take equity in a start-up company where Stanford people had any involvement. The incident was the formation of a biotech company by some Harvard people virtually within the university, apparently using university resources for the benefit of the start-up company. This caused Stanford's President to call a conference of university presidents at the Pajaro Dunes Conference Center, the result of which was a strong statement that universities should not be providing resources for start-up companies or acquiring equity that might create conflict-of-interest situations. This policy remained in effect at Stanford until 1992, and resulted in almost no equity from the licensing of start-up companies.

Since 1992, the policy has shifted, to where in 2001 the OTL was encouraged to take equity when licensing start-up companies. Of about 75 start-up companies providing equity to the OTL, 36 were in the period 2001–3. This may reflect the change in policy in 1998. Prior to 1998, all proceeds from the sale of equity went to a graduate student fellowship fund. None went to the OTL or to the inventors, whose goodwill and support is so crucial to the success of the OTL. For the OTL, this created a very difficult dilemma when negotiating a licence to a start-up and balancing taking cash versus taking equity as the licence issue fee. Clearly it was in the best interest of the inventors to take cash over equity and there was even the possibility of legal action by inventors if a significant amount of income was at stake – because, if they chose to take equity instead of cash, both the OTL 15 per cent and the inventor's one-third share would disappear. The policy changed in 2001. From that year, the OTL has been encouraged to take equity when licensing start-up companies. Now OTL and the inventors receive the proceeds from equity as if it was cash. The change produced immediate results. Of some 75 start-up companies providing equity to the OTL, 36 were in the period 2001–3.

Louisville, Kentucky

Louisville and the Kentucky 'Bucks for Brains' programme

The case of Kentucky provides an example of a state harnessing its universities' research and teaching activities as a key element in its economic strategy. Its strategy is driven by political will, and hype and hope (Glasner 2004) abound. There are interesting parallels with the strategy adopted by Georgia, another Southern state, with a strategy preceding that of Kentucky (see Tornatzky *et al.* 2002, Shapira 2005b). (The Georgia Research Alliance has helped endow 37 eminent scholars at one of Georgia's universities. The emphasis is on hiring individuals with an industrial background and often with an entrepreneurial orientation (Tornatzky *et al.* 2002, 22).)

The University of Louisville can date its history to 1798 with the establishment of an early medical school but it is 50 years old in modern guise. It began as a private university, part city-funded, until 1972, when there were financial problems, as a result of which it became part of the state system. From 1997, the university, along with Kentucky's other universities, became part of the state's new regional development strategy.

There are two stories about the Louisville economy. The first is that it is an economy in crisis. The second is that it is the most entrepreneurial location in the US and that Kentucky's universities will be the driving force for its new economic prosperity. The 'Bucks for Brains' programme is funding research but it is not clear how this will translate into economic development given the unpromising context. Louisville was ranked 45th out of 49 metropolitan areas (populations of over one million) in Florida's creativity index (see Florida 2002).

First the bad news. In 2003 the City of Louisville and Jefferson county consolidated to form the 16th largest city in America with nearly 700,000 people. Louisville is the economic driver of the state. Over a quarter of the state population lived in Jefferson county. It is an economy based on manufacturing, distribution and healthcare. Trucks are made in Louisville in two Ford plants which employ 9,800 people. Georgetown has Toyota. Other major manufacturers include GE, also employing 9,800 people – making dishwashers and refrigerators although manufacturing has been moved overseas. In the 1980s the company employed 25,000 people. UPS, which has its main hub in Louisville, employs over 20,000 people, and Norton Healthcare employs 7,500. Greater Louisville Inc. (GLI), a consortium of business players, not a government agency, has responsibility for economic development – attracting inward development and local growth (www.greaterlouisville.com/economic/indust/default.htm).

A review for the Brookings Institution by Katz (2002) bears many similarities to that undertaken of Georgia (Tornatzky *et al.* 2002, Shapira 2005b). Katz concluded that

- the new Regional City's workforce is relatively limited in size and skill, which hampers the region's ability to mature its economy
- it lost more young adults than the US on average and neighbouring counties

- metropolitan Louisville ranks near the bottom on national high school and college attainment
- the Regional City workforce lacks the education necessary to compete in today's 'knowledge economy'
- university R&D expenditure in the Louisville metropolitan area remains low
- metropolitan Louisville ranks low among peers and others in overall high-tech presence
- the Regional City of Louisville's population is decentralizing
- the Regional City is also home to a large concentration of poor workers who cluster near the old City of Louisville
- the Regional City is struggling to build a workforce to support and expand the economy
- the Regional City has a relative weakness in 'knowledge' industries with the potential for high-quality growth
- decentralization has spread the Regional City's population and resources into the suburbs
- the Regional City is growing in socially, racially, and economically divided ways.

Katz recommended that the strategy should be to:

- mobilize an 'amenities strategy' to attract and retain a talented work-force
- involve colleges and universities in long-term development strategy.

Next the good news. In 2003, Cognetics Inc ranked Louisville 9th among entrepreneurial hotspots, the best places in America to start and grow a company. *Entrepreneur, Inc* and *Business 2.0* have also drawn attention to the attractions of Louisville. These include a 500 per cent increase in the metropolitan area's venture capital pool, an intensive programme by the local chamber of commerce to support small business growth, and the city's establishment of a high-tech corridor (eMain US) adjacent to the medical centre. In 2003 the Governor appointed Dr Bill Brundage as the state's first 'New Economy Commissioner' to 'bring higher education, government and economic development together' (www.greaterlouisville. com/content/ed/business/rankings.pdf and www.louisville.edu/hsc/factsheets. pdf). Into this context came the 'Bucks for Brains' programme (Box 8.1).

The economic arguments are twofold and are based on a linear innovation process philosophy. First, the state's investment of $350 million will be worth $700 million when fully matched by private donors. The University of Louisville by 2005 had received $80 million. Second, research benefits translate into economic benefits. For example each $1 million in Federal funding for research generates $2.2 million for state and local economies. Discoveries made through research translate directly into business development opportunities. A further argument is based on the

---

Box 8.1 'Bucks for Brains' programme.

In 1997 the Kentucky legislature approved a bold plan to reform the state's system of higher education. The goal was to develop a 'seamless, integrated system of postsecondary education strategically planned and adequately funded to enhance economic development and quality of life'.

To that end, the state created the Research Challenge Trust Fund, a strategic investment in university research designed to create new jobs, new dollars and new opportunities for Kentucky citizens. Commonly known as 'Bucks for Brains', the programme uses state funds to attract and match private donations, effectively doubling the investment to support research in defined areas key to the state.

In 1998 Kentucky legislators invested $110 million in general fund appropriations to support 'Bucks for Brains' at the state's research and regional universities. They reinforced that commitment with an additional $120 million in 2000 and another $120 million in 2003.

This funding has allowed the University of Louisville to bring many prominent scholars to its campus to work alongside the school's already outstanding current faculty. In return, these pre-eminent faculty are creating economic opportunities, enhancing the education of students and drawing international attention to the university with significant breakthroughs, including numerous medical discoveries that will lead to a better quality of life for people everywhere.

Source: www.one-ky.com/bucksforbrains.html

---

eminence paradigm, that students gain from working with internationally recognized faculty.

As a consequence of the political economic objectives of the programme and the need to be involved in the decision-making process, the University of Louisville has established a Government Relations Department to 'Expand the university's presence in the offices of Kentucky's congressional presence and to help continue the unprecedented success of the university's challenge for Excellence'. Yet all is not well with the 'Bucks for Brains' programme. In 2004 there was not a funding round as the state dealt with a budget shortfall and not all the money from the last round was spent (personal communication, Alan Attaway, Professor of Accounting).

Biotechnology

Life sciences and the College of Business are major components of the links to the local economy. In the FY 1995, University of Louisville's expenditure on scientific research totalled $22.8 million. By 2000, expenditures had risen to $64.1 million – an increase of more than 180 per cent. In 2003, the total, which includes both external and internal funds allocated for research, was

$88.52 million, a further 38 per cent increase. The majority of the new funding for research was in life sciences. The medical school has over 1,100 professional places. The researchers attracted by the endowed chairs under the 'Bucks for Brains' programmes have brought in, and are expected to bring in, substantial amounts of Federal research dollars. In 2003, the University of Louisville grew at the fastest rate of any institution in the country for grant money supplied by the National Institutes of Health.

Although this is a major tobacco state, little of the tobacco settlement money has gone into the universities. Most of that money is going to projects in the state that will help tobacco farmers in some way. The state is trying to use natural products as springboards for economic development, for example through the state-funded Kentucky Natural Products Foundation which decides which companies will support. A condition of the award is that firms stay within Louisville. The state plan is to be a leader in that area. Two companies have been formed from the medical school, one of which uses tobacco in its research.

Indeed, the biotech industry is a major focus here, as in many universities throughout the US as well as in the UK. Louisville is starting from a very low base point and realistically cannot expect to generate large numbers of jobs. Cortright and Mayer (2002, 11) listed Louisville as having 'No significant Biotech Research or Commercialisation', reflected in Kentucky being an EPSCoR state. Yet the medical school and the life science departments are at the centre of the drive towards economic development. The Louisville Medical Centre, a partnership of three non-profit teaching hospitals plus the University of Louisville, formed the Louisville Medical Center Development Corporation, which at the time of writing is in the process of building a state-of-the art biomedical research park and technology centre. The hospital system is a major player in the Louisville innovation process. The Jewish hospital's corporate philosophy is that it is in its best interests to have strong medical research and has invested a lot of dollars in the university in the field of artificial hearts and hand transplants. It has been a major investor in the 'Bucks for Brains' programme.

A formalization of the commercialization of the outcomes of the research-to-innovation process is Metacyte, a consortium of business, the hospitals and the state of Kentucky (Box 8.2). Its objective is to foster local enterprise and to attract firms from other locations. Some $16 million has been spent on buildings in the medical area and $5 million by the state to build Metacyte. Land is still being acquired for a biotech park around the hospitals.

Four companies are listed as member companies on the Metacyte web page, not all of them spin-offs from Louisville's universities. For example NIRS was founded in Kansas and has an R&D office in Louisville. In 2004 the College of Business merged its technology incubator 'Ideas to Action' into Metacyte to increase efficiency. This partnership seems to be working well.

Box 8.2 Metacyte.

MetaCyte Business Lab LLC is the venture development subsidiary of Louisville Medical Center Development Corporation. MetaCyte Business Lab was incorporated by Jewish Hospital HealthCare Services, Inc., Norton Healthcare, Inc., UofL Health Care and the University of Louisville.

Located in the developing Louisville Life Science Research Park – within walking distance of the Louisville Medical Center – MetaCyte Business Lab is supported by the Commonwealth of Kentucky's Office for the New Economy and is a partner organization of The Innovation Group. In addition, Louisville/Jefferson County Metro Government supports the economic development efforts of MetaCyte Business Lab – the cornerstone of Louisville's and the Commonwealth's efforts to grow the life science and healthcare technology industry.

MetaCyte Business Lab identifies promising life science research and healthcare technology by prospecting within state universities, healthcare institutions, industry and the community, then drives that promising life science research and healthcare technology to market – and the clinic – by creating and assisting in the development of high-growth start-up companies.

Source: www.metacyte.biz

The entrepreneurial role

Like other universities, Louisville has measures to support entrepreneurial activity. The University Office of Technology Transfer employs a patent attorney, a licensing/start-up attorney with a BBA in finance, a contract attorney, a PhD with an MBA and a BS, who are responsible for soliciting disclosures, managing the patent process by outside attorneys and negotiating licences for University IP. The university has 13 university licences with equity provisions, three other licence agreements and three option agreements with companies.

Like most US universities, Louisville claims ownership of the IP of its staff and students. From 1998, the general rule is that, with certain exceptions, the University of Louisville Research Foundation, Inc. (ULRF), 'will hold all Legal Rights to all Intellectual Property conceived, first used or reduced to practice, discovered, or created, by any employee of the University, during his/her employment by the University'. Unlike at Oxford University, however, students who independently create IP arising out of their participation in programmes of study at the university, not resulting from their employment by the university, will retain the legal rights. Intellectual property created by students through the use of specialized resources or in connection with their employment by the university is owned by the ULRF.

In spite of the more entrepreneurial approach adopted by the university, the number of spin-offs, like that of patents and licences, has remained small. Within the university there is some scepticism about the university's strategy. Alan Attaway (Professor of Accounting, personal communication) for example said:

> Several in the community, including me, have been urging those in GLI and the Metro government that we cannot ignore our existing business base in pursuit of technology or biotech start-ups. Not that those efforts are not important but technology companies have a spotty track record with creating significant numbers of new jobs. We can launch 20 tech businesses – ten will fold in two years or less – because whatever they have figured out someone else has figured that out too and is doing it better; and 8 – if their ideas are any good those ideas will be bought out by bigger players. Very few technology companies are now waiting to do an IPO but are selling to the bigger players. This does not create new jobs. I'm not saying that the entrepreneurial efforts are not important – they are – but we need to be mindful of the type of ventures we are supporting. The name of the game is to back those who might create a significant number of new higher paying jobs in the area.

Massification of higher education and the training role

A much more extensive role within the economy is that of teaching and professional training. When the university became part of the state education system in 1970, the student body expanded and went from 6,000 students to 23,000. This is very much a 'local' university. Instate students comprise 83 per cent, and Jefferson county 55 per cent of all students. Out-of-state students are 17 per cent of enrolments and foreign students account for only 6 per cent of the population. The university's ranking for its doctoral programmes has risen so that, by 2003, the Carnegie Foundation placed the University of Louisville in the top tier of universities ranking it as 'Doctoral/research universities – extensive'.

In the early 1980s, the College of Business decided to make entrepreneurship its niche. In order to have a national name, the university has to find a niche. It has been recognized as being in the top 25 programmes for entrepreneurship in the last seven or eight years. The business school, which has a large proportion of graduate students, has a number of programmes designed to foster entrepreneurship. These include the Integrated MBA programme IMBA, which helps business start-ups from groups within the IMBA programmes. The Business School is involved by helping researchers write business plans. The goal is to have two start-ups per year out of that programme. In the early 2000s, 80 per cent of teams were working in dotcoms, creating business plans – web-based business programmes. This has dropped to zero. Now the focus is on biotech. Some ten companies have been formed in the past five or six years out of graduated classes who have launched a business of some kind. The most successful is a company called Genscape which has developed technology to monitor electricity flows – from generating plants to heating plants. When the national grid went down in 2002, this company was brought in as a consultant. One of the founders was from the first graduating class in the IMBA and another was from a later class. The company has been sold to a Californian group.

Whether the university takes an equity stake depends on the company and whether it is advantageous for a start-up to offer equity as part of a licensing deal. There are a lot of models. Two companies seem to be headed for success: one, started by faculty in the College of Arts and Science, Education and Medicine, is Neuronetrix. This company is developing a device that is put on a newborn baby and measures brain wave activity indicative of dyslexia at a week old. One of the IMBA teams worked with the company to develop the business plan. Another company, Othodata, has followed almost the same path. This company focuses on spine surgery and has developed a rod that has microchips so that healing can be monitored from the outside, eliminating unnecessary surgery. In this case, most of the science was done before the scientists came to the university on the 'Bucks for Brains' programme. The university does not have a stake in the transferred IP but will do in any improvements.

The College of Business has developed a partnership with UPS but much less with Ford or GE. UPS pays the university tuition fees, books, and a stipend to students who work for UPS doing shifts (midnight to 4 am, 4 am to 8 am). Alan Attaway (personal communication) recognizes that the college has a strategy of how to work with the old as well as the new economy and that not all efforts should go into fast growth sectors and the rest be ignored. The bulk of jobs in most places are SMEs; many have been there for years and provide a good base of employment. MBA teams are working with companies in the West End of the city where there is lots of unemployment and high crime rates. 'Jobs are the answer' may have an effect of reducing the crime rate if people are employed. This, however, is beyond the university's capacity to enthuse businesses. This is a role for the state. There is no funding for the university to liaise with local industry in the College of Business. It is all done by using student teams – free labour. The challenge is to get more organization, but this needs a full-time person – but there is no money yet. Little training is provided for companies – this is not popular. Many bigger companies have their own universities – e.g. Motorola, GE, Ford. The college is now trying a new initiative for executive training, which started in January 2005.

In the late 1980s to early 1990s, the College of Business ran very successful continuing education programmes while most of the university's attempts were losing money. The College took over Continuing Education for the whole university. Problems with the management of that facility led to the programme being closed and a distance-learning programme was offered instead. Currently the programme is being redeveloped under a new head. The college has also developed a programme on logistics and supply chain management, at graduate level. Most of the students work at UPS and other places in the town. This is not a degree programme but may develop as such.

The territorial role

According to Alan Attaway, Jim Ramsey, the current University President, came from state government but is an academic. His philosophy is that the university should be more involved in economic development and will be pushing this. Universities should be involved at different levels – law school, medical and dental schools. There may not be active links in the arts and sciences but they could get involved in the schools system. There is not enough money to make everything happen. 'At the same time, there are some people in the university who think that this is not what the university should be doing'.

Two bases for engagement with the local area are the School of Public Administration and the Urban Studies Institute, which has a partnership with the county working in environmental issues, sustainable environmental studies (see www.louisville.edu/opb/planning/stradirc.pdf). The university also houses the state data centre. In Alan Attaway's assessment, 'at the present time many of the local networks have not blossomed due to a lack of funding for such initiatives. The state's budget crisis leaves little money for such programmes'.

Princeton, New Jersey

Princeton is a small town with a population of only 14,000 people as of the 2000 census. The town lies in the west central portion of New Jersey about midway between Trenton and New Brunswick and about 50 miles from both New York and Philadelphia. Princeton University obtained its charter in 1746. It was known as the College of New Jersey until 1896 and it was British North America's fourth college. Princeton University retains traditional Vannevar Bush values of research and a commitment to undergraduate teaching, although a more recent engagement with economic development has focused on its contribution to national economic, cultural and social and political life. This is illustrated by Princeton's mission statement:

> Princeton University strives to be both one of the leading research universities and the most outstanding undergraduate college in the world. As a research university, it seeks to achieve the highest levels of distinction in the discovery and transmission of knowledge and

understanding, and in the education of graduate students. At the same time, Princeton aims to be distinctive among research universities in its commitment to undergraduate teaching. It seeks to provide its students with academic, extracurricular and other resources – in a residential community committed to diversity in its student body, faculty and staff – that will permit them to attain the highest possible level of achievement in undergraduate education and prepare them for positions of leadership and lives of service in many fields of human endeavor. Through the scholarship, research and teaching of its faculty, and the many contributions to society of its alumni, Princeton seeks to fulfill its informal motto: 'Princeton in the Nation's Service and in the Service of All Nations.'

www.princeton.edu/Siteware/aboutprinceton.shtml

Distributed innovation process

The changing profile of Princeton research – from a rarefied academic atmosphere with informal links to the neighbouring Institute for Advanced Studies to a university which now embraces collaborative activity with industry – is illustrated by the rapidly changing profile of research income. Since its inception in 1988, the University's Center for Photonic and Optoelectronic Materials (POEM) has marked a major change in university–industry relationships. POEM has demonstrated that the quality of its PhD students is as good or is better than any other PhD students. In 2003 the Princeton Institute for the Science and Technology of Materials (PRISM) was formed through the merger of the Princeton Materials Institute (PMI) and POEM. The goal of PRISM is 'to become the world leader in an area of materials science that is emerging as an important source of scientific discoveries and commercial opportunities' (www.princeton.edu/~seasweb/eqnews/winter03-04/feature4.html). In 1989 Princeton received only $11 million in external research income. The establishment of POEM changed the culture of collaboration, brought in external income and has given rise to academic entrepreneurship. The philosophy is that there should be a strong independent faculty – 'it is incumbent on industry to keep up' (personal communication, Joseph Montemarano, Director for Industrial Liaison (POEM)).

Since its formation, POEM has developed research and development partnerships with approximately 200 New-Jersey-based companies (including 40 start-ups) and entrepreneurs in a wide array of fields, ranging from aviation and environmental monitoring to medicine and telecommunications. POEM's focus is on companies with fewer than 50 employees. For example, Sensors Unlimited was recently acquired for $900 million, and Epitaxx was acquired for $450 million – both of these companies succeeding in large part because of POEM's assistance and technology. Organic electronics, biological imaging and bio-nano informatics are representative areas of forward-looking, interdisciplinary research led by POEM in partnership with industry and government. Also, POEM has launched an aggressive outreach effort to the venture and investment communities to make them aware of the valuable technology created by POEM and more broadly at Princeton University. POEM graduates work for start-ups and small companies for three to five years and many go on to start new companies. By 2005 around a dozen spin-offs had some student involvement.

POEM attracted some $12–14 million external dollars and became the second largest research unit on campus. Of this, 60 per cent was Federal grant, 15 per cent state, 25 per cent industry – half from large companies and half from small. One of the challenges for the university was to replace income from telecommunications industry, mainly AT&T. POEM was critical to the university's ability to attract the brightest and best faculty and students in opto-electronics. A university must have 'a combination of theoretical, applied, and entrepreneurial talent'. The quality of students has not been affected by industrially orientated research, according to Joseph Montemarano. POEM has demonstrated that the quality of PhD students is as good as or better than any other PhD students.

Alongside the more applied research, the university's national research role is reinforced with major Federal grants. In July 2004, the US Department of Energy announced that the US project office for ITER, a major international fusion experiment, will be located at the Princeton Plasma Physics Laboratory. Ever since fusion research began at Princeton University in 1951, PPPL, located on Princeton University's James Forrestal Campus, has been charged with developing the scientific understanding and key innovations that will lead to an attractive fusion energy source. PPPL, in partnership with DOE's Oak Ridge National Laboratory, will be responsible for overseeing the US ITER Project Office and providing it with the requisite staffing and facilities.

Defence and biotech

New Jersey, like Kentucky, is not one of the leading biotech or defence expenditure states. Life sciences are not one of Princeton's strengths. In 2002, New Jersey ranked 24th among all 50 states in NIH funding and received ten NIH grandest awards and contracts totalling $136.6 million. Yet the state is home to 19 of the 25 largest pharmaceutical and medical technology companies in the world, including Aventis Pharmaceuticals, Bristol-Myers Squibb (pharmaceutical research, oncology, immunology and inflammation drug discovery), Johnson & Johnson, Merck and Co. and Roche Pharmaceuticals. The big pharma companies in New Jersey focus mainly on manufacturing, but 17,300 people, one-quarter of their 69,200 employees, are engaged in R&D. An additional 120 or so biotech companies are clustered around a 48-mile research corridor stretching from Newark through New Brunswick to Princeton (Agres 2004). This is an example where the presence of a major research university and the co-location of pharmaceutical and biotech companies is coincidental.

Massification and the training role

Unlike at Oxford, at Princeton the undergraduate teaching focus and strong loyalty to the Alma Mater has remained, as is shown by the very high level of income from gifts. Princeton has begun to look outwards and has begun a number of initiatives, which, although not focused on applied research, may sensitize students to prevailing external agendas. The Oxford/Princeton Partnership, established in 2001, is one such initiative. It supports faculty research collaborations (including graduate student participation) and undergraduate student exchanges between Oxford University and Princeton University. Since the Partnership's inception, fifteen joint research projects have been approved for fixed-term internal seed funding. The university supports the Program in Continuing Education. In this programme, individuals become officially registered students, pay full tuition for each course they take, and receive a transcript and credit that may be used toward a degree at another institution of higher learning.

The entrepreneurial university

The entrepreneurial role, like the territorial role discussed below, is relatively recent. The Princeton University website lists only six spin-off companies, most of which started in the early 1990s. The majority of these are related to the photonics research area, and one is a bioscience company. For example, Global Photonic Energy Corporation development stage company was incorporated under the laws of the Commonwealth of Pennsylvania on 7 February 1994 by American Biomimetics Corporation ('Biomimetics'), a privately held new materials, science and technology venture company. It is based on 'organic thin film' technologies (the 'Energy Technologies') being developed by researchers at the University of Southern California and Princeton University. Cellular Genomics Inc. is a drug discovery and development company.

The recent more entrepreneurial stance of the university is illustrated by the work of PRISM. This initiative is designed to build on existing research expertise, to develop commercial applications and to strengthen ties with the regional economy. This interdisciplinary institute already has more than 65 faculty and 200 post-graduates. The new Institute will focus on research and education that combines expertise in 'hard' materials such as conventional semiconductors and ceramics with knowledge of 'soft' materials such as polymers and biological molecules. The objectives of the centre and kinds of cultural shifts that have been made within the university are illustrated by this quotation from the launch publicity:

The interdisciplinary aspect of PRISM research is complemented by a direct focus on industrial collaboration, particularly with companies in New Jersey. The Institute will promote an entrepreneurial style of research through support of far-reaching new ideas or 'seed' projects, involving researchers from different academic perspectives and external collaborations with industry and national laboratories. To cement its links with industry, PRISM will offer an enhanced technology infrastructure making it easy for companies to work with institute researchers, including an active affiliates program and ready access to the Institute's four state-of-the-art research facilities: the Nano/microfabrication Lab, the Ultrafast Laser Lab, the Imaging and Analysis Facility, and the Materials Computation Lab. For use by faculty, students and visitors, these facilities are designed to encourage the flow of people and ideas to Princeton's campus and central New Jersey.

The territorial role

Even as recently as the late 1980s, the state of New Jersey was not a partner of Princeton. The then University President William Bowen was reported as saying that Princeton was an accident of history and was not identified with the region. It was a national research institution (personal communication, Joseph Montemorano). Now there is a much stronger focus on local and regional economy and the university is seen as a force for growth. The rhetoric is all about partnership, and as in the case of University of Louisville, leverage of Federal funding. From being a different kind of university to Rutgers – a state university which has a role for economic development in its charter – this private university has found the territorial role to be beneficial in that it has brought in research income and has had a beneficial impact in the state. New Jersey, although it does not put tobacco settlement money into university research – that has gone in a bond to offset state deficit – has established the New Jersey Commission on Science and Technology (NJCST).

Wojciechowski (2004) reports that the NJCST has made a major impact on the economy through funding research, helping the state start and attract new companies and consolidation of activities at others – for example, Bristol-Myers Squibb's Magnetic Resonance Imaging R&D activities at its Lawrenceville site. PRISM is already home to four NJCST-supported programmes in organic electronics, large-area flexible displays and electronics, molecular and biomolecular imaging, and embedded system-on-a-chip design. Each has a number of industrial partners. Princeton researchers have become world leaders in the area of 'organic' and 'flexible' electronics, where conventional crystalline semiconductor devices are replaced with materials that are potentially cheaper, printable, and energy efficient. This work has led to several productive collaborations with companies that licensed discoveries from Princeton and now work closely with faculty members and graduate students.

Further, at Princeton alone, the infrastructure made possible by NJCST R&D programmes in emerging areas has led to Federal and industrial research funds over ten times the initial state investment, and led to the establishment of Princeton as a driver of Central New Jersey's 'Route 1 Research Corridor', a regional link which did not exist before the Commission's programmes took effect. Support from the Commission has enabled Princeton researchers to provide significant benefit to New Jersey companies: assisting more than 250 companies (including more than 50 start-ups), thereby creating new jobs and yielding in a single year (2002) over $500 million in capital gains from private investment in the companies partnered with Princeton – generating New Jersey income tax payments in excess of $15 million. Cumulatively, NJCST-supported activities at Princeton have resulted in more than $25 million in income and payroll taxes (surpassing total direct state grants and bond money provided), and leveraged more than $50 million in Federal grants and over $25 million in industry resources. Moreover, Princeton University has long played an important role in attracting prestigious international corporations to central New Jersey, particularly to the university-developed Forrestal Center properties in Plainsboro and South Brunswick.

The impact of these initiatives is to increase the attractiveness of the local economy to business. According to the *Moody's Investor Service Municipal Credit Research* report, the university's positive effect on the local economy and the stability of its presence is the dominant factor in the Triple A bond rating for Princeton Township and the Princeton Regional School District, and the Double A bond rating for Princeton Borough (www.princeton.edu/pr/facts/profile/04/32.htm).

Conclusions

The case studies show that each of the universities is positioned differently within international and national innovation systems, a variety of mechanisms by which universities engage in innovation and economic development, and that there can be more than one version of history. Stanford has a very long history of contributing to economic development in Silicon Valley in the context of the heritage of earlier technological revolution, which laid the basis for an environment in which the electronics industry could flourish. This transformation was aided by the ownership of vast tracts of land which gave the freedom for the university to capitalize on those assets through both the science park and the income from rent, and crucially by Federal defence expenditure. One version has it that Frederick Terman was the right man in the right place at the right time to capitalize on both assets. His vision was to maximize the returns on the very best talent he could attract to the university and set the terms of trade with government and industry at a time when the university was able to do so because of its expertise that was so useful in the Second World War and the Cold War. Once established, those terms laid the foundation for the future, building high-quality research and linked to graduate and professional education programmes through which entrepreneurship flourished. Told this way, the Silicon Valley/Stanford story illustrates Florida's (1999) point that what industry wants most from universities is 'talent not technology'. Another version is that similar developments were occurring through co-evolution of attitudes and practices in industry and in premier universities on the east coast, particularly at MIT.

The University of Louisville is located in a much less promising setting. The state has been suffering from the effects of de-industrialization in its traditional manufacturing industries, and its service industries are not natural collaborators with universities. It is a state with an already heavily polarized economy. Moreover, although Louisville has expertise in its hospitals, the University of Louisville has not had a history of research expertise in life sciences that the state sees as the sector most likely to produce jobs. Although the 'Bucks for Brains' programme has brought considerable funds into the university, the agenda is entirely one of economic development and does not appear to have the graduate programmes as central for sustaining links with industry and as a source of revenue. Issues of human resources, which take the longest to change here as elsewhere, are hence the most neglected part of technology-based development (Tornatzky *et al.* 2002). Rather, the terms of trade are that this money is for leverage of other income. On the other hand, the city is judged to be a fertile ground for entrepreneurship but it is not clear at this stage where the two connect. As the example of Georgia shows, states can make considerable gains in technology industries over a short period of time, but for a state to be transformed can take decades.

Princeton University, one of the world's most eminent universities, on the other hand, has the research base on which to build a regional economic strategy. A long history of top-quality research has provided the university with the leverage to dictate the terms on which it engages in economic development.

Hence the territorial role of each university and its associated accountability are different. Stanford University, through whichever version of history, has long been associated with the growth of Silicon Valley. As a private university, it has no formal requirement to form part of a regional economic governance system but is part of the social, economic and cultural fabric of the region. The University of Louisville, a state university on the other hand, like Princeton has recently been recruited into the regional governance system through a state-wide initiative. It and its staff have the most difficult task in delivering economic development as expectations are so high, and the opportunities for its graduates to contribute to raising the skill base of the region in the short term are limited. For Princeton, the academic as well as the commercial advantages of engagement with the region have been successfully translated into new models of research and research application which are reinforcing its premier status.

9 Conclusions

Introduction

This book has taken as its theme how, in the early twenty-first century, universities in Europe and the US are increasingly driven by political normative agendas that have innovation and economic development at their heart. It has shown that, although universities have long been involved in innovation and economic development, what is recent is their role as territorial actors. The rhetoric of the discourse around the economic agenda is revealing, not all of it having favourable connotations. Academic observers have used such epithets to describe universities' current place in innovation and economic development as 'mechanistic' and 'instrumentalist' position, as 'academic capitalism', as 'factories'. The book explores the changes within higher education and is critical of the normative agenda behind the growing convergence in orientation between institutions and industry. It highlights how pressure both from the state and from industry has produced new paradigms of accountability that now include responsibilities for regional development. It argues that one of the weaknesses of the current policy agenda is the focus on the elite or research universities, misattributing directions of causality and unrealistic expectations. Only recently has there been more debate on the long-term adverse consequences of some aspects of the current agenda, particularly the sustainability of high-quality research in the context of an increasing reliance on industry funding for research.

Systemic changes in the relationship between universities and the economy are investigated through the framework of eight paradigms. These eight interconnected trends or paradigms represent the complexity of contemporary relationships which characterize universities' involvement in economic development. They are defined as:

- innovation processes being increasingly distributed between actors in public and private sectors, resulting in a greater integration of activity
- a series of systemic changes within national innovation systems dating back to at least the early part of the twentieth century

- the disproportionate impact of the eminence of particular individuals and universities
- systemic changes in the orientation of university systems: the still important role played by defence research in the construction of university systems and the rapid rise in biotech-orientated research
- new accountabilities to industry and society
- a rapid expansion in student numbers from the late 1990s onwards
- the legitimation and priorization of entrepreneurial activities
- most recently, an explicit territorial role.

Distributed innovation systems

The increasing emphasis on economic development being determined by knowledge production and utilization, and the university as a source of the former and instrumental in providing the framework for the latter, forms the basis for the prevailing policy agenda. Both are underpinned by funding programmes at international, national and regional level designed to increase the distribution power of innovation systems (David and Foray 1995) by encouraging universities to be more commercial and for firms to increase their capacity to absorb university research.

Evidence shows, however, that universities are not the major input to industrial innovation and are commonly ranked as ninth or tenth in importance, some way behind clients and customers – which are universally found, along with internal resources, to be the major sources of innovation. Studies also show that degrees of engagement between universities and industry are context-dependent, with marked national, sectoral and institutional country differences. These are strongly influenced by the traditional cultural and institutional modes of behaviour (see Senker 2005). This holds even at the continental level, with the EU as a whole some way behind the effectiveness of the US national system of innovation. Evidence shows that the biotechnology, life science and pharmaceutical sector disproportionately accounts for the volume of linkages and is more internationalized than industries such as chemistry and engineering, which hence have different appropriability conditions (Brusoni and Geuna forthcoming). On the other hand, studies also show that university–industry engagement is not confined to high-tech sectors and that firms in medium- and low-tech industries, which form the majority of businesses, often work closely with universities, albeit by different routes (see Smith 1997).

Moreover, methods and targets chosen to identify the scale and scope of the link between university research, innovation and economic performance vary and the practice of measurement is undertaken for different reasons to show different outcomes. Any data set also at best shows a partial picture when it is total links that matter (Lee and Walshok 2003). Not all contacts are measured, of course: as Betts and Lee (2005) point out, the focus on innovations directly linked to universities, such as patents, seriously undercounts the impact of individual university scientists and engineers through informal contacts and being recruited into industry. For example, faculty consulting is not tracked by formal university means. Moreover, comparisons of performance between countries are complicated by differences in national and regional innovation systems and the difficulties in demonstrating both direct and indirect impacts. Moreover, the current emphasis on short-term evaluation severely overlooks the impact of research on innovation and economic development over longer periods.

The current policy agenda on increasing the efficiency of the innovation process through cluster policies focuses on innovation as a social as well as a technological process. While it would not be disputed that there are personal interactions in which tacit knowledge is transmitted between personnel in universities and industry as Chapter 2 shows, there is much debate about the significance of local innovation networks, compared to more geographically extensive interactions, in the efficiency of the innovation process (see Malmberg and Power 2004, for example). The focus on the territorial role overlooks the fact that what matter most to firms are the benefits to that particular location such as residential attractiveness rather than their being flagship companies in a broader economic development agenda.

Moreover, proximity effects change over time. In some industries but not others, localized linkages are most prevalent at early stages in an industry's growth and decline over time. Not all areas can benefit equally from a university's presence because of the lack of match between the profile of a university's teaching and its research. Other caveats are that urbanization are more important than localization economies. Evidence to support localization effects, hence the justification for policies which attempt to foster local university–industry links on the basis of innovation efficiency, is at best mixed.

The case studies from Europe and the US illustrate how universities vary in their degree of integration within geographically extensive and localized innovation systems and how this variation is related to interdependent systemic technological, political and institutional changes. For example, Stanford is the most integrated into industrial innovation systems and Louisville the least. The Grenoble model of collaboration between universities, research laboratories, business and central and local state is one which is replicated in the US and is being adopted by the UK.

National innovation systems

Countries differ in the level of allocation of resources allocated for research in universities and national laboratories, for supporting strategic technologies, and also in the distributive aspects of the national innovation system such as the ownership of intellectual property in universities and other public research institutions and in the establishment of TTOs in order to facilitate the exploitation of public sector knowledge (Senker 2005). Chapters 4 and 5 also show that systemic change is faster in some countries than in others (see Bozeman 2000).

The comparison between Europe and the US forms a central theme of the book to illustrate how these different elements in national innovation systems have actual and potential consequences for the trajectories of research-to-innovation systems. The US has traditionally been the model for Europe. The Europeanization of the higher education system in both teaching and research is intended to challenge US hegemony by improving efficiency by increasing harmonization and strengthening the research base. Under the Lisbon Agenda the aim is to raise the average share of EU GDP invested in R&D from 2 to 3 per cent by 2010. Within the EU a huge variety in structure and compliance existed amongst the EU15, now further complicated by the expansion to EU25. Yet in mid-2005, EU finance ministers were proposing severe cuts to the Framework 6 programme (Lipsett 2005).

The European paradox, that the quality of Europe's science is not matched by the universities' ability to respond to industry's needs, is frequently blamed on the universities. The counter-argument is that it is industry's under-investment, for example in the UK, that is the most significant barrier to a greater degree of integration, a key conclusion from the UK's Lambert Report, and supported by David (2005) and Senker (2005). Policy makers in the UK and Europe look to the US for models for improving the quality of research-to-innovation systems, observing more flexibility, greater investment in research and the impact of legislative change in the US system. In respect of the last, some analysts, however, argue that it is unrealistic to try to replicate systemic changes such as the Bayh-Dole Act of 1980 which appears to have had a major impact on the entrepreneurial activities of universities. David (2005) is one of a number of authors who argue that its impact has been misunderstood (Chapter 5) and cannot be separated from the conditions in the US at the time of the Act.

Moreover, the book shows that the US hegemony is not constant. Some analysts indeed suggest that the US has moved from a position of dominance to one of first among equals in line with a more widely distributed pattern of science and technological capabilities (Malecki 2005). While the US maintains its lead over other nations in R&D performance, the US share of research output, but not relative to publications, continues to decline. In some sectors, such as pharmaceuticals, the US maintains leadership because of much higher degree of knowledge integration between universities and other research institutes and industry than in the EU (Brusoni and Geuna forthcoming).

Eminence

Recent league tables which rank the top research institutions on such criteria as publications cited, patents, spending on research endowment income and knowledge integration show that the US universities outperform those in the rest of world, with the two exceptions of Oxford and Cambridge.

Eminence, however, while associated with academic excellence and indicated by such measures as the number of Nobel Prizes, Fields medals won and so on, now has a utilitarian value. The added-value and income accruing to top universities through three kinds of 'Matthew effects' have both direct and indirect leverage effects both on the way national and increasingly internationally distributed innovation systems operate and on the production of localized effects. In the former, these are being reinforced by national government efforts to create elite institutions – for example Germany in emulating the US (Chapter 4) – and through the establishment of international elites of universities – the global elite 8 and the Universitas 21 (U21) which was launched in Australia in 2001. In the latter, Chapter 2 illustrated the disproportionate impact that many, but not all, leading universities have on their local economies and the technological profiles of their regions.

Yet the position of universities in relation to commercialization activities is not constant. In the US for example, Federal programmes such as EPSCoR and state investments in research such as those in Georgia and in Kentucky aimed at using universities to drive economic development have had some impact. For example, Powers (2003) finds that in the US if private and Land Grant universities ever had an advantage over public universities in commercialization, that has disappeared in recent years.

Defence and biotech

This paradigm proposes an equivalence between defence and biotechnology in the orientation of university systems. As Chapter 3 documented and other chapters discussed, the share of research in universities dedicated to biotech and life sciences is increasing while defence is declining. In the 1980s, much academic research focused on the role played by defence in stimulating the growth of high-tech industries in locations such as Silicon Valley and Route 128 in the US and the M4 corridor in the UK (albeit without major university involvement). That emphasis has largely, and in my opinion erroneously, disappeared. Defence funding for universities and public research laboratories in countries such as the US, the UK and France, although it has declined since the ending of the Cold War, still comprises a significant component of national R&D systems. It has a major influence on the direction of university research, has limited civil applications and potentially crowds out other areas of more 'useful' research and operates largely without publicity (Langley 2005).

By the early twenty-first century, biomedical science comprises the largest share of R&D in US and UK universities. Like defence research, it is concentrated in a small number of centres in the US and Europe, and like defence research it is being further concentrated with the building of regional 'megacentres' – centres of public and private sector research in which public authorities are actively engaged in their development. Even so, as a target for economic development and job generation, the university–biotech commercialization route through spin-offs, patents and licences is, with a few high-profile exceptions, extremely limited. Even in the US, it is only a few blockbuster patents and licences that make up the bulk of income derived from commercialization. Yet biotech is an industry where regions are competing with each other for the attraction of major corporate research establishment and new firms (Betts and Lee 2005). The relationship between universities, innovation and economic development is therefore complex. The cases of defence and potentially biotech illustrate both the geographical impact of major expenditure programmes on economic activity and failures of commercialization of university research (Senker 2005). All in all, there are over-optimistic expectations of biomedical science and the biotech sector on innovation and economic development in Europe under current conditions (see DTI 2005; Nightingale and Martin 2004).

Accountability

How a system allocates resources is interdependent with systems of accountability. The governance of public universities occurs at three policy levels: government, university administration and the individual faculty. What is important is where power is exerted on and in each of these three levels in the respective national innovation systems. And, in spite of the limited returns, the supposed commercial potential of university research is being matched by an increase in measures designed to evaluate and benchmark the outputs of universities, public laboratories and programmes designed to improve flows of knowledge between these bodies and industry (see for example OECD 2002a). Yet at the institutional level, many immeasurable variables account for differences in university performance including institutional culture and incentive systems, policies which legitimate this kind of entrepreneurial activity (Powers 2003).

In the US and in Germany as well as in the UK, a consequence of the combined drives towards the excellence and industrial support for research may well be a polarized system, in some cases along old and in others along new lines. In meeting political agendas, the book shows that universities in Europe and the US are faced with tensions between academic values of open science and meeting short-term industry objectives. Studies, however, find evidence to support claims both for adverse effects on the commitment to free inquiry and for no adverse effects on the long-term direction of academic research.

While the book has argued that the territorial role brings with it new sets of accountabilities, what is not resolved at the regional or local level is the tension raising from the fact that states, regions or localities do not have responsibilities for conflicts of interests between, on the one hand, universities' commercial activities and, on the other, their societal responsibilities of education, custodians of culture heritage, recorders of history and agents of debate on philosophical, scientific, literary debates and so on. Instead multiple accountabilities and stakeholders exist in which those responsible for regional or local territorial development now have a say on what universities should be doing to stimulate economic development. Yet the ethical implications of what that means for the direction of university research in general and in military and biotechnical activity have not yet been widely debated locally. It is not in the remit of states or regions to be concerned with such issues; rather they remain national and EU responsibilities.

Massification

The contribution of universities to innovation and economic development through the teaching role is one of the most neglected relationships in academic analysis. It has, however, now assumed major political significance. Europe's Bologna agreement, for example, is for a common framework designed to improve economic performance through human capital formation from undergraduate to professional development and to increase the mobility of staff and students. It is mobility in the form of foreign recruitment of staff and students that has been key to the continued renewal of research activities in the US (Chapter 6), although concerns have been raised about the over-reliance on foreign-born talent (Malecki 2005).

The quality, quantity and mobility of the workforce are connected to levels of investment in science and technology at the national (and EU) level. Although the number of scientists and engineers is increasing, a lack of opportunities for young researchers found in Germany, the UK and the US is hindering the sustainability of the research base and hence potential longer-term links with industry. The UK, for example, is still redressing the problems of the legacy of the under-funding from Conservative governments. The university system suffers from poor pay for academic staff, limited opportunities for graduates students within academia and few incentives to stay on to undertake a PhD. Combined, these factors restrict the intake to the next generations both of senior researchers and of people who will participate in industry-related activities such as industry-funded studentships and who can be recruited by industry. Chapter 5 shows that similar problems are currently being experienced in the US. Evidence from the US suggests also that there are cultural barriers to be overcome in encouraging students to seek careers in industry.

As the examples of Grenoble and Stanford show, in order to improve levels of university–industry linkage, teaching and research should take a greater account of how graduate and professional education programmes can work to the benefit of both. What is missing in Oxford and Louisville, but found in Grenoble, Stanford and Princeton, is the emphasis on graduate education as a research and industry resource and on CPD. Senker (2005) concludes that entrepreneurial programmes and courses in graduate science programmes would raise the interest of scientists to work with or for industry and help build links between the two communities. Moreover, CPD/industry courses can be important sources of income as the examples of Stanford and UCSD illustrate.

Yet there is another viewpoint: that it is at primary and secondary school level rather than at university level that education has the greatest impact on the economy (Wolf 2002). Moreover such an emphasis on vocational skills has little to do with social justice and quality of life, a sentiment supported by Bundy (2004) writing about the polarization of the educational system in the US. Both point to a confusion of objectives arising from placing so much emphasis on universities on training.

Entrepreneurial universities

This book shows the progression of the steps taken by many universities to appropriate the gains of commercially valuable research activities and the different models that exist (see also Powers and McDougall 2003). Stanford was one of the first entrepreneurial universities in the US. In the UK, Cambridge University was one of the first to be identified with academic enterprise (in the mid-1980s), as was Chalmers, a private university in Sweden, and by the early twentieth century, the University of Twente was a leading model of the Netherlands' entrepreneurial universities. Although the vast majority of universities in Europe and the US have instituted measures to respond to growing political expectations, not all can be entrepreneurial in the same ways. Evidence from several countries finds that many TTOs are not effective mediators between the university and industry and there is a need for institutional innovation which complements its HEIs with novel organizations that are better suited to commercializing the results of research (Senker 2005; David 2005), and evidence from the US and Europe shows that most universities do not make a profit from the activities of their technology transfer offices or through intellectual property rights (Geuna and Nesta 2003).

Yet efforts to establish science parks, TTOs and spin-offs and to produce patents and licences are ubiquitous but are as much for political as for economic reasons. For example, Powers (2003) argues of the US that, as long as economic development remains a central concern for state and Federal policy makers, then continuing to support Land Grant universities in their pursuit of core purposes seems wise, even though, on financial grounds, policy should suggest otherwise.

The territorial role

Universities and other colleges are becoming more closely involved with their territories. In so doing, they are emerging as key actors in governance systems, becoming the focal point for the formulation and delivery of policies on innovation, entrepreneurship and cluster development, and human capital formation and development. This is the paradigm of the university which Etzkowitz (2003) describes as the 'regional innovation organizer'. Higher education then not only provides potentially a core element of the knowledge base of cities and regions, but universities and colleges also have the potential through their teaching and research missions to play a leading role in joining up the separate strands of urban development policy and linking the global to the local (Goddard 2004). While the case studies have shown that universities have been actively involved in local economic development, the evidence on effectiveness is mixed. Boosterish agendas tend to overlook the unintended outcome of polarization within economies, for example in Atlanta, in which economic benefits of stimulating economic development through innovation are largely confined to the core.

More detailed academic analysis of the contributions of other kinds of universities across a wide range of contexts has begun to inform that debate. Rather than the discussion being confined to the purely economic, the engagement of universities in the cultural life of cities and of their broader governance role in addressing problems of regeneration and sustainability are becoming more common (see Glasson 2003). Yet in many countries there is a lack of strategic thinking about economic development capacity at the regional or local level to assess what contribution the various universities can play (Powers 2003). As Betts and Lee (2005) point out, while universities can and do play an important role in stimulating regional innovation, they cannot do this without a multi-faceted entrepreneurial structure being in place locally. Best practices might also include a greater willingness to break down the traditional barriers within hierarchical tertiary educational systems that are found in many countries. They see it as misguided to consider universities in isolation from other processes in the economy. They find that the literature tends to 'overplay the role of universities and underplay the role of the private sector in generating innovative technology clusters'.

To conclude, in reviewing Gibbons *et al.* (1994), Edqvist (2003, 220) concludes that the book gives science a too-important role in society, and that it should be seen not as the goose which lays the golden eggs but rather as an ordinary hen laying breakfast eggs. This analogy could equally apply to universities in innovation and economic development.

References and further reading

Abraham, J. (1997) 'The science and politics of medicines regulation' In Elston, M.A. (ed.) *The Sociology of Medical Science and Technology* Oxford, Blackwell Publishers

Acs, Z., Audretsch, D.B. and Feldman, M.P. (1994) 'R&D spillovers and innovative activity' *Managerial and Decision Economics* 15, 131–8

Acs, Z. and Armington, C. (2004) 'Employment growth and entrepreneurial activity in cities' *Regional Studies* 38 (8), 911–28

Adams, J.D. (2002) 'Comparative localization of academic and industrial spillovers' *Journal of Economic Geography* 253–77

Advisory Council on Science and Technology (ACST) (1999) University Research and the Commercialisation of Intellectual Property in Canada. http://acst-ccst.gc.ca/acst/comm/rpaper/home_e.html

Agrawal, A. and Henderson, R. (2002) 'Putting patents into context' *Management Science* January

Agres, T. (2004) 'New York – New Jersey life science nirvana' *The Scientist* 12 April

Allen, T.J., Utterback, J, Sirbu, M.A. and Holloman, J.H. (1978) 'Government influence on the process of innovation in Europe and Japan' *Research Policy* 7, 124–9

Angel, D.P. (1991) 'High-technology agglomeration and the labor market: the case of Silicon Valley' *Environment and Planning* A, 23, 1501–16

Anselin, L., Varga, A. and Acs, Z.J. (1997) 'Local geographic spillovers between university research and high technology innovation' *Journal of Urban Economics* 42, 422–48

Anselin, L. Varga, A. and Acs, Z. (2000) 'Geographic spillovers and university research: a spatial econometric approach' *Growth and Change* 31 (4), 501–15

Antonelli, C. (2000) 'Collective knowledge communication and innovation: the evidence of technological districts' *Regional Studies* 34 (6), 535–47

Antonelli, C. and Quere, M. (2002) 'The governance of interactive learning within innovation systems' *Urban Studies* 39 (5–6), 1051–63

Archibugi, D. (1996) Book Review, R.R. Nelson (ed.) 'National innovation systems: a comparative analysis' *Research Policy* 25 (5), 838–42

Archibugi, D. and Iammarino, S. (2002) 'The globalisation of technological innovation: definition and evidence' *Review of International Political Economy* 9 (1), 98–122

Arundel, A. and Geuna, A. (2001) 'Does proximity matter to knowledge transfer from public institutes and universities to firms?' *SPRU Electronic Working Paper Series* 73

Arundel, A. and Geuna, A. (2004) 'Proximity and the use of public science by innovative European firms' *Economics of Innovation and New Technology* 13 (6), 559–80

Arundel, A. and Kabla, I. (1998) 'What percentage of innovations are patented? Empirical estimates for European firms' *Research Policy* 27, 127–41

Arundel, A. and Steinmuller, W.E. (1998) 'The use of patent databases by European small and medium-sized enterprises' *Technology Analysis and Strategic Management* 10, 157–73

Association of University and Technology Managers (2003) *AUTM licensing survey, FY 2002* Northbrook, IL www.autm.net

Association of University and Technology Managers (2004a) AUTM Licensing survey FY 2002 www.autm.net/index_ie.html

Association of University and Technology Managers (2004b) Draft NIH Letter from AUTM (6 July 2004) www.autm.net/Announcements/DraftNIHLetter1.htm

Athreye, S. and Keeble, D. (2000) 'Sources_of increasing returns and regional innovation in the UK' ESRC Centre for Business Research – Working Papers WP158, Cambridge, ESRC Centre for Business Research

Audretsch, D. and Stephan, P.E. (1996) 'Company-scientists' locational links: the case of biotechnology' *American Economic Review* 86, 641–52

Audretsch, D.B., Bozeman, B., Combs, K.L., Feldman, M., Link, A.L., Siegel, D.S., Stephan, P., Tassey, G. and Wessner, C. (2002) 'The economics of science and technology' *Journal of Technology Transfer* 27 (2), 155–203

Autio, E., Hameri, A.-P. and Vuola, O. (2004) 'A framework of industrial knowledge spillovers in big-science centers' *Research Policy* 33 (1), 107–26

Bachtler, J. (2004) 'Innovation-led regional development: policy trends and issues' Paper presented at the OECD conference on Innovation and Regional Development: Transition Towards a Knowledge-based Economy. Florence, Italy, 25–6 November 2004 (Unpublished)

Bagchi-Sen, S., Lawton Smith, H. and Hall, L. (2004) 'The US biotech industry – policy and practice' *Environment and Planning C.* 199–216

Balconi, M., Breschi, S. and Lissoni, F. (2004) 'Networks of innovators and the role of academia: an exploration of Italian patent data' *Research Policy* 33, 127–45

BankBoston (1997) *MIT: the impact of innovation*, web.mit.edu/newsoffice/founders/

Bartel, A. and Lichtenberg, F. (1987) 'The comparative advantage of educated workers in implementing new technology' *Review of Economics and Statistics* 69, 1–11

Bathelt, H. (2001) 'Regional competence and economic recovery: divergent growth paths in Boston's high technology economy' *Entrepreneurship & Regional Development* 13 (4), 287–314

Battelle Memorial Institute and the State Science and Technology Institute (2001) *State Government Initiatives in Biotechnology* www.bio.org

Baty, P. (2005) '£300m Science Central aims to boost businesses and jobs' *Times Higher Education Supplement*, 15 July, 9

Baxter, C. and Tyler, P. (2004) 'Creating enterprising places: what makes for competitive high-technology places' Paper presented at Cambridge–MIT Competitiveness Forum on *Metrics: evaluating research and science-based programmes*, 18 June 2004

Beeson, P. and Montgomery, E. (1993) 'The effects of colleges and universities on local labor markets' *Review of Economics and Statistics* 75, 753–61

Beise, M. and Stahl, H. (1999) 'Public research and industrial innovations in Germany' *Research Policy* 28 (4), 397–422

Belt, B., Hentley, J., Charles, D., Jones, I. and Audas, R. (2000) 'North east graduate labour markets 1999–2000' Centre for Urban and Regional Development Studies (CURDS), University of Newcastle upon Tyne

Berens, T.R. and Gray, D.O. (2001) 'Unintended consequences of cooperative research: impact of industry sponsorhip on climate for academic freedom and other graduate outcome' *Research Policy* 30, 179–99

Berglund, D. (1998) *State Funding for Cooperative Technology Programs* Columbus, OH, State Science and Technology Institute

Berman, E., Bound, J. and Griliches, Z. (1994) 'Changes in the demand for skilled labor within US manufacturing industries: evidence from the annual survey of manufacturers' *Quarterly Journal of Economics* 113 (4), 1245–80

Betts, J.R. (1997) 'The skill bias of technological change in Canadian manufacturing industries' *Review of Economics and Statistics* 79 (1), 146–50

Betts, J.R. and Lee, C. (2005) 'Universities as drivers of regional and national innovation: an assessment of the linkages from universities to innovation and economic growth' In (eds) *Higher Education in Canada*, C.M. Beach, R.W. Boadway and R. Marvin McInnis, Kingston, Ontario, McGill-Queens University Press

Bils, M. and Klenow, P.J. (2000) 'Does schooling cause growth?' *American Economic Review* 90 (5), 1160–83

BIO (2003) www.bio.org/tax/battelle.pdf

Black, D. and Henderson, V. (1997) 'A theory of urban growth' *Journal of Political Economy* 107 (2), 252–84

Blueprint (2004) 'New investment in stem cell therapies' *Blueprint: The Newsletter of the University of Oxford* 4 (11), 3 June, 1 www.ox.ac.uk/blueprint

Blumenthal, D., Causino, N., Campbell, E. and Louis, K.S. (1996) 'Relationship between academic institutions and industry in the life sciences: an industry survey' *New England Journal of Medicine* 334 (6), 369–73

Blumenstyk, G.C. (2001) 'A vilified corporate partnership produces little change (except better facilities)', *Chronicle of Higher Education*, 22 June 2001. http://chronicle.com/free/v47/i41/41a02401.htm

Blumenthal, D., Campbell, E.G., Anderson, M.S., Causino, N. and Louis, K.S. (1997) 'Withholding research results in academic life sciences: evidence from a National Survey of Faculty' *Journal of American Medical Association* 277, 1224–8

Boddy, M. (1988) 'Defence spending and the north–south divide' *Town and Country Planning* 5 (7), 116–17

Boekholt, P. (2003) 'Evaluation of regional innovation policies in Europe' Chapter 13 in P. Shapira and S. Kulhman (eds) *Learning from science and technology policy evaluation: experiences from the United States and Europe* Cheltenham, Edward Elgar, 244–59

Bok, D. (2003) *Universities in the market place* Princeton, Princeton University Press

Bompard, P. (2003) 'Italy plunged into marketing frenzy' *Times Higher Education Supplement* 8 August, 10

Boyer, E. (1994) 'Scholarship reconsidered: priorities for a new century' Chapter 3 in *Universities in the twenty-first century* London, National Commission on Education and The Council for Industry and Higher Education

Bozeman, B. (2000) 'Technology transfer and public policy: a review of research and theory' *Research Policy* 29, 627–55

Bozeman, B. and Gaughan, M. (2000) 'Evaluating scientific and technical human capital: an event history approach' Chapter 8 in *Proceedings from the 2000 US–European Workshop on Learning from Science and Technology Evaluation*, edited by P. Shapira and S. Kuhlmann www.isi.frauhofer.de/p/bh-proceed/pdt

Branscomb, L.M., Kodama, F. and Florida, R. (eds) (1999) *Industrializing knowledge: university–industry linkages in Japan and the United States* Cambridge, MA and London, MIT

Bray, M. and Lee, J. (2000) 'University revenues from technology transfer: licensing fees vs equity positions *Journal of Business Venturing* 15, 385–92

Breheny, M. and McQuaid, R. (eds) (1987) *The development of high technology industries* London, Croom Helm

Breschi, S. and Lissoni, F. (2001) 'Knowledge spillovers and local innovation systems: a critical survey' *Industrial and Corporate Change* 19 (4), 975–1005

Brighton, R. (2004) 'Evaluation of TCS' Paper presented at the Metrics: Evaluating Research and Science Based Programmes seminar, Cambridge–MIT Institute 18 June, Cambridge, MA, SQW

Brisse-Sillon, C. (1997) *Universités Publiques aux Etats-Unis*, Paris: L'Harmattan

Brusoni, S. and Geuna, A. (forthcoming) 'The key characteristics of sectoral knowledge bases: an international comparison' Chapter prepared for inclusion in C. Antonelli, D. Foray, B. Hall and W.E. Steinmuller (eds) *New frontiers in the economics of innovation and new technology* Cheltenham, Edward Elgar

Bundy, C. (2004) 'We'd like to be like America' *Times Higher Education Supplement*, 9 July, 16

Bunnell, T.G. and Coe, N.M. (2001) 'Spaces and scales of innovation' *Progress in Human Geography* 569–89

Burt, R.S. (1992) *Structural holes, the social structure of competition* Cambridge, MA, Harvard University Press

Business Higher Education Forum (2001) *Working together, creating knowledge: the university–industry research collaboration initiative* Washington, American Council on Education www.acenet.edu/programs/bhef/bhef_publications.cfm?pubID=230

Calvert, J. and Patel, P. (2002) 'University–industry research collaborations in the UK' Report on Phase 1 of a project funded by EPSRC/ESRC (Analysis of University–Industry Research Collaborations in the UK) Brighton, SPRU

Campbell, D. (2003) 'The evaluation of university research in the United Kingdom and the Netherlands, Germany and Austria' In P. Shapira and S. Kuhlmann (eds) *Learning from science and technology policy evaluation: experiences from the United States and Europe* Cheltenham, Edward Elgar, 109–45

Candell, A.B. and Jaffe, A.B. (1999) 'The regional economic impact of public research funding: A case study of Massachusetts' Chapter 19 in L.M. Branscomb, F. Kodama and R. Florida (eds) *Industrializing knowledge: university–industry linkages in Japan and the United States* Cambridge, MA and London, MIT 510–30

Carlsson, B. (ed.) (1997) *Technological systems and industrial dynamics* Boston, Kluwer Academic Publications

Carlsson, B. and Stankiewicz, R. (1991) 'On the nature, function and composition of technological systems' *Journal of Evolutionary Economics* 1, 93–118

Carayol, N. (2003) 'Objectives, agreements and matching in science-industry collaborations: reassembling the pieces of the puzzle' *Research Policy* 32 (6), 887–908

Caspar, S. and Matraves, C. (2003) 'Institutional frameworks and innovation in the German and UK pharmaceutical industry' *Research Policy*

Castells, M. and Hall, P. (1994) *Technopoles of the world* London, Routledge

Caulkin, S. (2004) 'Take aim, you will always miss' *Observer*, 14 November, Management 11

Cesaroni, F. and Piccaluga, A. (2002) 'Patenting activity of European universities: Relevant? Growing? Useful?' Paper al Convegno SPRU NPRnet, Rethinking Science Policy: Analytical Frameworks for Evidence-Based Policy, SPRU University of Sussex

Chadwick, A., Glasson, J., Lawton Smith, H., Clark, G. and Simmie, J. (2003) *Enterprising Oxford: the growth of the Oxfordshire high-tech economy* Oxford, Oxfordshire Economic Observatory

Chapman, C. (2005) 'Bid to create German Ivy League receives a £1.3bn shot in the arm' *Times Higher Education Supplement*, 15 July, 10–11

Chapple, K., Markusen, A., Schrock, G., Yamamoto, D. and Yu, P. (2004) 'High tech rankings, specialization and relationship to growth: a rejoinder' *Economic Development Quarterly* 18 (1), 44–9

Charles, D. and Conway, C. (2001) *Higher education–business interaction survey* Research Report 01/68 Newcastle, CURDS www.hefce.ac.uk

Charles, D. and Howells, J. (1992) *Technology transfer in Europe: public and private networks* London, Belhaven Press

Charles, D.R. (2003) 'Universities and territorial development: reshaping the regional role of UK universities' *Local Economy* 18 (1), 7–20

Cheney, T. (1997) 'Transferring technology to industrial partners at LETI's Grenoble Center' www.micromagazine.com/archive/97/07/facility.html

Clark, B.R. (1992) 'Graduate education and research training' Chapter 11 in T.G. Whiston and R.L. Geiger (eds) *Research and higher education: the United Kingdom and the United States* London, Society for Research into Higher Education, 138–52

Clark, B.R. (1998) 'Building the entrepreneurial university' *IAU Newsletter* 4 (2), May

Clark, G.L. (2004) 'Money flows like mercury: the geography of global finance' Paper presented at the Association of American Geographers Centennial Conference, Philadelphia, 16–19 March 2004

Clarysse, B.. Heinman, A. and Degroof, J.J. (2001) 'An institutional and resource-based explanation of growth patterns of research-based spin-offs in Europe' In OECD *Fostering high-tech spin-offs: a public strategy for innovation, STI Review* 26 Paris, OECD, 95–6

Cohen, W. and Levinthal, D. (1990) 'Absorptive capacity: a new perspective on learning and innovation' *Administrative Science Quarterly* 35 (1), 128–52

Cohen, W., Florida, R. and Goe, R. (1994) 'University–industry research centers in the United States' Report to the Ford Foundation, Carnegie Mellon University

Cohen, W.M., Florida, R., Ransazzese, L. and Walsh, J.P. (1998) 'Industry and the academy: uneasy partners in the cause of technological advance' Chapter 7 in

R. Noll (ed.) *Challenges to research universities* Washington DC, Brookings Institution Press, 171–200

Cohen, W.M., Nelson, R.R. and Walsh, J.P. (2002) 'Links and impacts: the influence of public research on industrial R&D' *Management Science* 48, 1–23

Collinson, S. (2000) 'Knowledge networks for innovation in small Scottish software firms' *Entrepreneurship and Regional Development* 12, 217–44

Cook, M. 'From Bologna to Berlin' www.naric.org.uk/pps/Malcolm%20Cook%20Bologna-Berlin.pps

Cook-Deegan, R.M. (2000) 'Medical biotechnology, United States policies influencing its development, In *Encyclopedia of ethical, legal, and policy issues in biotechnology*, Volume 1, New York, John Wiley and Sons, 798–809

Cooke, P. (1998) 'Introduction: origins of the concept' In H.-J. Braczyk, P. Cooke and M. Heidenreich (eds) (2000) *Regional innovation systems* London, UCL Press, 2–27

Cooke, P. (2002) 'Biotechnology clusters as regional, sectoral innovation systems' *International Science Review* 25 (1), 38–62

Cooke, P. (2004) 'The molecular biology revolution and the rise of bioscience megacentres' *Environment and Planning C Government and Policy* 22 (2), 161–78

Coombs, R. and Metcalfe, S. (2000) 'Universities, the science base and the innovation performance of the UK' CRIC Briefing Paper 5, November, Manchester, University of Manchester & UMIST

CORDIS (2003) *European innovation scoreboard 2003* Luxembourg, European Commission www.cordis.lu/trendchart

Cortright, J. and Mayer, H. (2002) *Signs of life: the growth of biotechnology centers in the US* Washington DC, The Brookings Institution, Center on Urban and Metropolitan Policy

Cosh, A.D. and Hughes, A. (2001) *Innovation and R&D in SMEs in enterprises in Europe, a sixth report* Luxembourg, Eurostat

Cowan, R. and Jonard, N. (2003) 'The workings of scientific communities' In A. Geuna, A. Salter and E. Steinmueller (eds) *Science and innovation: rethinking the rationales for funding and governance* Cheltenham, Edward Elgar, 309–34

Cowan, R., David, P.A. and Foray, D. (2000) 'The explicit economics of knowledge codification and tacitness' *Industrial and Corporate Change* 9, 211–54

Cozzens, S. (2003) 'Frameworks for evaluating S&T policy in the United States' Chapter 4 in P. Shapira and S. Kulhman (eds) *Learning from science and technology evaluation: experiences from the United States and Europe* Cheltenham, Edward Elgar, 54–65

Crespi, G. and Geuna, A. (2004) 'The productivity of science: an international comparison' a report prepared for the Department of Trade and Industry, Brighton, Sussex University, SPRU

Crow, M.M. and Tucker, C. (2001) 'The American research university system as America's *de facto* technology policy' *Science and Public Policy* 28 (1), 2–10

CURDS (2000) North East Graduate Labour Market Report Executive Summary 1999–2000, Newcastle upon Tyne, CURDS www.campus.ncl.ac.uk/unbs/curds/Keywords2.asp?T1=Labour+Markets

Curtis, P. (2004) 'Dire warnings as chemistry departments close' *Education Guardian*, 2 February, http://education.guardian.co.uk/universitiesincrisis/story/0,12028,1137231,00.html

Dankbaar, T. (2004) 'Embeddedness, context, proximity and control' *European Planning Studies* 12, 691–701

David, P. (1984) 'On the perilous economics of modern science' paper presented at the TIP Workshop Stanford University, August 1984 mimeo

David, P. (2005) 'Innovation and universities' role in commercialising research results: second thoughts about the Bayh-Dole experiment' SIEPR Discussion Paper 04-27 http://siepr.stanford.edu/programs/OpenSoftware_David/NSFOSF_Publications.html

David, P.A. and Foray, D. (1995) 'Accessing and Expanding the Science and Technology Knowledge Base' *STI. Review* 16, 13–68

David, P., Mowery, D.C. and Steinmuller, W.E. (1994) 'University–industry research collaborations: managing missions in conflict' Paper presented at the CEPR/AAAS conference 'University Goals, Institutional Mechanisms, and the "Industrial Transferability" of Research', sponsored by the American Academy of Arts and Sciences and the Centre for Economic Policy Research at Stanford University, held at Stanford, CA, 18–20 March 1994

Davies, J.L. (1997) 'The regional university: issues in the development of an organisational framework' *Higher Education Management* 9 (3), Paris, OECD, 29–42

Davis, C. (2003) 'London to incubate bioscience' *Times Higher Education Supplement*, 1 August, 4

Davis, E. (2004) 'Massive rises needed to save Oxford' www.oxfordstudent.com/2004-02-19/news/8

Davis, H.G. and Diamond, N. (1997) *The rise of American research universities: elite and challenges in the post-war era* Baltimore, Johns Hopkins University Press

De Bernardy, M. (1999) 'Reactive and proactive local territory: cooperation and community in Grenoble' *Regional Studies* 33 (4), 343–52

De Fontenay, C. and Carmel, E. (2004) 'Israel's Silicon Wadi: the forces behind cluster formation' In T. Bresnahan and A. Gambardella (eds) *Building high-tech clusters: Silicon Valley and beyond* Cambridge, Cambridge University Press, 40–77

Dicken, P. and Malmberg, A. (2001) 'Firms in territories: a relational perspective' *Economic Geography* 345–63

Di Gregorio, D. and Shane, S. (2003) 'Why do some universities generate more start-ups than others?' *Research Policy* 32, 209–27

DfES (2003) *The future of higher education* London, DfES www.dfes.gov.uk/highereducation/hestrategy/heandb.shtml

Dosi, G. (1988) 'The nature of the innovation process' Chapter 11 in G. Dosi, C. Freeman, R. Nelson, G. Silverberg and L. Soete (eds) *Technical change and economic theory* London, Pinter 221–38

Doutriaux, J. (2003) 'University–industry linkages and the development of knowledge clusters in Canada' *Local Economy* 18 (1), 63–79

Druilhe, C. and Garnsey, E. (2000) 'High-tech activity in Cambridge and Grenoble' *Entrepreneurship and Regional Development* 12 (2), 163–77

Druilhe, C. and Garnsey, E. (2004) 'Do academic spin-outs differ and does it matter?' *Journal of Technology Transfer* 29 (3–4), 269–85

DTI (1988) *DTI – The department for enterprise* London, Department of Trade and Industry

DTI (1993) *Realising our potential: a strategy for science, technology and engineering* London, Department of Trade and Industry

DTI (1998) *Our competitive future* London, Department of Trade and Industry

DTI (2000) *Excellence and opportunity: a science and innovation policy for the 21st century* London, HMSO

DTI (2001) *Business clusters in the UK – a first assessment* www.dti.gov.uk/clusters/map/

DTI (2003) *Bioscience 2015: Improving national health, increasing national wealth* Department of Trade and Industry, London, HMSO

DTI (2004) *Universities mean business* Higher Education Business Interaction Survey 2001/2 P/2004/64

DTI (2005) *Comparative statistics for the UK, European and US biotechnology sectors: analysis year 2003* Report prepared by Critical I Limited for the Department of Trade and Industry, London, DTI

Dunford, M. (1989) 'Technopoles, politics and markets: the development of electronics in Grenoble and Silicon Glen' Chapter 4 in M. Sharp and P. Holmes (eds) *Strategies for new technologies: case studies from Britain and France* London, Philip Allan

Edquist, C. (1997) 'Systems of innovation approaches – their emergence and characteristics' Chapter 1 in C. Edquist (ed.) *Systems of Innovation* London, Pinter, 1–35

Edqvist, O. (2003) 'Layered science and science policies' *Minerva* 41, 207–21

EEDA (2002) *East of England framework for regional employment and skills action* Histon, Cambridge, EEDA

Eisinger, P. (1988) *The rise of the entrepreneurial state: state and local economic development policy in the US* Madison, University of Wisconsin Press

Enders, J. (2001) 'Serving many masters: the PhD on the labour market' Paper prepared for the CHER conference, 2–4 September, Dijon

Engelstoft, S., Jensen-Butler, C., Smith, I. and Winther, L. (2002) 'The economics of industrial clusters and an examination of their performance in Demark' Paper presented at the Regional Science Association International British & Irish Section 32nd Annual Conference, Brighton and Hove, 21–3 August 2002

Etzkowitz, H. (1983) 'Entrepreneurial scientists and entrepreneurial universities in American academic science' *Minerva* 21, 198–233

Etzkowitz, H. (1999) 'Bridging the gap: the evolution of industry–university links in the United States' Chapter 8 in L.M. Branscomb, F. Kodama and R. Florida (eds) *Industrializing knowledge: university–industry linkages in Japan and the United States* Cambridge, MA and London, MIT, 203–33

Etzkowitz, H. (2003) 'Research groups as "quasi-firms": the invention of the entrepreneurial university' *Research Policy* 32 (1), 109–21

Etzkowitz, H. and Leydesdorff, L. (1995) 'The triple helix university–industry–government relations: a laboratory for knowledge-based economic development' *EASST Review* 14 (1), 14–19

Etzkowitz, H. and Leydesdorff, L. (1997) Introduction: universities in the global knowledge economy. In H. Etzkowitz and L. Leydesdorff (eds) *Universities and the global knowledge economy: a triple helix of university–industry–government relations* London, Pinter, 1–8

Etzkowitz, H. and Leydesdorff, L. (2000) 'The dynamics of innovation: from national systems and "Mode 2" to a triple helix of university–industry–government relations' *Research Policy* 29 (2), 109–23

Etzkowitz, H., Webster, A., Gebhardt, C. and Cantisano Terra, B.R. (2000) 'The future of the university and the university of the future: evolution from ivory tower to entrepreneurial paradigm' *Research Policy* 29 (2), 313–30

European Commission (1994) *The European report on S&T indicators 1994* EUR 15897 EN, Luxembourg, Office for Official Publications of the European Communities

European Commission (1996) *Green paper on innovation* Brussels, European Commission

European Commission (1997) *Second European report on S&T indicators 1997* Appendix EUR 17639, Luxembourg, Office for Official Publications of the European Communities

European Commission (2001a) *2001 innovation scoreboard* Commission Staff Working Paper SEC (2001) 1414, Brussels

European Commission (2001b) *Communication from the Commission: the regional dimension of the European research area* Brussels, 3 October 2001 COM (2001) 549 final

European Commission (2002) *University spin-outs in Europe – overview and good practice* Directorate General for Enterprise EUR 17046, Brussels, European Commission

European Commission (2003a) 'Communication from the Commission: the role of the universities in the Europe of Knowledge' Brussels COM (2003) 58 final

European Commission (2003b) *Third European Report on S&T indicators 2003: towards a knowledge-based economy* Luxembourg, Office for Official Publications of the European Communities 2003 EUR 20025 EN www.cordis.lu/indicators/third_report.htm

European Commission (2003c) *Communication from the Commission life sciences and biotechnology – a strategy for Europe, progress report and future orientations* SEC (2003) 248, Brussels

European Commission (2004) 'Innovation in Europe, Iceland and Norway: overview of the third Community Innovation Survey', Luxembourg, CEC www.cordis.lu/innovation-smes/src/cis.htm

Evans, R., Butler, N. and Goncalves, E. (1991) *The campus connection: military research in campus* London, CND

Faulkner, W. and Senker, J. (1995) *Knowledge frontiers: public sector research and industrial innovation in biotechnology, engineering ceramics, and parallel computing* Oxford, Clarendon Press

Fazackerley, A. (2003) 'EU "red tape" baffles the UK' *Times Higher Education Supplement*, 8 August

Fazackerley, A. (2004) 'Last biotech moves GM research to US' *Times Higher Education Supplement*, 2 July 2004, 52

FDA (2004) 'Innovation or stagnation? www.fda.gov/oc/initiatives/criticalpath/whitepaper.html

Feldman, M.A. (1985) 'Biotechnology and local economic growth: the American pattern' Chapter 5 in P. Hall and A. Markusen (eds) *Silicon landscapes* Winchester, MA, Allen & Unwin

Feldman, M. (1994) *The geography of innovation* Dordrecht, Kluwer Academic

Feldman, M.P. (1999) 'The new economics of innovation, spillovers and agglomeration: a review of empirical studies' *The Economics of Innovation and New Technology* 8, 5–25

Feldman, M. (2001) 'Location and innovation: the new economic geography of innovation, spillovers, and agglomeration' Chapter 20 in G. Clark, M. Feldman and M. Gertler (eds) *The Oxford Handbook of Economic Geography* Oxford, Oxford University Press, 373–94

Feldman, M.P. and Ronzio, C. (2001) 'Closing the innovative loop: moving from the laboratory to the shop floor in biotechnology manufacturing' *Entrepreneurship and Regional Development* 13, 1–16

Feldman, M. and Schreuder, Y. (1996) 'Initial advantage: the origins of the geographic concentration of the pharmaceutical industry in the Mid-Atlantic region' *Industrial and Corporate Change* 5, 839–62

Feller, I. (1999) 'The American university system as a performer of basic and applied research' Chapter 3 in L. M. Branscomb, F. Kodama and R. Florida (eds) *Industrializing knowledge: university–industry linkages in Japan and the United States* Cambridge, MA and London, MIT, 65–101

Feller, I. (2000) cherry.iac.gatech.edu/e-value/bh-proceed/02-Frameworks.pdf

Feller, I. (2004) 'The public research university' American Association for the Advancement of Science Presentation to the AAAS 29th Forum on Science and Technology Policy, Washington DC, 22 April 2004 www.aaas.org/spp/rd/feller 404/pdf

Felsenstein, D. (1994) 'Large high technology firms and the spatial extension of metropolitan labor markets: some evidence from Israel' *Urban Studies* 31 (6), 867–83

Firn, D. (2004) 'Safety fears could drive research abroad' *Financial Times*, 29 July, 3

Florida, R. (1999) 'The role of the university: leveraging talent, not technology' *Issues in Science and Technology* (Summer) www.nap.edu/issues/15.4/florida.htm

Florida, R. (2002) *The rise of the creative class* New York, Basic Books

Florida, R. and Cohen, W. (1999) 'Engine or infrastructure? The university role in economic development' Chapter 23 in L.M. Branscomb, F. Kodama and R. Florida (eds) *Industrializing knowledge: university–industry linkages in Japan and the United States* Cambridge, MA and London, MIT, 589–610

Fogarty, M.S. and Sinha, A.K. (1999) 'Why older regions can't generalise from route 128 and Silicon Valley: university–industry relationships and regional innovation systems' Chapter 18 in L.M. Branscomb, F. Kodama and R. Florida (eds) *Industrializing knowledge: university–industry linkages in Japan and the United States* Cambridge, MA and London, MIT, 473–509

Foray, D. (1997) 'Generation and distribution of technological knowledge' Chapter 3 in C. Edquist (ed,) *Systems of innovation* London, Pinter, 64–85

Freeman, C. (1987) *Technology and economic performance: lessons from Japan* London, Pinter

Freeman, C. (1988) 'Japan: a new national system of innovation?' Chapter 16 in G. Dosi, C. Freeman, R. Nelson, G. Silverberg and L. Soete (eds) *Technical change and economic theory* London, Pinter, 330–48

Freeman, C. (1995) 'The "national system of innovation"' *Cambridge Journal of Economics* 19 (1), 5–24

Frenz, M., Michie, J. and Oughton, C. (2005) 'Innovation and cooperation: the role of absorptive capacity' Birkbeck Working Paper Series, Birkbeck, University of London

Gardner, R. (2003) 'Don't concentrate, its bad for research health' *Times Higher Education Supplement*, 5 September, 14

Garnsey, E. and Lawton Smith, H. (1998) 'Proximity and complexity in the emergence of high technology industry: the Oxbridge comparison' *Geoforum* 29 (4), 433–50

Geiger, R.L. (1986) *To advance knowledge: the growth of American research universities, 1900–1940* Oxford, Oxford University Press

Geiger, R.L. (2003) 'Universities and the production of knowledge for industry' Paper presented at the SCANCOR conference 'Universities and the Production of Knowledge', Stanford University, 25–6 April 2003

Georghiou, L. and Kuhlmann, S. (2002) 'Future policy instruments: evaluation of the socio-economic effects of the European research area' In W. Polt, J. Rojo, K. Zinöcker, G. Fahrenkrog and A. Tübke (eds) *RTD Evaluation Tool Box – Assessing the Socio-Economic Impact of RTD-Policies* Brussels and Luxembourg (European Commission, Joint Research Centre, Institute for Prospective Technological Studies, CSC-EEC-EAEC) (IPTS Technical Report Series, EUR 20382 EN), 203–10 (see http://epub.jrc.es/docs/EUR-20382-EN.pdf)

Georghiou, L. and Metcalfe, S. (2002) *Evolutionary foundations of technology policy* Cheltenham, Edward Elgar

Georghiou, L. and Roessner, D. (2000) 'Evaluating technology programs: tools and methods' *Research Policy* 29 (4–5), 657–78

Gertler, M. (1997) 'Globality and locality: the future of "geography" and the nation state' in P.J. Rimmer (ed.) *Pacific geographies: integration and globalisation in the Asia-Pacific economy* St Leonards, Allen and Unwin, 12–34

Gertler, M.S. and Wolfe, D.A. (eds) (2002) *Innovation and social learning: institutional adaptation in an era of technological change* Basingstoke, Macmillan/Palgrave

Geuna, A. (1998) 'Determinants of university participation in EU-funded R&D cooperative projects' *Research Policy* 26, 677–87

Geuna, A. (2001) 'The changing rationale for European university research funding: are there negative unintended consequences?' *Journal of Economic Issues* XXV, 607–32

Geuna, A. and Martin, B.E. (2003) 'University research evaluation and funding: an international comparison' *Minerva* 41 (4), 277–304

Geuna, A. and Nesta, L. (2003) 'University patenting and its effects in academic research' SEWPS Working Paper 99, June

Geuna, A., Salter, A.J. and Steinmueller, W.E. (2003) 'General introduction' In A. Geuna, A.J. Salter and W.E. Steinmueller (eds) *Science and innovation: rethinking the rationales for funding and governance* Cheltenham, Edward Elgar, xv–xxi

Gibbons, M., Limoges, C., Nowotny, H., Schwartman, S., Scott, P. and Trow, M. (1994) *The production of knowledge: the dynamics of science and research in contemporary societies* London, Sage

GLA Economics (2004) *World city, world knowledge* London, GLA

Glasmeier, A. (2000) *Manufacturing time* New York, Guildford Press

Glasner, P. (2004) 'Genomic potentials: promise to product in the post-genomic era' Presentation at the Bio-Link Seminar, Cardiff University, 5 July

Glasson, J. (2003) 'The widening local and regional development impacts of the modern universities – a tale of two cities (and North–South perspectives)' *Local Economy* 18 (1), 21–37

Goddard, A. (2003) 'Capital's colleges converge' *Times Higher Education Supplement*, 1 August, 4

Goddard, J. (2004) Keynote address to the OECD Institutional Management in

Higher Education (IMHE) General Conference on Choices and Responsibilities: Higher Education and the Knowledge Society, Paris, September 2004

Goddard, J., Charles, D., Pike, A., Potts, G. and Bradley, D. (1994) *Universities and communities* London, Committee of Vice Chancellors and Principals

Godden, A. (2003) 'Regional productivity clarified' Unpublished mimeo, September

Godin, B. and Gingras, Y. (2000) 'The place of universities in the system of knowledge production' *Research Policy* 29 (2), 273–8

Goldstein, H. and Luger, M.I. (1992) 'University-based research parks as a rural development strategy' *Policy Studies Journal* 20 (2) (Spring), 249–64

Goldstein, H.A. and Renault, C.S. (2004) 'Contributions of universities to regional economic development: a quasi-experimental approach' *Regional Studies* 38 (7), 733–46

Goldstein, H.A., Maier, G. and Luger, M.I. (1995) 'The university as an instrument for economic development: U.S. and European Comparisons' In D. Dill and B. Sporin (eds) *Emerging patterns of social demand and university reform: through a glass darkly* Oxford, Pergamon

Goodman, S. (2003) *Twin peaks Rhône-Alpes* www.nature.com/nature/journal/v426/n6964/full/nj6964-366a.html

Granovetter, M. (1973) 'The strength of weak ties' *American Journal of Sociology* 78 (6), 1360–80

Gregerson, B. and Johnson, B. (1999) 'Learning economies, innovation systems and European integration' *Regional Studies* 31 (5), 470–90

Griliches, Z. (1979) 'Issues in assessing the contribution of R&D to productivity growth' *Bell Journal of Economics* 10, 92–116

Griliches, Z. (1992) 'The search for R&D spillovers' *Scandinavian Journal of Economics* 94, S29–47

Grossman, G. and Helpman, E. (1991) *Innovation and growth in the global economy* Cambridge, MA, MIT Press

Grossman, J.H., Morgan, R.P. and Reid, P.P. (2001), 'Contributions of academic research to industrial performance in five industry sectors' *Journal of Technology Transfer* 26 (1–2), 143–52

Grudkova, V. (2001) *The technology economy: why do tech companies go where they go?* Washington DC, EDA National Forum, 30 May

Grupp, H. (1995) 'Science, high-technology and the competitiveness of EU countries' *Cambridge Journal of Economics* 19 (1), 209–23

Guillaume, H. (1998) *Rapport de Mission sur la technologie et l'innovation* Paris, MRET

Gummett, P. and Gibbons, M. (1978) 'Government research for industry: recent British developments' *Research Policy* 7 (3), 268–90

Hague, D. and Oakley, K. (2000) *Spin-offs and start-ups in UK universities* London, CVCP

Haines, I. (2003) 'Concentrating too much' Invited article, *Save British Science Newsletter* 37, July, London, Save British Science www.savebritishscience.org.uk

Halkier, H. (2003) 'Discourse, institutionalism and public policy: theory methods and a Scottish case study' Centre for International Studies, Aalborg University, Discussion Paper 23/2003

Hall, B.H., Link, A. and Scott, T.J. (2000) 'Barriers inhibiting industry from partnering with universities: evidence from the Advanced Technology Programme' *Journal of Technology Transfer* 26, 87–98

Hall, P. (1984) 'The geography of the Fifth Kondratiev' Chapter 1 in P. Hall and A. Markusen (eds) *Silicon landscapes* Winchester, MA, Allen & Unwin, 1–19

Hall, P., Breheny, M., McQuaid, R. and Hart, D. (1987) *Western sunrise* London, Allen & Unwin

Hansard (2003) 18 March 2003, *Column 630W* http://www.publications.parliament.uk/pa/cm200203/cmhansrd/v0030318/text/30318w04/htm

Hart, D.M. (1988) *Forged consensus: science, technology and economic policy in the United States 1921–1953* Princeton, Princeton University Press

Haugh, P. (1995) 'Formation of biotechnology firms in the Greater Seattle region: an empirical investigation of entrepreneurial, financial and educational perspectives' *Environment and Planning A* 27, 249–76

HEFCE (2003) The Third Annual Higher Education–Business Interaction Survey www.hefce.ac.uk/pubs/hefce/2003/03_11.htm

Henley, J. (2004) 'Top French scientists in threat to quit' *The Guardian* 13 January, 14

Henry, N. and Pinch, P. (2000) '(The) industrial agglomeration (of Motor Sport Valley): a knowledge, space, economy approach' In J. Bryson, P. Daniels, N. Henry and J. Pollard (eds) *Knowledge Space Economy* London, Routledge

Herbst, M. (2004) 'The production–morphology nexus of research universities: the Atlantic split' *Higher Education Policy* 17, 5–21

Hicks, D. (1995) 'Published papers, tacit competencies and corporate management of the public/private character of knowledge' *Industrial and Corporate Change* 4 (2), 401–24

Hill, P. (2004) 'Lambert to draft model IP contracts' *Times Higher Education Supplement*, 28 May, 60

HM Treasury (2003) *Lambert review of business–university collaboration* (The Lambert Report) www.hm-treasury.gov.uk/consultations_and_legislation/lambert/consult_lambert_index.cfm

House Committee on Science (1998) 'Unlocking our future toward a new national science policy: a report to Congress by the House Committee on Science', 24 September www.house.gov/science/science_policy_report.htm

House of Commons Health Committee (2005) 'The Influence of the Pharmaceutical Industry Fourth Report of Session 2004–5' Volume 1 House of Commons London, The Stationery Office Limited

House of Commons Science & Technology Committee (2004) *Scientific publications: free for all?* www.publications.parliament.uk/pa/cm200304/cmselect/cmsctech/399/39902.htm

Howells, J.R.L. (1985) 'Product sophistication, industrial organisation, and location: the UK pharmaceutical industry' *Environment and Planning A* 17, 1045–62

Howells, J. (1999) 'Regional systems of innovation?' In D. Archbugi, J. Howells and J. Michie (eds) *Innovation policy in a global economy* Cambridge, Cambridge University Press 67–93

Howells, J. (2000) 'Innovation collaboration and networking: a European perspective' Chapter 3 in P. Healey (ed.) *European research, technology and development: issues for a competitive future* Key research findings from the ESRC Research Programme *The European Context of UK Science Policy* London, SPSG, 35–52

Howells, J.R.L. (2002) 'Tacit knowledge, innovation and economic geography' *Urban Studies* 39, 871–84

Hsu, D. and Bernstein, T. (1997) 'Where do leads from licenses come from? Source data from six institutions' *Journal of the Association of the University Technology Managers* 9, 1–33

Hughes, A. (2003) 'Knowledge transfer, entrepreneurship and economic growth: some reflections and implications for policy in the Netherlands' ESRC Centre for Business Research, University of Cambridge Working Paper 273

Huttner, S. (1999) 'Knowledge and the biotech economy: a case of mistaken identity' Paper presented at the High-Level CERI/OECD/NSF Forum on Measuring Knowledge in Learning Economies and Societies, May, Arlington, VA

Institute of Higher Education, Shanghai Jiao Tong University (2004) ed.sjtu.edu.cn/ranking.htm

Jacob, M., Lundqvist, M. and Hellsmark, H. (2003) 'Entrepreneurial transformations in the Swedish university system: the case of Chalmers University of Technology' *Research Policy*

Jacobsson, S. (2002) 'Universities and industrial transformation' SPRU Electronic Working Paper Series Paper 81 www.sussex.ac.uk/spru

Jacobsson, S. and Rickne, A. (2003) 'The Swedish "academic paradox" – myth or reality: how strong is really the Swedish "academic" sector?' Paper presented at the Conference in Honour of Keith Pavitt 'What Do We Know About Innovation', The Freeman Centre, University of Sussex, 13–15 November 2003

Jaffe, A.B. (1989) 'Real effects of academic research' *The American Economic Review* 88, 957

Jobbins, D. (2004) 'EUA to look at UK's top-up model' *Times Higher Education Supplement*, 9 April, 10

Jobbins, D. (2005) 'Oxford may join global elite 8' *Times Higher Education Supplement*, 15 July, 6

Katz, B. (2002) *Beyond merger: a competitive vision for the regional city of Louisville* Washington DC, the Brookings Institution, Center on Urban and Metropolitan Policy

Katz, J.S. and Martin, B.R. (1997) 'What is research collaboration?' *Research Policy* 26, 1–18

Keeble, D., Lawson, C., Lawton Smith, H., Moore, B. and Wilkinson, F. (1997) 'Internationalisation processes and networking and local embeddedness in technology-intensive small firms' ESRC Centre for Business Research, Cambridge University WP 53, March

Keep, E. and Mayhew, K. (2004) 'Dead end for the vocational route?' *Times Higher Education Supplement*, 9 July, 16

Kenney, M. (1986) *Biotechnology: the university–industry complex* New Haven, Yale University Press

Klevorick, A.K., Levin, R.C., Nelson, R.R. and Winter, S.G. (1995) 'On the sources and significance of interindustry differences in technological opportunities' *Research Policy* 24, 185–205

Kodama, F. and Branscomb, L.M. (1999) 'University research as an engine for growth: how realistic is the vision?' Chapter 1 in L.M. Branscomb, F. Kodama and R. Florida (eds) *Industrializing knowledge: university–industry linkages in Japan and the United States* Cambridge, MA and London, MIT

Kreijen, M. and Van der Laag, A. (2003) 'Spin-offs as a bridge between two worlds: a policy perspective' In A. van der Laag and J. Snijder (eds) *Entrepeneurship in the Netherlands: knowledge transfer, developing high-tech ventures* The Hague, Ministry of Economic Affairs and EIM Business and Policy Research

Krugman, P. (1991) *Geography and trade* Cambridge, MA, MIT Press

Kuhlmann, S. (2003) 'Evaluation as a source of "strategic intelligence"' Chapter 18 in P. Shapira and S. Kuhlmann (eds) *Learning from science and technology policy evaluation: experiences from the United States and Europe* Cheltenham, Edward Elgar, 352–80

Kung, Shiann-Far (1995) *The role of science parks in the development of high technology industries, with special reference to Taiwan* Doctoral dissertation, St Catharine's College, Cambridge University

Laafia, I. (2002) *Statistics in focus SCIENCE AND TECHNOLOGY THEME 9* 3/2002 www.eucomed.be/docs/Employment%20in%20high-tech%20-%20 Europe%209500.pdf

Lanciano-Morandat, C. and Nohara, H. (2002a) 'The scientific labour market in international perspective: a "bridging institution" between academia and industry for the co-operation and transfer of knowledge and competences' SASE 2002 Conference Work and Labour in the Global Economy, University of Minnesota, Minneapolis, Minnesota, 27–30 June 2002

Lanciano-Morandat, C. and Nohara, H. (2002b) 'Academic spin-offs in France: the construction of the societal between national and local. First comparative approach' SASE 2002 Conference Work and Labour in the Global Economy, University of Minnesota, Minneapolis, Minnesota, 27–30 June 2002

Langley, C. (2005) *Soldiers in the laboratory: military involvement in science and technology – and some alternatives* Scientists for Global Responsibility www.sgr.org.uk

Lanza, R. and Piccaluga, A. (1995) 'Top-down and bottom-up approaches for technology transfer' *Technology Review* 83, 115–21

Lawton Smith, H. (1990) *The location and development of advanced technology in Oxfordshire in the context of the research environment* Unpublished DPhil thesis, University of Oxford

Lawton Smith, H. (2000) *Technology transfer and industrial change in Europe* Basingstoke, Macmillan

Lawton Smith, H. (2002) 'The context for science and technology regulation' In H. Lawton Smith (ed.) *The regulation of science and technology* Basingstoke, Palgrave

Lawton Smith, H. (2003a) 'Maximising the benefits from a concentration of universities' Paper presented at SEEDS Conference, the Barbican, 11 July

Lawton Smith, H. (2003b) 'Local innovation assemblages and institutional capacity in local high-tech economic development: the case of Oxfordshire' *Urban Studies* 40 (7), 1353–69

Lawton Smith, H. (2003c) 'Knowledge organisations and local economic development: the cases of Oxford and Grenoble' *Regional Studies* 37 (2), 899–90

Lawton Smith, H. (2005) 'The biotechnology industry in Oxfordshire: enterprise and innovation' *European Planning Studies* 12 (7), 985–1002

Lawton Smith, H. and De Bernardy, M. (2000) 'University and public research institute links with regional high-technology SMEs' In D. Keeble and F. Wilkinson (eds) *High-technology clusters, networking and collective learning in Europe* London, Ashgate Publishing, 90–117

Lawton Smith, H. and Glasson, J. (2005) *Public Research High-tech Spin-offs:*

Measuring Performance and Growth in Oxfordshire, Oxford: Oxfordshire Economic Observatory

Lawton Smith, H. and Ho, K.W. (2005) 'Measuring the performance of Oxford University, Oxford Brookes University and the government laboratories' spin-off companies' Fifth Triple Helix Conference, Turin, May 2005

Lawton Smith, H., Glasson, J. and Chadwick, A. (2005) 'The geography of talent: entrepreneurship and local economic development in Oxfordshire' *Entrepreneurship and Regional Development* 17, 449–76

Lawton Smith, H., Glasson, J., Simmie, J., Chadwick, A. and Clark, G. (2003) *Enterprising Oxford: the growth of the Oxfordshire high-tech economy* Oxford, Oxford Economic Observatory

Lazzeroni, M. and Piccaluga, A. (2003) 'Towards the entrepreneurial university' *Local Economy* 18 (1), 38–48

Lécuyer, C. (2002) www.stanford.edu/dept/HPS/TimLenoir/Startup/QuarterlyRpts/ProgressReportJan02.pdf

Lee, C.W.B. and Walshok, M.L. (2002) 'Critical path analysis of California's S&T education system: alternative paths to competency through continuing education and lifelong learning' a Report prepared for the California Council on Science and Technology, Sacramento, California Council on Science and Technology

Lee, C.B. and Walshok, M.L. (2003) 'Total links matter: the direct and indirect effects of research universities in regional economies' Paper prepared for University of California's Industry–University Cooperative Research Programme, UCSD

Leifner, I., Schatzl, L. and Schroder, T. (2004) 'Reforms in German higher education: implementing and adapting Anglo-American organizational and management structures at German universities' *Higher Education Policy* 17, 23–8

Lenoir, T. and Ueyama, T. (2002) www.stanford.edu/dept/HPS/TimLenoir/Startup/QuarterlyRpts/ProgressReportJan02.pdf

Lenoir, T., Rosenberg, N., Rowen, H., Sandelin, J., Lécuyer, C., Colyvas, J., Ueyama, T. and Sheehan, R. (2002) *Stanford start-up project quarterly report* www.stanford.edu/dept/HPS/TimLenoir/Startup/QuarterlyRpts/ProgressReport-Jan02.pdf

Leone, A., Vamos, J., Keeley, R. and Miller, W.F. (1993) 'A survey of technology based companies founded by members of the Stanford University Community' Stanford, Office of Technology Licensing, Stanford University

Liebeskind, J.P., Oliver, A.L., Zucker, L.G. and Brewer, M. (1996) 'Social networks, learning and flexibility: sourcing scientific knowledge in new biotech firms' *Organisational Science*, 7 February

Lindholm, A. (1994) *The economics of technology-related ownership changes – a study of innovativeness and growth through acquisitions and spin-offs* PhD dissertation, Department of Industrial Management and Economics, Chalmers University of Technology, Gothenburg, Sweden

Lindholm Dahlstrand, A. (1997) 'Growth and inventiveness in technology-based spin-off firms', *Research Policy* 26 (3), 331–44

Lindholm Dahlstrand, A. and Jacobsson, S. (2003) 'Universities and technology-based entrepreneurship in the Gothenburg region' *Local Economy* 18 (1), 80–90

Lindholm Dahlstrand, A. and Lawton Smith, H. (2003) 'Science parks and economic development' In *Encyclopedia of life support systems* (EOLSS), developed under the auspices of the UNESCO, Oxford, Eolss Publishers, www.eolss.net

Link, A.N. and Scott, J.T. (2003) 'The growth of the Research Triangle Park' *Small Business Economics* 20, 167–75

Lipsett, A. (2005) 'Europe recruits UK trio' *Times Higher Education Supplement*, 22 July, 5

Llerena, P. and Meyer-Krahmer, F. (2003) 'Interdisciplinary research and the organization of the university: general challenges and a case study' In A. Geuna, A.J. Salter and W.E. Steinmueller (eds) *Science and innovation: rethinking the rationales for funding and governance* Cheltenham, Edward Elgar, 80–1

Llerena, P., Matt, M. and Schaeffer, V. (2003) 'Evolutions of the French innovation policies and the impacts on the universities' In A. Geuna, A.J. Salter and W.E. Steinmueller *Science and innovation: rethinking the rationales for funding and governance* Cheltenham, Edward Elgar

Louis, K.S., Jones, L.M., Anderson, M.S., Blumenthal, D. and Campbell, E.G. (2001) 'Entrepreneurship, secrecy, and productivity: a comparison of clinical and non-clinical faculty' *Journal of Technology Transfer* 26 (3), 233–45

Lovering J. (1991) 'The changing geography of the military industry in Britain' *Regional Studies* 25 (4), 279–95

Lowen, R.S. (1998) *Creating the Cold War university: the transformation of Stanford* Berkeley, University of California Press

Lucas, R. (1988) 'On the mechanics of economic development' *Journal of Monetary Theory* 22, 3–39

Luger, M. and Goldstein, H. (1991) *Technology in the garden: research parks and regional economic development* Chapel Hill and London, The University of North Carolina Press

Lundvall, B.-A. (1988) 'Innovation as an interactive process – from user–producer interaction to national system of innovation' Chapter 17 in G. Dosi, C. Freeman, R. Nelson, G. Silverberg and L. Soete (eds) *Technical change and economic theory* London, Pinter, 349–69

Lundvall, B.-A. (ed.) (1992) *National systems of innovation: towards a theory of innovation and interactive learning* London, Pinter

Lundvall, B.-A. (1999) 'Technology policy in the learning economy' In D. Archibugi, J. Howells and J. Michie (eds) *Innovation policy in a global economy* Cambridge, Cambridge University Press, 19–34

Lundvall, B.-A. (2002) 'The university in the learning economy' DRUID Working Papers 02-06, DRUID, Copenhagen Business School, Department of Industrial Economics and Strategy/Aalborg University, Department of Business Studies

Lundvall, B.-A. and Maskell, P. (2000) 'Nation states and economic development' Chapter 18 in G.L. Clark, M. Feldman and M. Gertler (eds) *The Oxford handbook to economic geography* Oxford, Oxford University Press 353–72

McCann, P. and Shepherd, S. (2001) 'Public investment and regional labour markets: the role of UK Higher Education' Chapter 9 in D. Felsenstein, R. McQuaid, P. McCann and D. Shefer (eds) *Public investment and regional economic development* Cheltenham, Edward Elgar, 135–53

MacKinnon, I. (1998) 'What exactly is economic development?' *Economic Development* 60, 6

Malecki, E. (1997) *Technology and economic development: the dynamics of local, regional and national competitiveness* 2nd edition London, Addison Wesley Longman

Malecki, E. (2005) 'The United States: still on top?' Paper presented at Association of American Geographers Annual Conference, Denver, 4–9 April 2005

Malerba, F. and Orsenigo, L. (1997) 'Technological regimes and sectoral patterns of innovative activities' *Industrial and Corporate Change*, Special Issue on Technological Regimes and the Evolution of Industrial Structures 6, 83–177

Malerba, F. and Orsenigo, L. (2002) 'Innovation and market structure in the dynamics of the pharmaceutical industry and biotechnology: towards a history-friendly model' *Industrial and Corporate Change* 11 (4), 667–703

Malinowski, M.J. (2000) 'Biotechnology in the USA: reponsive regulation in the life science industry' 2 *International Journal of Biotechnology* 16–26

Malmberg, A. and Power, D. (2004) 'On the role of global demand in local innovation processes' In P. Shapiro and G. Fuchs (eds) *Rethinking regional innovation and change* Dordrecht, Kluwer Academic Publishers

Malo, S. and Geuna, A. (2000) 'Science–technology linkages in an emerging research platform: the case of combinatorial chemistry and biology' *Scientometrics* 47 (2), 303–21

Mansfield, E. (1991) 'Academic science and industrial innovation' *Research Policy* 20, 1–12

Mansfield, E. (1998) 'Academic science and industrial innovation: an update of empirical findings' *Research Policy* 26, 773–6

Mansfield, E. and Lee, J.-Y. (1996) 'The modern university: contributor to industrial innovation and recipient of industrial R&D support' *Research Policy* 25, 1047–58

Marklein, M.B. (2003) 'Universities lose state aid when benefactors step in' *US Today*, 26 August

Markusen, A., Hall, P. and Glasmeier, A. (1986) *High-tech America: the what, how, where and why of the sunrise industries* Bosten, Allen & Unwin

Marshall, E. (1999) 'Two former grad students sue over alleged misuse of ideas' *Science* 284, 23 April, 562–3

Marshall, E. (2000) 'Patent suit pits postdoc against former mentor' *Science* 287, 2399–401

Martin, B.R. (2003) 'The changing social contract for science and the evolution of the university' Chapter 1 in A. Geuna, A.J. Salter and W.E. Steinmueller (eds) *Science and innovation: rethinking the rationales for funding and governance* Cheltenham, Edward Elgar, 7–29

Martin, R. and Sunley, P. (2003) 'Deconstructing clusters: chaotic concept or policy panacea?' *Journal of Economic Geography* 3, 5–35

Martin, R., Miller, P. and Syas, S. (2003) 'The "new" economy: myths, realities and regional dynamics' Paper presented at Workshop on High-Tech Businesses: Clusters, Constraints and Economic Development, Robinson College, Cambridge www.cbr.cam.ac.uk/news/pdf/martin.pdf

Maskell, P. and Tornqvist, G. (2003) 'The role of universities in the learning region' Chapter 7 in R. Rutten, F. Boekma, and E. Kuijpers (eds) *Economic geography of higher education: knowledge infrastructure and learning regions* London, Routledge

Mason, G. (2000) 'High-level technical skills, labour mobility and knowledge transfer in Western Europe' Chapter 2 in P. Healey (ed.) *European research, technology and development: issues for a competitive future* Key research findings from the ESRC. Research Programme *The European Context of UK Science Policy* London, SPSG, 25–34

Mason, G. and Wagner, K. (1994) 'Innovation and the skill mix: chemicals and engineering in Britain and Germany' *National Insititute of Economics Review* 148, 61–72

Mason, G., Beltramo, J.-P. and Paul, J.-J. (2004) 'External knowledge sourcing in different national settings: a comparison of electronics establishments in Britain and France' *Research Policy* 33 (1), 53–72

Massey, D. (1995) *Spatial divisions of labour* Basingstoke, Macmillan

Massey, D., Quintas, P. and Wield, D. (1992) *High-tech fantasies: science parks in society, science and space* London, Routledge

Merton, R. (1968) 'The Matthew effect in science' *Science* 159, 56–63

Metcalfe, S. (1997) 'Technology systems and technology policy in an evolutionary framework' In D. Archibugi and J. Mitchie (eds) *Technology, globalisation and economic performance* Cambridge, Cambridge University Press

Meyer, M. (2002) 'Tracing knowledge flows in innovation systems – an informetric perspective on future research on science-based innovation' *Economic Systems Research* 14 (4), 323

Meyer, M. (2003) 'Are academic patents an indicator of useful university research?' *Research Evaluation* 12 (1), 17–27

Meyer-Krahmer, F. and Schmoch, U. (1998) 'Science-based technologies: university–industry interactions in four fields' *Research Policy* 27 (8), 835–51

Miles, N. and Lawton Smith, H. (2004) 'SEEDA – Structure and dynamics of the South East economy reducing intra-regional disparities: Oxfordshire "phenomenon" case study' a Report to SEEDA and GOSE, Guildford, Government Office of the South East

Miller, J. (2003) 'Sealing the coffin on the experimental use exception' *Duke Law and Technology Review* 0012 7 May www.law.duke.edu/journals/dltr/articles/2003dltr0012.html

Miller, J. and Senker, J. (2000) 'International approaches to research policy and funding: university research policy in different national contexts' Final report prepared for the Higher Education Funding Council for England (HEFCE), April, Brighton, SPRU

Miller, W.L. and Morris, L. (1999) *Fourth generation R&D, managing knowledge, technology and innovation* New York, John Wiley and Sons

Minshall, T. and Wicksteed, B. (2005) *University spin-out companies: starting to fill the evidence gap* A report on a pilot research project commissioned by the Gatsby Charitable Foundation

Monjon, S. and Waelbroek, P. (2003) 'Assessing spillovers from universities to firms: evidence from French firm-level data' *International Journal of Industrial Organization* 21, 1255–70

Moore, G. and Davis, K. (2001) 'Learning the Silicon Valley way' Stanford Institute for Economic Policy Research (SIEPR) Discussion Paper 00-45

Morgan, K. and Nauwelaers, C. (eds) (1999) *Regional innovation strategies: the challenge for less-favoured regions* London, HMSO in association with Regional Studies Association

Mowery, D.C. (1983) 'Economic theory and government technology policy' *Policy Sciences* 16, 27–43

Mowery, D.C. (1998) 'Collaborative R&D: how effective is it? Issues in science and technology online' http://205.130.85.236/issues/15.1/mowery.htm

Mowery, D.C. and Langlois, R.N. (1986) 'Spinning off and spinning on (?): the federal government role in the development of the US computer software industry' *Research Policy* 27, 639–45

Mowery, D.C. and Sampat, B.N. (2001) 'Patenting and licensing university inventions: lessons from the history of the research corporation' *Industrial and Corporate Change* 10 (2), 317–55

Mowery, D.C. and Sampat B.N. (2002) 'International emulation of Bayh-Dole: rash or rational?' Paper presented at American Association for the Advancement of Science symposium on International Trends in the Transfer of Academic Research, Boston, February 2002

Mowery, D.C. and Ziedonis, A.A. (2002) 'Academic patent quality and quantity before and after the Bayh-Dole Act in the United States' *Research Policy* 31 (3), 399–418

Mowery, D.C., Nelson, R.R., Sampat, B.N. and Ziedonis, A.A. (1999) 'The effects of the Bayh-Dole Act in U.S. university research and technology transfer' Chapter 11 in L.M. Branscomb, F. Kodama and R. Florida (eds) *Industrializing knowledge: university–industry linkages in Japan and the United States* Cambridge, MA and London, MIT, 269–306

Muizer, A. (2003) 'Knowledge transfer to innovative start-ups' In A. van der Laag and J. Snijder (eds) *Entrepeneurship in the Netherlands: knowledge transfer, developing high-tech ventures* The Hague, Ministry of Economic Affairs and EIM Business and Policy Research

Musselin, C. (1990) 'Structures formelles et capacités d'intégration dans les universités françaises et allemandes' *Revue Française de Sociologie* 31, 439–61

Narin, F., Hamilton, K.S. and Olivastro, D. (1997) 'The increasing linkage between U.S. technology and public science' *Research Policy* 26, 317–30

National Institute General Medical Sciences, National Institutes of Health (NIGHMS/NIH) (1997) *Why do basic research?* www.nigms.nih.gov/news/science_ed/whydo.html

National Science Foundation (2000) *Science and Engineering Indicators 2000*, vol. 2, 2.49–2.52, 2.58

Nelson, R. (1988) 'Institutions supporting technical change in the US' Chapter 15 in G. Dosi, C. Freeman, R. Nelson, G. Silverberg and L. Soete (eds) *Technical change and economic theory* London, Pinter, 312–29

Nelson, R. (ed) (1993) *National innovation systems: a comparative analysis* New York, Oxford University Press

Nelson, R. and Rosenberg, N. (1993) 'Technical innovations and national systems' Chapter 1 in R. Nelson (ed.) in *National innovation systems: a comparative analysis* New York, Oxford University Press, 3–27

Nightingale, P. and Martin, P. (2004) 'The myth of the biotech revolution' *Trends in Biotechnology* 22 (11), 564–69

NIH (2003) National Institutes of Health Press Release for the FY 2003 President's Budget www.nih.gov/news/budgetfy2003/2003/NIHPressbudget.htm

Noble, D.F. (1977) *America by design: science, technology, and the rise of corporate capitalism* New York, Knopf

Noisi, J. (2003) 'Alliances are not enough: explaining rapid growth in Canadian Biotechnology' *Research Policy* 32, 737–50

Noll, R.G. (1998) 'The American research university: an introduction' Chapter 1 in *Challenges to research universities* Washington DC, Brookings Institution Press, 1–30

Nooteboom, B. (1999) 'Innovation, learning and industrial organisation' *Cambridge Journal of Economics* 23, 127–50

Nooteboom, B. (2000) *Learning and innovation in organisations and economies* Oxford, Oxford University Press

North, D. (1990), *Institutions, institutional change & economic performance* Cambridge, Cambridge University Press

NSB (2003) National Science Board, *The science and engineering workforce: realizing America's potential* Arlington, VA, National Science Foundation (NSB 03-69)

NSF (2002) *Academic research and development expenditures: fiscal year 2002* www.nsf.gov/sbe/srs/nsf04330/start.htm

NSF (2004) *Science and engineering indicators 2004: academic research and development* www.nesf.gov/sbe/srs/seind04/c5/c5s1.htm

Nülle, G.M. (2004) 'A little market, a lot of state' www.mises.org/fullstory.aspx?control=1448&id=65

OECD (1998) *The university in transition* Paris, OECD

OECD (1999/IHME) *The response of higher education institutions to regional needs* Paris, OECD

OECD (2001a) *Science, technology innovation scoreboard* Paris, OECD

OECD (2001b) *Fostering high-tech spin-offs: a public strategy for innovation* STI REVIEW 26 Paris, OECD

OECD (2002a) *Benchmarking industry–science relationships* Paris, OECD

OECD (2002b) 'Draft final report on the strategic use of intellectual property by public research organisations in OECD countries' DSTI/STP (2002) 42/REV, Paris, OECD

OECD (2002c) *Main science and technology indicators* Paris, OECD

OECD (2002d) *Questionnaire on the patenting and licensing activities of PRO's* Paris, OECD

OECD (2003) *The STI scoreboard: creation and diffusion of knowledge* www.oecd.org

OECD (2004) *Innovation-led policies for regional competitiveness* Paris, OECD

Oinas, P. and Malecki, E.J. (2002) 'The evolution of technologies in time and space: from national and regional to spatial innovation systems' *International Science Review* 25 (1), 132–48

Oughton, C., Landabaso, M. and Morgan, K. (2002) 'The regional innovation paradox: innovation policy and industrial policy' *Journal of Technology Transfer* 27, 97–110

Owen-Smith, P. and Powell, W.W. (2001) 'To patent or not: faculty decisions and institutional success at technology transfer' *Journal of Technology Transfer* 26, 99–114

Owen-Smith, P. and Powell, W.W. (2003) 'The expanding role of university patenting in life sciences: assessing the importance of experience and connectivity' *Research Policy*

Owen-Smith, P. and Powell, W.W. (2004) 'Knowledge networks as channels and conduits: the effects of spillovers in the Boston biotechnology community' *Organisation Science* 15, 5–21

Oxford University Gazette (1999) 'Regional liaison director appointed' www.ox.ac.uk/gazette/1999-00/weekly/071099/news/story_4.htm

Pammolli, F., Riccaboni, M., Gambardella, A., Mariani, M. and Orsenigo, L. (2001) 'Innovation and competitiveness in the European biotechnology industry'

Report Commissioned by the European Commission, DG Enterprise, as a Background Paper for the Competitiveness Report 2001

Patel, P. (2002) *Measuring third stream activities* Final Report to the Russell Group of Universities www.clo.cam.ac.uk/final_russell_report.pdf

Pavitt, K. (1984) 'Sectoral patterns of technical change: towards a taxonomy and a theory' *Research Policy* 13, 343–73

Pavitt, K. (1998a) 'The social shaping of the national science base' *Research Policy* 27, 793–805

Pavitt, K. (1998b) 'Do patents reflect the useful research output of universities?' *Research Evaluation* 7 (2), August, 105–12

Pavitt, K. (2003) Commentary in A. Geuna and W.E. Steinmueller (eds) (2003) *Science and innovation: rethinking the rationales for funding and governance* London, Edward Elgar, 89–93

Pearson, R., Jagger, N., Connor, H., Perryman, S. with de Grip, A., Marey, P., Corvers, F. (2001) *Assessing the supply and demand for scientists and technologists in Europe* IES Report 377 www.employment-studies.co.uk/summary/summary.php?id=377

Peck, F. and McGuinness, D. (2003) 'UK competitiveness and the regional agenda: making sense of clusters in the North of England' *Local Economy* 18 (1), 49–62

Pedersen, R. (2004) 'Can't stem progress: the UK could benefit from the US' politicking with basic biomedical research' *Times Higher Education Supplement*, 26 March

Philips, D. (1994) 'The research mission and research manpower' Chapter 3 in *Universities in the twenty-first century* London, National Commission on Education and The Council for Industry and Higher Education

Pirnay, F., Surlemont, B., Nlemvo, F. (2003) 'Toward a typology of university spin-offs' *Small Business Economics* 21 (4), 355–69

Polt, W. (2001) *Benchmarking industry science relations: the role of framework conditions* Final report for the EC–DG Enterprise

Porter, M. (1990) *The competitive advantage of nations* London, Macmillan

Porter, M. (1998) 'Clusters and the new economics of competitiveness' *Harvard Business Review* 77, 1–10

Potts, G. (2002) 'Regional policy and the "regionalization" of university–industry links: a view from the English regions' *European Planning Studies* 10 (8), 987–1012

Potts, G. (2003) 'Collaboration on graduate utilisation efforts in North East England' Unpublished mimeo, gareth.potts@neweconomics.org

Powers, J. (2003) 'Do Land-Grant and private universities enjoy a performance premium in the technology commercialisation game?' Association of the Study of Higher Education Conference, Portland Oregon, November 2003

Powers, J.B. and McDougall, P.P. (2003) 'University entrepreneurship: testing a typology and its performance effects on technology licensing to firms that go public' www.babson.edu/entrep/fer/BABSON2003/XXIV/XXIV-P2/XXIV-P2.html

Poyago-Theotoky, J., Beath, J. and Siegal, D.S. (2002) 'Universities and fundamental research: reflections on the growth of university–industry partnership' University of St Andrew's, Department of Economics Discussion Paper Series 0201

Pressman, L. (ed) (2000) *AUTM licensing survey: FY 2001* Northbrook, IL, Association of University Technology Managers

Pressman, L. (ed.) (2001) *AUTM licensing survey: FY 2001 Survey Summary* North-brook, IL (AUTM) www.autm.net/surveys/01/01summarypublicversion.pdf

Pressman, L., Guterman, S., Abrams, I., Geist, D., Nelsen, L. (1995) 'Pre-production investment and jobs induced by MIT exclusive patent licenses: a preliminary model to measure the economic impact of university licensing' *Journal of Association University of Technology Managers* 7, 77–90

Quigley, J.M. and Rubinfeld, D.L. (1993) 'Public choices in public higher education' In C. Clotfelter and M. Rothshild (eds) *Studies of supply and demand in higher education* Chicago, University of Chicago Press

Rahm, D. (1993) www.stanford.edu/dept/news/pr/94/940329Arc4357.html

Rahm, D. (1994a) 'Academic perceptions of university–firm technology transfer' *Policy Studies Journal* 22 (2), Summer, 267–78

Rahm, D. (1994b) 'Rethinking technology transfer policy' *Southeastern Political Review* 22 (4), December, 707–28

Reed, T.J. (2004) 'Just growing' *Oxford Magazine* 227 Oxford, Oxford University Press

Riccaboni, M., Powell, W.P., Pammolli, F. and Owen-Smith, J. (2003) 'Public research and industrial innovation: a comparison of US and European innovation system in the life sciences' Chapter 6 in A. Geuna, A.J. Salter and W.E. Steinmueller (eds) *Science and innovation: rethinking the rationales for funding and governance* Cheltenham, Edward Elgar, 169–201

Rickne, A. (2000) *New technology based firms and industrial dynamics: evidence from the technological systems in Sweden, Ohio and Massachusetts* Department of Industrial Dynamics, Chalmers University of Technology, Gothenburg, Sweden

Roberts, E.B. and Wainer, H.A. (1968) 'New enterprises on Route 128' *Science Journal*, December

Roberts, G. (2002) *SET for success* The Roberts Review for HM Treasury www.hm-treasury.gov.uk/Documents/Enterprise_and_Productivity/Research_and_Enterprise/ent_res_roberts.cfm

Romer, P. (1986) 'Increasing returns and long run growth' *Journal of Political Economy* 94, 1002–37

Romer, P. (1990) 'Endogenous technological change' *Journal of Political Economy* 98, S71–S102

Romer, P. (1999) 'Should the government subsidize supply or demand in the market for scientists and engineers?' NBER Working Paper 7723 www.nber.org

Rosenberg, P. (2000) *Patent law fundamentals* St Paul, West Group

Rosenberg, N. and Colyvas, J. (2002) *Rosenberg/Colyvas first quarter report* Quarterly Reports www.stanford.edu/dept/HPS/TimLenoir/Startup/QuartlerlyRpts/ProgressReportJan02.pdf

Rosenberg, N. and Nelson, R.R. (1994) 'American universities and technical advance in industry' *Research Policy* 23, 323–48

Rosenweig, R. (1998) 'The Cold War era and the modern university' www.stanford.edu/dept/news/stanfordtoday/ed/9807/9807fea4.html

Rowen, H.S. and Sheehan, R. (2002) 'First quarter report: the GBS and Silicon Valley' www.stanford.edu/dept/HPS/TimLenoir/Startup/QuarterlyRpts/ProgressReportJan02.pdf

Royal Society (2003) 'Keeping science open: the effects of intellectual property policy on the conduct of science' Report prepared by the Royal Society working group on intellectual property, London, Royal Society

Ruivo, B. (1994) '"Phases" or "paradigms" of science policy?' *Science and Public Policy* 21 (3), 157–64

Rutten, R.P.J.H., Boekema, F.W.M. and Kuijpers, E. (2003) 'HEIs, regions and the knowledge-based economy' In R.P.J.H. Rutten, F.W.M. Boekema and E. Kuijpers (eds) *Economic geography of higher education* (Studies in Business Organization and Networks, 23), 244–52, London, Routledge

Sabato, J. (1975) *El pensamiento latinoamericano en la problematic ciencia-tech-nologia-desarrollo-dependencia* Buenos Aires, Paidos

Sainsbury Report (1999) *Biotechnology clusters: report of a team led by Lord Sainsbury, Minister for Science* London, Department of Trade and Industry

Salter, B. and Frewer, L. (2002) 'The changing governance of biotechnology – the politics of public trust' Working paper from current ESRC project: 'The governance of human genetics', funded by the ESRC as part of its Innovative Health Technologies Programme, University of East Anglia www.uea.ac.uk/~x514/research/governance/BIOGOV3.pdf

Salter, A.J., Martin B.R. (2001) 'The economic benefits of publicly funded basic research: a critical review' *Research Policy* 30, 509–32

Salter, B. and Smith M.E. (2002) 'The UK's stake in the biotechnology debate: global competition and regulatory politics' Working paper from current ESRC project: 'The governance of human genetics', funded by the ESRC as part of its Innovative Health Technologies Programme, University of East Anglia www.uea.ac.uk/~x514/research/governance/UK'sstakeinthebiotechnologydebate. pdf

Salter, A., Este, P., Martin, B., Guena, A., Scott, A., Pavitt, K., Patel, P. and Nightingale, P. (2000) *Talent not technology: investing in universities and colleges for global success. Public funded research and innovation in the UK.* London, Report for CVCP

Sandelin, J. (2002) www.stanford.edu/dept/HPS/TimLenoir/Startup/Quarter-lyRpts/ProgressReportJan02.pdf

Saperstein, J. and Rouach, D. (2002) *Creating regional wealth in the innovation economy* American University, Kogod, November www.escp-eap.net

Saviotti, P.P. (1998) 'Industrial structure and the dynamics of knowledge genera-tion in biotechnology' In J. Senker (ed.) *Biotechnology and competitive advant-age* Cheltenham, Edward Elgar

Saxenian, A. (1983) 'The genesis of Silicon Valley' *Built Environment* 9, 7–17

Saxenian, A. (1994) *Regional advantage* Cambridge, MA, Harvard University Press

Saxenian, A. (1999) *Silicon Valley's new immigrant entrepreneurs* San Francisco, Public Policy Institute of California

SBS (2003) 'Investing in the future' *Save British Science Newsletter* 37, July, London, Save British Science www.savebritishscience.org.uk

SBS (2004a) 'Science and the economy' *Save British Science Newsletter* 39, January, London, Save British Science www.savebritishscience.org.uk

SBS (2004b) 'Bologna declaration' *Save British Science Newsletter* 39, January, 8, London, Save British Science www.savebritishscience.org.uk

Schell, A. (2001) *IEEE-US R&D Policy Committee testimony on behalf of the American Association of Engineering Societies before the House Appropriations Subcommittee on Defense*, 28 March 2001www.ieeeusa.org/forum/POLICY/2001/01march28.html

Scherer, F.M. and Ross, D. (1990) *Industrial market structure and economic performance* Boston, Houghton Mifflin Company

Schumpeter, J.A. (1949) 'The historical approach to the analysis of business cycles' In J.A. Schumpeter, *Essays on entrepreneurs, innovations, business cycles, and the evolution of capitalism*, edited by R.V. Clemence and introduced by R. Swedberg, New Brunswick, NJ and London, Transaction, 1989, 322–29

Schwerin, J. (2004) 'The evolution of the Clyde region's shipbuilding innovation system in the second half of the nineteenth century' *Journal of Economic Geography* 4, 83–101

Scott, A. (1988) *New industrial spaces* London, Pion

Scott, A. and Storper, M. (1987) 'High technology industry and regional development: a theoretical critique and reconstruction' *International Science Journal* 112, 215–32

Segal Quince (1985) *The Cambridge phenomenon* Cambridge, Segal Quince and Partners

Senker, J. (1996) 'National systems of innovation, organisational learning and industrial biotechnology' *Technovation* 16 (5), 219–29

Senker, J. (2005) 'Assessing the capitalisation of knowledge: the need for a broad policy approach' Paper presented at the Fifth Triple Helix Conference, Turin, 18–21 May 2005

Shane, S. (2004) *Academic entrepreneurship: university spinoffs and wealth creation* Cheltenham, Edward Elgar

Shapira, P. (2005a) *US national innovation system: science, technology and innovation policy* Developments BETA, 28 February, cherry.iac.gatech.edu/beta/xoutline.htm

Shapira, P. (2005b) 'Innovation challenges and strategies in catch-up regions: Developmental growth disparities in Georgia, USA' In G. Fuchs and P. Shapira (eds) *Rethinking regional innovation: path dependency or regional breakthrough* New York, Springer

Shapira, P. and Kuhlman, S. (eds) (2003) *Learning from science and technology policy evaluation: experiences from the United States and Europe* Cheltenham, Edward Elgar

Sharpe, E. (1991) 'The life of Frederick Terman' *SMEC Vintage Electrics* 3 (1) (now SMECC) www.smecc.org/frederick_terman_-_by_ed_sharpe.htm

Siegel, D.S., Waldman, D. and Link, A. (1999) *Assessing the impact of organizational practices on the productivity of university technology transfer offices: an exploratory study*, NBER Working Paper Series, No. 7256

Siegel, D.S., Waldman, D. and Link, A. (2003) 'Assessing the impact of organisational practices on the relative productivity of university technology transfer offices: an exploratory study' *Research Policy* 32 (1), 27–48

Siegel, D.S., Waldman, D., Atwater, L. and Link, A.N. (2002) 'Improving the effectiveness of commercial knowledge transfers from universities to firms' *Journal of High Technology Management Research*

Simmie, J. and Sennett, J. (1999) 'Innovative clusters: global or local linkages?' *National Institute Economic Review* 170, 87–98

Simmie, J., Sennett, J., Wood, P. and Hart, D. (2002) 'Innovation in Europe: a tale of networks, knowledge and trade in five cities' *Regional Studies* 36 (1), 47–64

Sine, W.D., Shane, S. and Di Gregorio, D. (2003) 'The halo effect and technological licensing: the influence of institutional prestige on the licensing of university inventions' *Management Science* 1–19

Slaughter, S. and Leslie, L. (1999) *Academic capitalism: politics, policies, and the entrepreneurial university* Baltimore, Johns Hokpins University Press

Slaughter, S. and Rhoades, G. (1996) 'The emergence of a competitiveness research and development policy coalition and the commercialization of academic science and technology' *Science, Technology and Human Values* 21 (3), 303–39

Smith, K. (1997) 'Economic infrastructures and innovation systems' Chapter 4 in C. Edquist (ed.) *Systems of innovation: technologies, institutions and organisations* London, Pinter, 86–106

Smith, K. (2000) 'What is the "knowledge economy"? Knowledge-intensive industries and distributed knowledge bases' Paper prepared as part of the 'Innovation Policy in a Knowledge-Based Economy' Commissioned by the European Commission STEP. Group, Oslo

Sonnert, G. and Holton, G. (2002) *Ivory bridges: connecting science and society* Cambridge, MA, MIT Press

Stanford University News Service (1994) 'University, government role in technology transfer analyzed', 29 March www.stanford.edu

Steed, G.P.F. and De Genova, D. (1983) 'Ottawa's technology-oriented complex' *Canadian Geographer* 27 (3), 263–78

Steinmueller, W.E. (2003) 'Commentary' In A. Geuna, A.J. Salter and W.E. Steinmueller (eds) *Science and innovation: rethinking the rationales for funding and governance* Cheltenham, Edward Elgar, 236–43

Stephan, P.E. (2001) 'Educational implications of university–industry technology transfer' *Journal of Technology Transfer* 26 (3), 199–205

Stephan P.E. (2003) 'Commentary' In A. Geuna, A.J. Salter and W.E. Steinmueller (eds) *Science and innovation: rethinking the rationales for funding and governance* Cheltenham, Edward Elgar

Stephan, P.E. and Everhart, S.S. (1998) 'The changing rewards to science: the case of biotechnology' *Small Business Economics* 10, 141–151

Stephan, P.E., Gurmu, S., Sumell, A.J. and Black, G. (2002) 'Patenting and publishing: substitutes or complements for university faculty?' Paper presented at NBER Higher Education Meeting, 3 May

Sternberg, R. (1996) 'Regional growth theories and high-tech regions' *International Journal of Urban and Regional Planning* 518–38

Sternberg, R. (1999) 'Innovative linkages and proximity: empirical results from recent surveys of small and medium-sized firms in German Regions' *Regional Studies* 33 (6), 529–40

Stevenson, L. (2002) 'Innovation and entrepreneurship: Dutch policy in an international context' In A. van der Laag and J. Snijder (eds) *Entrepeneurship in the Netherlands: knowledge transfer, developing high-tech ventures* The Hague, Ministry of Economic Affairs and EIM Business and Policy Research

Stodder, J. (undated) 'Scientific and engineering workers: education supplies, occupational demands' www.rh.edu/~stodder/EdSupply.htm

Stokes, D.E. (1997) *Paster's quadrant: basic science and technological innovation* Washington DC, Brookings Institution Press

Stoneman, P. (1987) *The economic analysis of technology policy* Oxford, Blackwell

Sturgeon, T.J. (2000) 'How Silicon Valley came to be' Chapter 2 in M. Kenney (ed.) *Understanding Silicon Valley: the anatomy of an entrepreneurial region* Stanford, Stanford University Press

Swann, G.M.P. and Prevezer, M. (1996) 'A comparison of the dynamics of industrial clustering in computing and biotechnology' *Research Policy* 25, 1139–57

Swann, G.M.P., Prevezer, M. and Stout, D. (1998) *The dynamics of industrial clustering: international comparisons in computing and biotechnology* Oxford, Oxford University Press

Tajnai, C. (1996) 'From the valley of heart's delight to the Silicon Valley: a study of Stanford University's role in the transformation' Stanford Computer Forum http://forum.stanford.edu/carolyn/valley_of_hearts

Taylor, T. (1985) 'High-technology industry and the development of science parks' Chapter 9 in P. Hall and A. Markusen (eds) *Silicon landscapes* Winchester, MA, Allen & Unwin, 134–43

Thanki, R. (1999) 'How do we know the value of regional development to higher education?' *Regional Studies* 33, 84–9

THES (2003a) 'A. dilemma in the way of science' *Times Higher Education Supplement*, 18 July, 12

THES (2003b) 'EU ruling in stem cells smooths research path' *Times Higher Education Supplement*, 18 July, 14

THES (2004) 'World university rankings' *Times Higher Education Supplement*, 5 November

Thomson, A. and Goddard, A. (2003) 'Anger after DFES' *Times Higher Education Supplement*, 1 August, 2

Thursby, J.C., Jensen, R., and Thursby, M.C. (2001) 'Objectives, characteristics and outcomes of university licensing: a survey of major U.S. universities *Journal of Technology Transfer* 26, 59–72

Tornatzky, L.G. (2003) 'Benchmarking university–industry relationships: a user-centred evaluation approach' Chapter 12 in P. Shapira and S. Kuhlman (eds) *Learning from science and technology policy evaluation: experiences from the United States and Europe* Cheltenham, Edward Elgar

Tornatzky L.G., Waugaman, P.G. and Grayt, D.O. (2002) *Innovation U.: new university roles in a knowledge economy* Southern Growth Policies Board, www.southern.org/pubs/innovationU/default.asp

Townsend, M. (2003) 'Probe into "bullying" of GM panel scientists' *Observer* 24 August, 4

Tracey, P. and Clark, G. (2003) 'Alliances, networks and competitive strategy: rethinking clusters of innovation' *Growth and Change* 34 (4), 508–11

Traore, N. and Rose, A. (2003) 'Determinants of biotechnology utilization by the Canadian industry' *Research Policy* 32 (10), 1719–35

Trune, D. and Goslin, L. (2000) 'Assessment of technology transfer profitability within US universities' *European Biopharmaceutical Review*, September, 56–62

Tushman, M.L., Anderson, P.C. and O'Reilly, C. (1997) 'Technology cycles, innovation streams, and ambidextrous organizations: organization renewal through innovation streams and strategic change' In M.L. Tushman and P.C. Anderson (eds) *Managing strategic innovation and change* New York, Oxford University Press 3–23

Tysome, T. (2003a) 'Skills flagship fails to inspire' *Times Higher Education Supplement*, 8 August, 2

Tysome, T. (2003b) 'Strategy "ignores" HE role in skills provision' *Times Higher Education Supplement*, 5 September, 10

Tysome, T. (2004) 'Club together to get more cash, Oxford colleges told' *Times Higher Education Supplement*, 16 July, 8

US Council on Competitiveness (1998) *Going global: the new shape of American Innovation* Washington

Utley, A. (2003) 'Man United hits home straight' *Times Higher Education Supplement*, 1 August, 2

Van Hoorebeek, M. (2004) 'Are the economic hounds at the gates of the ivory towers? The experimental use defence and Madey v Duke University' *Industry and Higher Education* 18 (3), 145–56

Van Reenan, J. (2002) 'Economic issues for the U.K. biotechnology sector' Lexcon/University College London Working Paper, February www.lexecon.co.uk/profiles/articles/biotech5.pdf

Veugelers, R. and Cassiman, B. (2003) 'R&D cooperation between firms and universities: some empirical evidence from Belgian Manufacturing' Center for Economic Policy Research (CEPR) Discussion Paper series 3951 www.ecpr.org

Viale, R. and Ghiglione, B. (undated) *The triple helix model: a tool for the study of European regional socio economic systems* www.jrc.es/pages/iptsreport/vol29/english/REG1E296.htm

Vorley, T.R. (2004) A *geography of London's biotechnology* Unpublished MSc Thesis, Department of Geography, University of Leicester

Waasdorp, P. (2002) 'Innovative entrepreneurship: a Dutch policy perspective' In A. van der Laag and J. Snijder (eds) *Entrepeneurship in the Netherlands: knowledge transfer, developing high-tech ventures* The Hague, Ministry of Economic Affairs and EIM. Business and Policy Research

Walcott, S. (2001) 'Growing global: life cycle of a life science cluster' *Growth and Change* 32, 511–32

Walcott, S. (2002) 'Analysing an innovative environment: San Diego as a bioscience beachhead' *Economic Development Quarterly* 16, 99–114

Walshok, M. (1994) 'Rethinking the role of research universities in economic development' *Industry and Higher Education* 8, March, 8–18

Walshok, M.L. (2002) 'Introduction' *Industry and Higher Education* 16 (1), 7–8

Walshok, M.L., Furtek, E., Lee, C.W.B. and Windham, P.H. (2002) 'Building regional innovative capacity: the San Diego experience' *Industry and Higher Education* 16 (1), 27–42

Warden, R. (2003) '... As Spain fights to woo students' *Times Higher Education Supplement*, 8 August, 11

Waters, R. and Lawton Smith, H. (2002) 'RDAs and local economic development: scale and competitiveness in Oxfordshire and Cambridgeshire' *European Planning Studies* 10 (5), 633–49

Webster, A. and Rappert, B. (1997) 'Regimes of ordering: the commercialisation of intellectual property in industrial–academic collaborations' *Technology Analysis and Strategic Management* 9, 115–19

Wever, E. and Stam, E. (1999) 'Clusters of high technology SMEs: the Dutch case' *Regional Studies* 33 (4), 391–400

Whitely, R. (2003) 'Competition and pluralism in the public sciences: the impact of institutional frameworks on the organization of academic science' *Research Policy* 32 (6), 1015–29

Wilkinson, F. (1983) 'Productive systems' *Cambridge Journal of Economics* 7, 413–29

Winterhager, M. and Weingart, P. (1997) *Forschungsstatus Schweiz 1995 Publikationsaktivität und Rezeptionserfolg der schweizerischen Grundlagenforschung im internationalen Vergleich 1981–1995* Bern, Schweizerischer Wissenschaftsrat, FOP 45/1997

Wojciechowski, F. (2004) 'A new research institute for the science and technology of materials' *Princeton Research* New Jersey (April), 24–5

Wolf, A. (2002) *Does education matter? Myths about education and economic growth* London, Penguin

Wolfe, D. (2003) 'Commentary' In A. Geuna, A.J. Salter and W.E. Steinmueller (eds) *Science and innovation: rethinking the rationales for funding and governance* Cheltenham, Edward Elgar

Wolfe, D.A. and Gertler, M. (2003) 'Cluster old and new: lesson from the ISRN study of cluster development' In D.A. Wolfe and M.S. Gertler (eds) *Clusters old and new* Montreal and Kingston, School of Policy Studies Queen's University and McGill–Queen's University Press

Wong, C. (2003) 'Indicators at the crossroads: ideas, methods and applications' *Town Planning Review* 74 (3), 253–79

Woods, M. (undated) http://sciencecareers.sciencemag.org/feature/cperspec/eurocar.shl

World Economic Forum (2004) *The global competitiveness report 2004–2005* www.weforum.org

Woznaik, G. (1984) 'The adoption of interrelated innovations: a human capital approach' *Review of Economics and Statistics* 66, 70–9

Yarrow, G. (1993) with Lawton Smith, H. *Social security and friendly societies: options for the future* London, National Conference of Friendly Societies, June 1993

Young, S. and Brown, R. (2002) 'Globalisation and the knowledge economy' In N. Hood, J. Peat, E. Peters and S. Young (eds) *Scotland in a global economy: the 20:20 vision* Basingstoke, Palgrave Macmillan

Zhou, P.-L., Tang, Z.-N., Wang, J.-T. and Yang C.-X. (2004) 'Mathew effect in artificial stock market' *International Journal of Modern Physics* B http://xxx.lanl.gov/PS_cache/cond-mat/pdf/0406/0406365.pdf

Zucker, L.G. and Darby, M.R. (1996) 'Star scientists and institutional transformation: patterns of invention and innovation in the formation of the biotech industry' *Proceedings of the National Academy of Science* 93 (12), 709–16

Zucker, L.G. and Darby, M.R. (2001) *Commercialising knowledge: university science, knowledge capital and firm performance in biotechnology* NBER Working Paper 8499, Cambridge, MA, NBER

Zucker, L.G. and Darby, M.R. and Armstrong, J. (1998a) 'Geographically localized knowledge: spillovers or markets?' *Economic Inquiry* 36, 65–86

Zucker, L.G. and Darby, M.R. and Brewer, M.B. (1998b) 'Intellectual human capital and the birth of US biotechnology enterprises' *American Economic Review* 88, 290–306

Zucker, L.G, Darby, M.R. and Terero, M. (2002) 'Labor mobility from academe to commerce' *Journal of Labor Economics* 20 (3), 629–60

Index